GW01100170

A Special Flame
The Music of Elgar and Vaughan Williams

based on
the proceedings of an International Symposium
jointly organised by
The Elgar and RVW Societies

held at
The British Library,
Euston Road
London

Saturday 29 & Sunday 30 March 2003

Elgar Editions

Published in Great Britain by

Elgar Editions

the publishing imprint of

Elgar Enterprises
20 High Street, Rickmansworth, Herts WD3 1ER
(e-mail : editions@elgar.org)

© individual contributors, 2004

First Published : August 2004

All rights reserved.
No part of this publication may be reproduced, stored in a retrieval system,
or transmitted in any form or by any means, electronic or mechanical,
including the Internet, without the prior permission in writing of Elgar Enterprises.

British Library Cataloguing in Publication Data
A Catalogue record for this book
is available from the British Library

ISBN 0 9537082 9 2 (Elgar Editions)

Printed and bound in Great Britain by
Antony Rowe Ltd,
Bumper's Farm, Chippenham, Wiltshire

Contents

	Foreword	v
1.	**Elgar and Vaughan Williams: A 21st Century Celebration** Michael Kennedy	1
2.	**"It looks all wrong, but it sounds all right"**: The social background to the life and music of Elgar and Vaughan Williams Andrew Neill	10
3.	**Dreamers of Dreams**: The songs of Elgar and Vaughan Williams Claire-Louise Lucas & Jonathan Darnborough	23
4.	**Battle Songs & Elegics**: Elgar, Vaughan Williams & British music 1914–1918 Lewis Foreman	42
5.	**What Have We Learnt from Elgar?**: Vaughan Williams and the ambivalence of inheritance Byron Adams	70
6.	**Stanford, Elgar and Vaughan Williams**: Influences and reflections Michael Pope	78
7.	**"My Dear Elgar"**: The letters of Elgar and Vaughan Williams Hugh Cobbe	85
8.	**From *The Apostles* to *Sancta Civitas***: The oratorios of Elgar and Vaughan Williams Charles McGuire	99
9.	**"Sheer early morning loveliness"**: Ralph Vaughan Williams and *The Poisoned Kiss* Stephen Connock	116
10.	**'Immemorial Ind'**: Elgar's score for *The Crown of India* Robert Anderson	130
11.	**Eleven Symphonies : Do They Travel?** If not, why not? Panel discussion: Byron Adams, Lewis Foreman, Charles McGuire & David Owen Norris; chairman Andrew Neill	136
12.	**Evening Concert**	152
	Contributor Biographies	158
	Notes and References	162
	Index	177

In memory of
Margaret Kay (1946–2003)

Acknowledgments

The success of the symposium, on the proceedings of which this book is based, was entirely due to the contributions of those who gave presentations. Owing to the sudden illness of Margaret Kay it was not possible for us to express our thanks at the time and we would like to record our appreciation to the contributors and for the high quality of their papers. We also remain grateful to the staff of the British Library for ensuring that the proceedings for the weekend ran smoothly and that the support systems functioned perfectly. In particular we wish to thank Chris Banks, Hugh Cobbe and Ken Shirreffs for their considerable help before, during and after the event.

As organisers of this event we were very grateful to John Norris for his help in many areas, not least in publishing, in short order, the programme for the weekend. John has also kindly agreed to edit this book which we hope will not only be of use to future students but also a reminder of a memorable weekend. Our thanks are also due to Ann Vernau for her editorial assistance in various ways in the preparation of this book for publication.

Foreword

Following the conclusion of this symposium we were asked by many who had attended when we would be arranging another one! It is clear, and this was emphasised during the symposium, that Elgar and Vaughan Williams remain eternally fascinating as subjects for study and discourse. We both felt, though, that we had perhaps exhausted the possibilities of running a seminar devoted exclusively to these two composers whose music, inspiration and lives had so little in common.

Few would disagree with Michael Kennedy's assertion that Britten, Elgar and Vaughan Williams were the recent giants of British music, with their creative lives spanning a period of eighty three years from Elgar's *Serenade for Strings* to Britten's *Phaedra*. All three composers were more than aware of their musical heritage and legacy. If it is accepted that these were the dominant composers in British music of the time, it remains a constant source of astonishment that we in Britain do not have a higher opinion of our place in 20th century music. What other country can boast three composers of such quality and variety working throughout most of the last century? Furthermore, if we accept David Owen Norris's contention, expressed in this symposium, that Elgar and Vaughan Williams (at least) are bigger than their music, then we were right in exploring some of the political and social issues, such as the Delhi Durbar of 1911, with which they were associated.

We were lucky in finding a series of sympathetic presenters who could draw the right connections between Elgar and Vaughan Williams whenever this was possible. Inevitably there was some repetition, but we believe this did not mar the nature of the presentations overall. The warmth of response at the end of the second day and in the post afterwards was confirmation that the content and arrangements were largely right.

Although a weekend like this cannot please everyone, there is no doubt that most attendees went away with something to treasure and we received few criticisms. Indeed there were some memorable moments, including the opportunity to meet with Lady Evelyn Barbirolli and Ursula Vaughan Williams when they joined us on the second day. Few will forget, either, David Owen Norris playing Vaughan Williams's little known transcription of J S Bach's Chorale *Ach blieb' bei uns, Herr Jesu Christ* and the concert that ended the Saturday when the dry acoustic of the British Library's lecture theatre did not spoil music making of the highest quality.[1]

Vaughan Williams once wrote: "The history of English music has been one continual struggle between the natural musical proclivities of the English people and the social and artistic conditions which have prevented these national tendencies from pursuing their natural course." [2] Elgar, too, instinctively realised the elements of what Vaughan Williams calls a 'struggle'. Nothing demonstrates more clearly the differences between Elgar and Vaughan Williams than the way in which they tackled the resolution of this dichotomy. However, we can be grateful that they both tried to find an answer and, in the process, left us with much great music.

This book publishes all the papers presented at the Symposium, with one exception. Those who know the work of David Owen Norris will not be surprised to learn that his fascinating lecture, *Elgar and Vaughan Williams: Their Musical Legacy* was as much a performance as a lecture.[3] We have come to the conclusion that it is not really possible to transcribe this and sustain the essence of the original. Consequently, we have not included it in this volume.

During the discussion, at the end, the symposium was sadly marred by the collapse and subsequent death of Margaret Kay. Her enthusiasm for the music of both Elgar and Vaughan Williams and her work at the Elgar Birthplace Museum and for The Elgar Society was an inspiration to many. We are happy to dedicate this publication to her memory.

Stephen Connock (Chairman, RVW Society)
Andrew Neill (Chairman, The Elgar Society)

July 2004

1 – Notes for this chapter appear on page 162.

Elgar and Vaughan Williams:
A 21st Century Celebration

Michael Kennedy

For most of us in this room, I suspect, Edward Elgar and Ralph Vaughan Williams are the two greatest English composers of the past 150 years. I put it like that because comparisons with Tallis, Byrd, Purcell and others of their epochs are misleading and in some ways impossible. Perhaps only Benjamin Britten challenges Vaughan Williams's place in the top two. League tables are objectionable, anyway, so let's just say that Britten is England's greatest opera composer and leave it at that.

Fifteen years separate the births of Elgar and Vaughan Williams, not quite enough to put them in different generations and, indeed, as far as their composing careers are concerned they are contemporaries from about 1897. We know that Elgar first dawned on Vaughan Williams's consciousness when he went to an early performance of the 'Enigma' Variations. I deduce that this was in October 1899 when Richter conducted it in London for the second time and therefore Vaughan Williams heard the first London performance of the revised ending. He had gone to the concert, it seems, to hear a work by Dohnányi but the Variations put it out of his mind. Considering how much interest the Variations had aroused among musicians as well as the general public at the first performance in June of that year, it is curious that a composer like VW went to St James's Hall *not* to hear the Elgar. Never mind, the music did its work, as it had done for Bernard Shaw who also heard 'Enigma' as it were by accident and sat up and said "Phew! We've got it at last". What impressed Vaughan Williams so much? We can guess it was the variation labelled 'R.P.A.', because he tells us in a 1932 essay 'The Evolution of the Folk Song' that this fifth variation appealed to him as something peculiarly English. He wrote: "The knowledge of our folk songs did not discover for us something new, but uncovered for us something which had been hidden by foreign matter." He goes on to say that the fifth variation gave him the same "sense of familiarity, the same sense of the something peculiarly belonging to me as an Englishman which I also felt when I first heard 'Bushes and Briars' or 'Lazarus'. In other works of Elgar I feel other influences not so germane to me and I cannot help believing that that is the reason why I love, say, the 'Be merciful' chorus from *Gerontius* more and the prelude to the same work less". This is understandable – 'Be merciful' would have suggested the influence of English church music to Vaughan Williams while the Prelude would have suggested *Parsifal* and Strauss's *Death and Transfiguration*. Let's hear the fifth variation conducted by Elgar and also the start of 'Be merciful' immediately afterwards.

Examples 1 & 2 [§]

Elgar of course would have, or perhaps I should say *might* have, repudiated the folk-song parallel since he took no or little interest in the folk-song revival and once said to his friend, the architect Troyte Griffith, "*I* am folk-song".

We may take it, from his discovery of 'Enigma', that Vaughan Williams had not heard Elgar's choral works of the 1890s, *The Black Knight, King Olaf, The Light of Life* and *Caractacus*. These were produced by Midlands and Northern choral societies or at the Three Choirs Festival between 1893 and 1898 while Vaughan Williams was at the Royal College of Music or at Trinity College, Cambridge. At both places he would have been under the influence of Stanford and therefore not likely to be exposed to Elgar. But the 'Enigma' Variations put him on the scent enough for him to go to Birmingham in October 1900 for the first performance of *The Dream of Gerontius* and it even led him to write to Elgar asking for lessons in orchestration. In his famous 1935 essay *What Have We Learnt From Elgar?*, Vaughan Williams answers his own question with the words "Of course, orchestration". And although Elgar would not give him lessons he could not stop him spending hours at the British Museum studying the full score of the Variations or *Gerontius*.

In that essay, Vaughan Williams gives specific examples of what he himself learned from Elgar and what he specially admired in Elgar. He makes the point that Elgar's choral technique developed from his orchestral technique and cited as example how he would add altos to tenors – I quote – to "reinforce the tone and enrich the colour just as he might add the violas to the cellos". He then gave this example from *Gerontius:*

Example 3

§ – See page 9 for a list of the musical examples accompanying this lecture.

He also gives examples of what he calls Elgar's "orchestral daring, the outcome of an absolutely sure touch". One of them – which he always liked to mention and which he spoke about to me at the time of Elgar's centenary in 1957 – was the muted horn's counter-melody at the beginning of the First Symphony. Vaughan Williams said he was sure that if a student had taken this passage to a teacher, the teacher would have crossed it out and told the student he did not know the elements of orchestral balance. Yet, VW says, "Elgar has so placed it that it comes through with entire clearness", as you can hear:–

Example 4

The other point he makes is orchestral scoring. Elgar's orchestration sounds so full, he says, that subtlety is the last thing we expect. He then gives an example which I will quote in full from the climax to 'Praise to the Holiest' in *Gerontius*. Here, says VW, "one would expect every instrument to blaze away and that orchestral subtlety was out of place and that Elgar would be content to let the instruments double the voices". But he then cites the outline of the trumpet and trombone parts in this passage. I quote:

> For the first four bars the third trombone and tuba double the bass voice, except for a thoughtful rest in the third trombone part. After a blaze for all the brass on the first bar, the first and second trombones are silent for two bars, the voices are too high to need the heavy tone of trombones. In the fourth bar the trumpets leave off because the sopranos are high and do not need their support and the trombones are added to give weight to the middle parts. On the last beat of bar four the brass is silent (except the fag-end of the tuba dotted minim) partly because the chorus is there momentarily less forcible and partly to give breath for another blaze in the sixth bar.

I don't know how much of that you can identify, but here is the passage concerned:

Example 5

This shows, incidentally, how closely Vaughan Williams studied the Elgar score. He later remarks that he had found as a conductor that you could dispense with extra instruments without damage to the texture. You could do this in Wagner, but in Elgar, even in the accompaniments to choral movements, there was hardly anything that could be left out without leaving a hole in the texture.

So what about the influence on Vaughan Williams's own music of the close study of Elgar scores? Cribbing, VW called it and found nothing reprehensible about it. Real cribbing he defined as "when one composer thinks with the mind of another even when there is no mechanical similarity of phrase... One is so impressed by a certain passage in another composer that it becomes part of oneself". He confessed that the Elgar phrase which influenced him most was Gerontius's 'Thou art calling me'. Let's hear it:–

Example 6

But he said it was not so much the phrase as originally sung there, but when it occurs later in combination with another theme, like this:–

Example 7

Vaughan Williams then provides proof of this cribbing or, as it might be more polite to put it, absorption. The first example he gives is from *A Sea Symphony*.

Example 8

and from *A London Symphony*:

Example 9

Here is another example which he does not mention, but I will. It comes from the *Five Mystical Songs*, the song called 'Easter':–

Example 10

And I would suggest that, while not straightforward cribbing, there is a deliberate tribute to Elgar in another of VW's works written after Elgar's death when VW conducted what everyone said was a memorable performance of *Gerontius*, so that work must have been much in his mind. I mean the *Five Tudor Portraits*. There is an Elgarian connection here anyway, because it was Elgar who suggested to Vaughan Williams that he should set Skelton's poems. "Make an opera out of Elinor Rumming", he said. Sadly Elgar did not live to hear the result of his prompting, not an opera but a vivid and vivacious choral movement. However, the single greatest movement of the *Tudor Portraits* is the fourth, the lament of Jane Scroop over the death of her pet sparrow killed by a cat. Without any hint of parody, Vaughan Williams builds a most touching requiem on this charming poem. And his model for it was, in my opinion, the Angel's Farewell from *Gerontius*, also a setting for mezzo-soprano, choir and orchestra. Here is part of the Elgar:–

Example 11

and now part of Jane Scroop:–

Example 12

All that is sufficient, I think, to show how much Vaughan Williams admired Elgar. He had certain reservations. He did not subscribe to the view of *Falstaff* as Elgar's greatest orchestral work, feeling that the music was being judged by literary standards. And he certainly felt that *The Apostles* and *The Kingdom* were patchy, even saying to me once that someone ought to make a selection from the two as one work, a suggestion that I am sure will be regarded as outrageous and was perhaps made half in jest to tease me. But only half!

Elgar's attitude to Vaughan Williams, indeed to most other composers who were his contemporaries or near-contemporaries, was much more complex. There is no reference to the younger man in Elgar's letters or in Alice Elgar's diary in the years before 1914 when Vaughan Williams began to make his mark. The *Tallis Fantasia* had its first performance in 1910 in a Three Choirs Festival concert at Gloucester when it immediately preceded a performance of *Gerontius*. Each composer conducted his own work so presumably they must have met in the conductors' room on that occasion. We don't know, though we do know that Vaughan Williams sat next to Lady Elgar at a Three Choirs performance of the Second Symphony, presumably in 1911. That was at Worcester, when Kreisler played the Elgar Violin Concerto and Vaughan Williams conducted the first performance of the *Mystical Songs*, but again there is no documentary evidence of either a meeting or of an opinion. We know that Elgar did not go to the Leeds Festival in 1910 when *A Sea Symphony* had its triumphant first performance. He had said in a letter to Alice Stuart Wortley that he was not attending because he had not been asked. "My popularity shows, in dismal relief, the popularity of someone else! They propose to ruin the Variations, to travesty the accompaniments to *Sea Pictures* and conventionalise *Go Song of Mine*. The festival has gone steadily down in interest and is now a dull affair of only Kapellmeister interest." Heaven knows what he was talking about! The reason for this rather sour attitude was, of course, the "someone else". The chief conductor of the Leeds Festival was Stanford. He and Elgar had not spoken to each other since Elgar's appointment as professor at Birmingham in 1905 and his somewhat disparaging remarks about British composers in his inaugural lecture there. But there had been coolness before that, even though Stanford had been the leading advocate for Elgar being made an honorary Doctor of Music at Cambridge in 1900 and had also seconded him for membership of The Athenaeum. Elgar no doubt knew of Stanford's alleged comment after hearing *Gerontius*: "It stinks of incense." In any case, Elgar was almost paranoid about academic musicians, although always making an exception for Parry. Elgar knew that Vaughan Williams was a pupil of Stanford and that was enough to damn him and to make him an object of suspicion. He cannot have known that Stanford and Vaughan Williams often quarrelled and that Stanford was a highly critical teacher. Nor can he have known that Vaughan Williams was not a man to join cliques.

VW was further damned in Elgar's eyes because he was a Cambridge man and Elgar knew that Cambridge was the epicentre of anti-Elgarian prejudice, Stanford's animosity being carried on by E J Dent, another known friend of Vaughan Williams, and by C B Rootham, the unfortunate minor composer whose setting of *For the Fallen* was eclipsed by Elgar's. Percy Young has recounted somewhere that you could practically be sent down or at any rate ostracised for expressing admiration of Elgar in inter-wars Cambridge. Rootham gave a lecture in Cambridge on the morning that Elgar's death was reported in the papers. He began by saying: "Well, gentlemen, I see that a would-be English country gentleman has died." I'm glad to say that the whole class then got up and left, so perhaps there were more closet Elgarians than Cambridge suspected. At any rate, Vaughan Williams was never associated with that sort of thing and in about the mid-1920s Elgar came to realise it. Before that, though, at the first Three Choirs performance of the Cello Concerto at Hereford in 1921, he had gone up to VW and said: "I'm surprised, Dr Vaughan Williams, that you should come to hear vulgar music like this."

This perhaps is the point at which to say something about the different and contrasted backgrounds of Elgar and Vaughan Williams. Elgar was born into a lower middle-class home, not poor but certainly not affluent. He was one of a large family and he was brought up as a Roman Catholic, although his father was not Catholic. His father kept a music shop and that made him a tradesman, socially demeaning in Victorian times. He left school at 15 and had no musical training beyond a few violin and piano lessons. The rest he found out by himself, by reading and performing and listening. He never lost a feeling of social inferiority and that he was a victim of the class system even though he married an Indian Army General's daughter, was taken up by titled and fashionable women, often dined with the King, was knighted at the age of 47 and appointed OM at 54. He was and remained ultra-suspicious and contemptuous of academic and university musicians and made taking offence into an art form! He sought out honours – he was still angling for a peerage when he died – and he more or less proposed himself as Master of the King's Musick.

Vaughan Williams, on the other hand, was a descendant of Darwins and Wedgwoods. He was always quite well off, not extravagantly but comfortably. He went to public school, to the Royal College of Music and to Trinity College, Cambridge. From 1899, when he was 27 and took his degree, he was always called Dr Vaughan Williams. His teachers were Parry, Stanford and other university musicians. Politically leaning towards socialism and liberalism, he had no desire for honours, accepting only the OM. He refused a knighthood, probably more than once, and also the post of Master of the King's Musick. He taught at the Royal College of Music, but otherwise was a free-lance composer most of his life and so, despite his relative lack of money, was Elgar, whose only job, until about 1900, was teaching the violin to schoolgirls.

There is enough in that brief comparison to show why Elgar would make such an ungracious remark to Vaughan Williams as "I'm surprised you come to hear such vulgar music". The thaw seems to have begun with Vaughan Williams's *Sancta Civitas*, first performed in 1926, two years after Stanford's death. After hearing it, Elgar said to him that he was glad he hadn't written his third oratorio, *The Last Judgment*, because Vaughan Williams had done it for him in *Sancta Civitas*. There are indeed distant echoes of *The Apostles* – I do *not* suggest these were deliberate; I'm sure they weren't – in the Alleluias of *Sancta Civitas*. They must have struck a chord with Elgar:

Example 13

So for the last ten years or so of Elgar's life those two great men seem to have had a friendly relationship. They saw each other each year at the Three Choirs Festivals and we may assume Elgar came to know some of Vaughan Williams's music. One of my most precious possessions is the postcard of Christmas greetings Elgar sent to VW in December 1933. He was too ill to write it himself. It is in Elgar's daughter Carice's handwriting but Elgar has signed it and it begins "My dear Ralph" – this at a time when men of their generation would still address their friends by their surnames *tout court*.

There was another personal and rather piquant link at that time, too. Elgar's last feminine muse, the violinist Vera Hockman, was also a friend of Vaughan Williams. As Kevin Allen's book recounts, Vera played in the orchestra at what became a memorial performance of *Gerontius* that Vaughan Williams conducted at Dorking in April 1934. He had written to Elgar about the proposed performance, as part of the Leith Hill Festival, just before Elgar's death. He had not conducted it before and he said that "it will be one of the great moments of my life when I stand with trembling baton to conduct it". Vera liked Vaughan Williams's article *What Have We Learnt From Elgar?* and wrote to tell him so. He replied to "Dearest Vera" that her letter was "the only one he had received which said anything nice about it".

So, what do we learn about Elgar and Vaughan Williams as the twin giants of English music in the first quarter of the 20th century? First that paradoxically they had little in common yet had a lot in common. They could be compared, almost, with Mahler and Strauss. Mahler said that he and Strauss were both tunnelling from opposite sides of the same mountain and would one day meet in the middle, but they never did. Elgar had no interest in folk-song and not much, as far as we know, in the early English composers such as Byrd and Tallis. He belongs to the European tradition, Wagner, Brahms, Strauss, and a little to the French composers Bizet, Saint-Saëns and Massenet, although Vaughan Williams thought the germs of the Elgarian idiom could be found in the, to quote him, "small but rather charming music" of organists such as Henry Smart and John Goss. I have never investigated the validity of that claim. Vaughan Williams, on the other hand, drew inspiration from folk-song and from Tallis, Byrd and Weelkes but also from Ravel and Debussy. Both are considered quintessentially English, yet the puzzle of what constituted English music becomes even more enigmatic when we think that Elgar's Violin Concerto, one of his most 'English' works, owes much to Bruch, Brahms and Saint-Saëns and that Vaughan Williams's *Pastoral Symphony* owes equally much to Ravel. Vaughan Williams identified Elgar's "peculiar kind of beauty" as giving us, his fellow-countrymen, "a sense of something familiar – the intimate and personal beauty of our own fields and lanes".

He also remarked that such Elgar compositions as 'Nimrod', 'W.N.' or the 'Angel's Farewell' have become so much a part of our national consciousness that we cease to criticise them. "It falls to the lot of very few composers, and to them not often, to achieve this bond of unity with their contemporaries. Elgar has achieved this more than most and, be it noted, not when he is being deliberately popular, as in *Land of Hope and Glory* or *Cockaigne*, but at those moments when he seems to have retired into the solitude of his own sanctuary." Vaughan Williams did not strike that deliberately popular note with anything comparable to *Land of Hope*. It is through his hymn-tunes and the *Greensleeves Fantasia* that he has achieved that particular slot, as we would say today, in the hearts of his fellow-countrymen and perhaps even more in the *Tallis Fantasia*, where he links hands across the centuries with one of the founts of his own inspiration. But there is one other work where he stands shoulder to shoulder with Elgar in discerning that all the apparent certainties of the world before 1914 were about to be shaken to their foundations. At the start of the *finale* of *A London Symphony*, Vaughan Williams sounds an Elgarian note of foreboding. In these pages more than any others, the orchestration he had learned by studying the scores of the *Variations* and *Gerontius* reveals him not as would-be pupil of the master but as the master's equal in expressing something personal and something national – and something eternal.

Example 14

List of Musical Examples Played

1. Elgar: 'Enigma' Variations – R.P.A.
2. Elgar: *The Dream of Gerontius* – 'Be merciful'
3. Elgar: *The Dream of Gerontius* (excerpt)
4. Elgar: Symphony no.1 – beginning of first movement
5. Elgar: *The Dream of Gerontius* – excerpt from Part 2
6. Elgar: *The Dream of Gerontius* – 'Thou art calling me'
7. Elgar: *The Dream of Gerontius* (excerpt)
8. Vaughan Williams: *A Sea Symphony* (excerpt)
9. Vaughan Williams: *A London Symphony* (excerpt)
10. Vaughan Williams: *Five Mystical Songs* – Easter
11. Elgar: *The Dream of Gerontius* – 'Angel's Farewell'
12. Vaughan Williams: *Five Tudor Portraits* – 'Jane Scroop'
13. Vaughan Williams: *Sancta Civitas* (excerpt)
14. Vaughan Williams: *A London Symphony* –
    excerpt from the final movement

"It looks all wrong, but it sounds all right"
The social background to the life and music of Elgar and Vaughan Williams

Andrew Neill

I cannot remember the first time I heard the opening of Vaughan Williams's *Tallis Fantasia* with that G major chord spread seductively across five octaves, but it has become part of me for over forty or more years. I am listening to something that is simultaneously contemporary and also very old. It is far more than a tribute to the music of Thomas Tallis or English music of the 16th century; it is rooted in my soul and the soil of my country. It is both timeless and timely and tells of vast cathedrals, ancient people and a time when our lives were governed by the seasons, the harvest and the quest for survival. If this sounds whimsical I hope these preparatory comments will become clear during the course of this session.

It is arguable that Elgar and Vaughan Williams had little in common, but the nature of their artistic contribution to the music of this country means that this assertion is not that simply made. On the other hand their differences can become blurred, as they did for me when living far away. I can vividly recall, shortly after I went to live in Sydney in 1986, listening to Vaughan Williams's Fifth Symphony. As that rapturous ending filled the concert hall of the Opera House I had a vision of home. The tears poured, uncontrollably, down my cheeks for, as Ivor Gurney put it: "Only the wanderer knows England's graces." It is easy to become sentimental the farther and longer one is away and, at the risk of being labelled insular, my consideration today will begin by looking at the legacy Elgar and Vaughan Williams inherited as English artists.

Nowadays we are more aware of our past, particularly that part long obscured, than any previous generation. In recent years, much work has enabled us to understand England in the Dark Ages and the time before the Roman invasion. If at times our vision is faint, this is sufficient to allow us to trace some links with our ancient culture and how this developed over time to influence us today. We now understand pre-Roman England to have been more sophisticated, more populous and more in contact with its European neighbours than was previously appreciated. We now know more than ever about the time between the end of Roman England and the Norman invasion. We can understand the importance of the cultural activity centred on the North East of England, and its influence on the Continent, and we can mourn the passing of Anglo-Saxon England, just as we can shed a tear for Caractacus as he is sent to Rome in chains. To me this is important as we consider the intuitive appreciation both composers had for their past; historically and musically.

As a nation we can be inclined towards a cultural inferiority. We can become over-awed by the musical heritage of Austro-Germany, the Italian Renaissance, the art of the Low Countries and the self-confidence of France in its self-belief. Even when we confront the riches of a master we honour him, as in the case of Turner, by awarding an annual prize to those who seem to have no idea of his legacy. If they have awareness then they hardly honour him, even if they satisfy the artistic establishment as to their credentials. Artists can surprise and mystify as well as turn our conceptions on their head, but to shock for the sake of it invites an artist to be condemned to either a short artistic life or to a very narrow band of support. Vaughan Williams, in his Indian summer, provided a role model, as should all great artists. We find him exploring new ways of expressing himself in the opening to his last symphony, the flugelhorn and saxophones adding colour to his music in a way never previously tried. This is a great artist challenging us to think again and look at the world with a fresh eye.

Nevertheless, it seems to me that as a nation we have confidence in only one world-class artist, one which even our European peers acknowledge; but Shakespeare cannot carry the culture of a whole country on his back! Those opening bars of the *Tallis Fantasia* are not just an example of masterly construction, for the piece shows how the hand of one generation can reach across centuries to a heritage which is respected, understood and loved. Within recorded memory the serious shocks (what I think are now known as 'seismic') which have buffeted the population of these islands can almost be counted on the fingers of one hand. This is not an exhaustive list, but I would suggest these were the Roman invasion and occupation from AD 43, the Norse raids of the Dark Ages, the Norman invasion, the Black Death of the 14th century, the break with Rome, the Civil War 100 hundred years later and the massive loss of life of the Great War. Compared to much of the rest of Europe this was a relatively stately traverse across 2000 years. Time allowed invaders to mingle and breed, even if it took about 300 years in the case of the Normans to absorb or be absorbed. At the expense of the existing culture we know this allowed the development of the English language and the emergence of an artistic tradition that became recognisably English.

Both Elgar and Vaughan Williams recognised their debt to this tradition. Nowhere is this more obvious than in Vaughan Williams's work in collecting folk-song and the way this permeated much of his music for the remainder of his life. We probably all agree that Elgar's musical heritage lies elsewhere, but I am not so sure this is as clear cut as we tend to believe. Although he joined the Folk Song Society when it was inaugurated in 1898, it seems that this heritage did not really interest him. "I write the folk songs of this country," he said. Clearly Elgar did not; but as Michael Kennedy has already pointed out, sufficient of his music had already become "part of the national consciousness" to see what Elgar might have meant.

Elgar understands the English pastoral in such music as the interludes from *Falstaff*, the 'river' music in the A flat Symphony and much of *Caractacus*, where his historical awareness is acute too. To me, he intuitively understood the destruction of a way of life that came with the Romans. Although the ending of *Caractacus* might be anomalous, much of the rest of the work seems to be a cry of love, by Caractacus, for his country: its subtle light, greenness, tolerance and essential peace. It was, and is, something worth preserving, as I think Elgar shows in his setting of his eponymous hero's opening aria in Scene 1:

> The air is sweet, the sky is calm,
> All nature round is breathing balm,
> The echo of our warfare falls
> Faint, — distant, — on these grassy walls,
> O spirits of the hill, surround
> With waving wings this holy ground,
> And from your airy censers show'r
> Strength to me in this lonely hour.

Perhaps there is something of the second Act of *Tristan* there, and if so it begs the question as to what is Englishness in music. In 1958 Vaughan Williams wrote, referring to Elgar and Parry: "the same circumstances which produced our beautiful English folk-songs also produced their music, founded as it should be on our own history, our own incomparable landscape, even perhaps our undependable weather and our abominable food." [1] I feel I know what Vaughan Williams meant, and Elgar was in despair when the weather was bad; but we readily disparage what has been a fundamental ingredient in shaping the people of these islands and the 20 million or so who became that diaspora which formed other nations around the world.

1 – Notes for this chapter appear on pages 162–3.

In recognising the intuitive, if different, 'Englishness' of Elgar and Vaughan Williams we can overlook Hubert Parry's desire to establish a national school of music in England. In his biography of Parry, Jeremy Dibble suggests: "His development of such a language had the effect of establishing and consolidating diatonicism as a quintessential element of a future national style." [2] Dibble goes on to say: "A detailed study of Elgar's earlier cantatas and the 'Enigma' Variations (particularly Nimrod and the Finale) shows that, besides the various continental influences of Wagner, Massenet, and Delibes, diatonicism and its techniques are central to his language." [3]

I am not really sure it is possible to describe English art or culture and most particularly English music as opposed to German or French music without becoming diverted by a subject which will distract us far beyond the restrictions of this symposium. I do not intend to go much further into the subject for it is easy, if not dangerous, to generalise. Three pieces perhaps demonstrate this point. Does William Byrd's *Come pretty babe* sound English when performed, for example, by Montserrat Figueras who is certainly not from these shores? Secondly, the slow movement from Stanford's Second Symphony shows how long the shadow of German music could be. Lastly, the wedding procession of Fenton and Nannetta from the third act in Verdi's *Falstaff* gives us a foreigner's view of English rusticity. Now Byrd was an English recusant and we know Stanford, who was Irish, settled and composed in England. Verdi, elsewhere in *Falstaff*, gets close to one aspect of Englishness very successfully: its bawdiness through innuendo and suggestion. Despite Falstaff's interest in seduction, this becomes incidental to the drama, the pastoral atmosphere of which comes through at the end. It is funny, unkind and irreverent but never erotic. In itself perhaps this is, after all, rather English!

Michael Kennedy has already mentioned the meeting between Elgar and Vaughan Williams after the first performance of *Sancta Civitas*. Perhaps Elgar recognised the visionary in Vaughan Williams at this moment, like the flame he lit in *The Dream of Gerontius* 27 years before. However, it is difficult to believe that Elgar could have rekindled in 1926 that magical other-worldliness that was a touchstone of his masterpiece. The importance of Vaughan Williams's report of the meeting lies in the meeting itself not in what we might have missed. But the hope for something eternal repeated at the end of *Santa Civitas*: "I am the bright and the morning star. Surely I come quickly" echoes the sentiment at the end of *The Dream of Gerontius*, 'Swiftly shall pass thy night of trial here,

And I will come and wake thee on the morrow'. However, to make such a link will not make us all content. In her book, *Paradise Remembered*, Ursula Vaughan Williams writes of the 1956 Three Choirs Festival, "There was the usual *Gerontius*, to which Ralph went; by now my Elgar allergy was common knowledge to my friends, so I was exempt ..." [4]

Despite the fact that virtually all the great Elgar conductors were and are equally at home with the music of Vaughan Williams, Ursula Vaughan Williams exposes the different musical voices with which Elgar and Ralph Vaughan Williams speak. Furthermore we confront a paradox: Elgar the outsider who became a conservative insider with a lasting sense of inferiority contrasted with the socially confident insider who became an independent, liberal-minded discoverer and promoter of England's musical heritage. Vaughan Williams was big enough morally and a great enough musician to recognise Elgar's achievement and originality in a work such as the A Flat Symphony. In 1957, in his centenary tribute to Elgar Vaughan Williams said: "In the introduction to Elgar's First Symphony the melody is given to fairly heavy woodwind and violas; the violoncellos and double basses play the bass détaché while the harmony is left to two soft muted horns. When I think of a student *bringing* the score to any composition teacher he would have put his blue pencil through it and would have said that this could not be heard. And to my mind when I look at it still, it looks all wrong but it sounds all right. There indeed we have a mystery and a miracle." [5]

Here is a symphony with a motto theme, which is developed by its creator in ways almost without precedence, with scoring of great virtuosity on the one hand and extreme delicacy on the other. It is, of course, more than that as Neville Cardus acknowledged in 1970, as he looked back 62 years to the first performance. "The great thing about the A flat Symphony, when we who were young first heard it, was that it liberated English music at the turn of the century from parochialism, from a 'folky' nationalism." [6] Although contradicting any implication that Elgar was a member of any national school, "liberated" is the key word here. For without Elgar's symphonies our confidence in our music would be diminished. But, all the same, even though his face sits uncomfortably on our £20 note and his music is now commonly played in this country, it is Elgar who is more the outsider of the two composers. It is his journey to acceptance and respectability which is in such contrast to that of Vaughan Williams that makes the combining of these twin tales of such interest.

Sir Adrian Boult, in a posthumous tribute to Vaughan Williams in 1958, said: "Great men are often thought to be distant and aloof. Some may be; but I can assure you that Ralph Vaughan Williams was one of the most approachable in the world. His home in Regent's Park was the centre of the greatest activity: meetings, rehearsals, gatherings to sing, gatherings to talk were constantly being organised by his charming wife; and all were welcome there. The day before he died he saw and gave advice to a young composer. A week earlier he spent an hour with me reading through the score of his Ninth Symphony and playing me a recording to help me to get to know the work. He never spared himself, even though he must often have hated encroachments on his time by others when he would prefer to be quiet and compose. He looked every inch a great man, and it was wonderful to see a packed audience in the RFH rise to its feet on seeing him come in. Somehow everyone felt that here was a man who was doing for British greatness just what Shakespeare or Milton had done in their days." [7]

Now some of this might equally apply to Elgar. However, in suggesting that I am in danger of making a generalisation which, when we are considering two great men, is all too easy. To make any valid comparisons we need to make distinctions. Elgar, to Roy Henderson, was always *Sir Edward*, whilst Vaughan Williams was *Uncle Ralph*.[8] Some time ago a commentator (it may have been Hans Keller) remarked on how differently one should approach Haydn and Mozart when putting their music into context. With Mozart it is necessary to know his health at the time, his state of mind and his pecuniary circumstances and whether he was in favour at Court or with the Archbishop of Salzburg. With Haydn we barely need to comment; Haydn was always ... well just Haydn. Perhaps there is something in making a comparison today by substituting, in our minds, the neurotic conservative Edward Elgar for Mozart and the liberal flexible Ralph Vaughan Williams for Haydn as we look at their development from youth to that moment when they made their respective marks on the mind of the public.

There is a photograph from 1937 which demonstrates the social gap which separated Elgar and Vaughan Williams. It was taken outside Lord's cricket ground on the day of the Eton-Harrow match. Two boys on the left, in their top hats, are from Vaughan Williams' circle and the boys from the town are on the right in their grey flannel shorts gazing in a mixture of awe and amusement at these figures from a privileged other world.

Asa Briggs suggests that the Victorian era can be divided into three rough phases. The first, between the Queen's accession in 1837 and The Great Exhibition of 1851, covered a period of social instability which included the working-class Chartists and the anti-corn-law leaguers. A more balanced period followed, "punctuated by the Crimean War", covering the boom years of stability and growth in the 1860s. Britain was then "the richest country in the world with a per capita income 50 per cent higher than that of France and almost three times that of Germany in 1860".[9] In 1859 Darwin published his *The Origin of Species* and John Stuart Mill his *Essay on Liberty*, two works which questioned religious and social fundamentals. The final period from the 1870s until the end of the century covers the collapse of the Victorian boom, the rise of organised political parties, the extension of the franchise and the constant issue of Irish Home Rule.

If we accept Briggs's rough definitions we can see that, although Elgar was only separated from Vaughan Williams by 15 years, he grew up in a different time. In 1857 Lord Palmerston, perhaps the last of the Whigs, was Prime Minister but by 1872 Gladstone, the new Liberal, was in command of his first administration and, although not yet permanently, control of government was passing, inexorably, to the House of Commons. Elected in 1868, Gladstone's first administration has been described as the most competent government of the century, despite the background of increasing social unrest, the Franco-Prussian war and Irish issues.[10]

Elgar may well have been fortunate to be born in Worcestershire. The county, despite the presence of aristocratic families such as the Beauchamps and dowager Queen Adelaide at Witley Court, was not dominated by large landowners; it was a county of yeoman farmers and people who could make a living from independent work in the city of Worcester. The environment enabled people like Elgar's father, William, to run a business and bring up a family with some success. A talented child could find his feet and eventually climb the social ladder and achieve the greatest honours, through hard work combined with natural genius.

In contrast Vaughan Williams was brought up in a class which did not require him to work and, as Ursula Vaughan Williams points out in her biography, he was rarely short of money.[11] Let me remind you of Vaughan Williams's ancestry. One great-great-grandfather was Josiah Wedgwood, founder of the renowned pottery, and another Erasmus Darwin, author of *The Botanic Garden*. Furthermore, his great uncle was Charles Darwin. These were the ancestors of the Wedgwoods, his mother's family, who lived at their Surrey home, the substantial Leith Hill Place with its four-acre kitchen garden. Sir Edward and Lady Vaughan Williams's family lived nearby at Tanhurst. Arthur Vaughan Williams, their third son, married the second Wedgwood daughter, Margaret in 1868. They soon moved to Down Ampney in Gloucestershire where he had accepted the post of vicar. Ralph, their third child, was born on 12 October 1872, but his life at the home of his birth was little longer than that of Elgar at Broadheath for, on the death of his father in February 1875, he was taken back to Surrey and Leith Hill Place where he would be brought up by his mother and her family assisted by twelve servants.

Both composers owed much to their mothers. Ralph remembered his mother's common sense when he asked about *The Origin of Species*; she replied "The Bible says God made the world in six days. Great Uncle Charles thinks it took a little longer: but we need not worry about it, for it is equally wonderful either way".[12] Ralph was therefore secure in a comfortable environment not wanting in much except for the presence of a father. It can hardly be said that the Elgar family wanted for the essentials of life either – even families of their standing employed two servants – but the reality of Victorian life also touched young Edward with the death of his brothers Henry and Joseph. Despite the similarities I mentioned earlier and the loving homes in which both composers were raised, the social and economic gap was enormous. At 15 years old Edward, by then the eldest son, had to earn a living whilst Ralph would benefit from a fine education: at Field House and Charterhouse Schools, the Royal College of Music and Cambridge University.

Charterhouse had moved to Godalming during 1872, the year in which Ralph was born. As he was to write in 1957: "You know I learned quite a lot of music at Charterhouse, though it was supposed to be the Philistine period of Public School life, and I and a ... friend once actually gave a concert of our own compositions...." Young Ralph's piece was a Piano Trio in G major and he recalled being congratulated by the Charterhouse mathematics master: "'Very good Williams, you must go on'. This was one of the few words of encouragement I have ever received."[13] We should not underestimate the quality of Elgar's education, nor his ability to absorb, interpret and develop information, but it is in the academic training young Ralph received that we find the greatest contrast of all with the older Edward. We need, I feel, to explore this further.

Elgar was clearly an exceptional child, for it was the sound of the orchestra which caught his imagination. Like Richard Strauss, who was brought up close to an orchestra, he felt how music should sound, instinctively. His maturity in music making came at the end of a long apprenticeship, and my brief today is to look at some of the roots of this achievement. Hunger is a spur to many things including work and to creativity in an artist. Elgar was no exception to this general rule and his years of earning a living through teaching the violin to reluctant girls in Malvern was but one of the crosses he had to bear before breaking free with The 'Enigma' Variations and *The Dream of Gerontius*.

Being self-taught, Elgar developed his sound from what he heard. This was from German and French sources which, with the visit of Dvořák to Worcester in 1884, added to his own instinctive understanding of how to use the instruments available to him. His 'university' was his musical friends, his work at Powick Asylum and the Three Choirs Festival orchestra all combined with an astonishing ear. From this mix emerged an individual voice and a talent which was to use the German orchestra with consummate skill in his self-confident world of sound. Thus he was able to create a form of Englishness which has a validity of its own.

Looking at the picture of the retired colonel, the image of conformity, it is almost impossible to appreciate how important this escape from academia was for Elgar. As an artist he needed to develop on his own and on his own terms. His insecurity manifested itself on a number of occasions, such as his rejection of an invitation to a formal luncheon in Malvern to celebrate Queen Victoria's Diamond Jubilee in 1897. This note was sent by Elgar to the organisers 1½ hours prior to the start of the festivities. "I am sure you would not wish your board to be disgraced by the presence of a piano tuner's son and his wife." [14] Now that *is* extraordinary; written by a man who had already established a local reputation with a wife from the top of the social order. The use of the word "disgraced" is a sign of deep insecurity, it is almost self-loathing! This is a side of Elgar's character we find almost impossible to understand. It is the man who was to forbid his wife to attend the Coronation of King George V and the man who wrote, shortly after her death, that "no single person was ever kind to me".

However, in that same letter to Sir Sidney Colvin, Elgar had also written "I am still at heart the dreamy child who used to be found in the reeds by Severn side with a sheet of paper trying to fix the sounds and longing for something very great".[15] Of course it is important to balance the impression of an insecure introvert with our appreciation of the gay "japester", the loyal friend, cartoonist extraordinary and generous supporter of fellow musicians. Does all this matter? For, after all, without Elgar's music we would not be sitting here today. I am sure it does, for we need to balance the character as Elgar was not just a writer of tunes: he became, for a short while, the dominant musician in the country, and therefore an artist of supreme importance.

As we know, Elgar developed slowly, but he put down his musical roots early. His 'tune from Broadheath' dates from 1867 but this simple motiv influenced his music for the rest of his life, and the emergence and maturing of Elgar's genius is something of a "mystery and a miracle". I am increasingly of the opinion that we might make a similar claim on Vaughan Williams's behalf, even as we look at his academic background. By this I mean the process by which he developed a voice as original as Elgar and a sound world that is entirely his own. His early academic life was dominated initially by two academics, one an Anglo-Irishman steeped in the music of Brahms and Schumann. Michael Pope will be reviewing the legacy of Stanford, but as far as his importance in the life of Vaughan Williams is concerned we have to acknowledge Stanford's role as a teacher, even if at times an uncomprehending one, and his influence as a composer of songs and church music. Parry, with whom Vaughan Williams began studying at the age of 17, became something of a father figure, widening his musical horizons not only to the disparate worlds of Brahms and Wagner, but by creating a sense of destiny as Vaughan Williams recalled: "We pupils of Parry have, if we have been wise, inherited from him the great English choral tradition, which Tallis passed on to Byrd, Byrd to Gibbons, Gibbons to Purcell, Purcell to Battishill and Greene, and they in their turn, through the Wesleys to Parry." [16]

And then there was another Cambridge man, Charles Wood, an Ulster Protestant who was only six years older than Vaughan Williams. His legacy today is mainly remembered in his contribution to church music, and in smaller choral works and song. He was, in his pupil's words, "the finest technical instructor I have ever known". At the time he was organist and scholar of Gonville and Caius College. This must have been an exceptionally rich time for Vaughan Williams as he befriended, amongst others, G E Moore, G M Trevelyan and Hugh Allen.

So we find that two of Vaughan Williams's largest musical influences were Parry and Stanford, both of whose musical roots lay in Germany. What is more he studied with Max Bruch in Berlin in 1897 and earlier, in 1892 he had been "deeply shaken" when he heard the first London performance of *Tristan and Isolde* conducted by Gustav Mahler. It would seem that Vaughan Williams was exposed as much if not more in his youth to the great influences of German music as Elgar. Because he studied within its world we should celebrate his natural musical integrity which allowed the development of his own musical voice. This integrity further manifests itself in the decision to study with Ravel in 1907, even after he had made his musical mark with works like *Toward the Unknown Region*. Ravel offered an alternative vision to 'teutonic contrapuntalism' by showing Vaughan Williams how to colour his orchestration. If his work with Ravel helped Vaughan Williams to produce *On Wenlock Edge* then we are all beneficiaries, but Ravel did say that Vaughan Williams was the only pupil who "did not write my music".

It is difficult to imagine Elgar establishing a similar relationship with Ravel or anyone else for that matter! In a recent lecture, Professor David Cannadine made the point that, in his view, Elgar was a typical product of the artisan class, fearing the working class once he had left their proximity.[17] He was fortunate in growing up in a city renowned for its loyalty to the Crown, and its inherent conservatism would have helped foster these characteristics in Elgar. Michael Kennedy has alluded to Elgar's sensitivity if anyone (including the likes of Sir Adrian Boult) dared to meddle with his scores. How different was the attitude of Vaughan Williams, who would do virtually anything to assist the performance of one of his works adapting, if necessary, to local needs. I realise that today I may have over-emphasised the dark side of Elgar's character, but the struggle for recognition left a deep scar and cannot be ignored, as in the recollection of the explanation Elgar gave to Boult, who had suggested conducting *Gerontius* with reduced woodwind, as an economy. "… it was the discovery that no one in that very wealthy city (Birmingham) – which always pretended to be proud of the production of *Gerontius* – cared a straw whether the work was presented as I wrote it or not …" [18]

Vaughan Williams's long experience manifests itself in something rather simple, yet profound, as the camera pans across the Canadian landscape at the beginning of the 1941 film *The 49th Parallel*. Here Vaughan Williams responded enthusiastically to the discipline of composing for a film in a long-limbed Elgarian melody. However, what makes this one of the most compelling of all film themes is that it seems to carry the weight of Vaughan Williams's memories of what he had seen and experienced when serving in the previous conflict; he just seems to 'tell it how it was'.

Without a broad and tolerant understanding of the roots of our culture we hardly create the environment whereby "your young men shall see visions, and your old men shall dream dreams". Both Elgar and Vaughan Williams saw visions and in their old age dreamt their dreams, the younger composer never stopping his work. Neville Cardus, in that article from 1970, asked a question: "But why is not Elgar taken as much to heart in Germany and Austria as we, in Britain, take Bruckner to heart? Each has symphonic characteristics in common. Technically, and as a symphonic thinker, Elgar is the more interesting composer over a long stretch, of the two. If it (the A flat Symphony) was good enough for Richter, it should be good enough for Karajan." [19] With nine symphonies to excite the modern conductor, much of Cardus's comment could now be brought up to date and applied to Vaughan Williams. Sadly it would seem that there are few beyond these shores who can be bothered to master the language and style (in all its variety) that Vaughan Williams lays before his interpreter. The need to redress this attitude must be one of the reasons why societies such as ours are formed. This extraordinary neglect (or is it disregard) is something we should bear in mind as we consider the legacy of two great creative artists.

Both Elgar and Vaughan Williams were, for a large part, Edwardians in attitude and temperament. They retained the courtesies of the age and flourished at a time when the hurly-burly had barely been invented. They lived in a world of graciousness and at a pace dictated by manners and the requirements of a lady to change her dress three or four times a day. This world was Parry's too, and Elgar being the new recruit (so to speak) was generous in his praise of Parry as a man and in particular of one work. He declared *Blest Pair of Sirens* to be one of the "noblest works of man" and Vaughan Williams's admiration extended to it being his "favourite piece of music written by an Englishman". Would both composers be surprised at Parry's neglect these days or would they secretly understand the fickleness of taste and keep their secret to themselves? Jeremy Dibble has referred to the "tight, organically driven musical structure, rich diatonic language of dissonance and multiple appoggiaturas, counterpoint redolent of Bach not to mention a heightened sense of choral pragmatism and accessibility, symbolised an English aesthetic".[20] Modern society is not much interested in aesthetics whether they are English or anyone else's!

In 1910 *A Sea Symphony* burst upon our shores. Yes, you can hear its debt to Elgar and Parry, but you can also feel something of what Elgar owed to his senior as Vaughan Williams distilled this joint inheritance. We do not need to look very far to see what an inheritance it was!

List of Musical Examples Played

1. Vaughan Williams: *Fantasia on a theme of Thomas Tallis* (LPO/Boult)
2. Vaughan Williams: Symphony no.9 in E minor (RLPO/Handley)
3. Elgar: *Caractacus* (Wilson-Johnson/LSO/Hickox)
4. Byrd: *Come Pretty Babe* (Figueras/Consort of Viols/Savall)
5. Stanford: Symphony no.2 in D minor (Ulster Orchestra/Handley)
6. Verdi: *Falstaff* (PO/Von Karajan)
7. Elgar: Symphony no.1 in A flat (LPO/Boult)
8. Vaughan Williams: *Fear no more the heat of the sun* (Rolfe Johnson/Keenlyside/Johnson)
9. Elgar: *Wand of Youth* Suite no.2: 'Fairies & Giants' (RLPO/Handley)
10. Elgar: *Falstaff* (LPO/Boult)
11. Vaughan Williams: Prelude to *49th Parallel* (NPO/Herrman)
12. Elgar: *The Kingdom* (Kenny/Hodgson/Gillett/Luxon/LPO/Slatkin)

Dreamers of Dreams
The Songs of Elgar and Vaughan Williams

Claire-Louise Lucas & Jonathan Darnborough

Both Elgar and Vaughan Williams wrote songs throughout their creative lives, including many fine works in each case. The purpose of this talk is to compare their approaches to song writing and we hope to demonstrate that, underlying the obvious differences in style, their approaches have a great deal in common.

Not surprisingly, in sixty minutes, we do not plan to discuss all 65 or so of Elgar's songs and the approximately 80 songs by Vaughan Williams. We will start with a brief survey of each composer's song output, highlighting characteristic features of their songs as well as drawing attention to areas of their output that have been neglected. We will then move on to the comparison of the two composers' approaches to song-writing, focussing in particular on their techniques of word setting.

The songs of Edward Elgar

It is often said of Elgar's songs that they are not the most important part of his repertoire and, set against the symphonies and other major works such as *Gerontius*, maybe that is true. But so often with composers the songs are little laboratories in which ideas can be tested out: the song is after all the perfect opportunity to write a miniature. We found, when we looked at Elgar's songs, that they exhibit countless foretastes of the larger works with which Elgar is more often associated and that many of them are little masterpieces in their own right.

One reservation frequently cited in respect of Elgar's songs is that there are no completed song cycles for voice and piano, or indeed any other recital combination. In the course of our studies, however, we have concluded that this reservation is, in fact, not strictly true. This is not to say that we have discovered any previously unknown songs – would that we had! – but we have established that Elgar's one completed song cycle, the orchestral *Sea Pictures*, enjoys a valid alternative existence as a recital work for voice and piano.

The orchestral song cycle *Sea Pictures* was written for the 1899 Norwich Festival and given its first performance by Clara Butt on 5 October 1899 with Elgar conducting. We started studying these pieces with a view to preparing them for performance with orchestra but were very pleasantly surprised to see how little the piano parts resembled the orchestral reductions that are such a nightmare to most pianists, where every note of the orchestral texture seems to have been dumped on the piano staves. On the contrary these looked like real piano parts.

The opening of 'Sea Slumber Song', for example, is a masterclass in the use of piano sonority. Elgar's pedal markings are very definite, summoning up a wonderful aura of sound from the instrument. Typical is the pedal mark over bars 4 and 5.

Ex 1. Elgar: *Sea Pictures* – 'Sea Slumber Song', bars 4 and 5

The whole thing coalesces into a gentle rocking which, of course, is highly appropriate to the idea of the motion of the sea. In this song, and throughout the whole set, we found that the piano writing was absolutely idiomatic, conjuring the very best and most interesting, vivid sounds from the instrument.

We then discovered that the London première of *Sea Pictures* was, in fact, given by Clara Butt, again accompanied by Elgar but this time at the piano. On that occasion they apparently only played four of the songs – and although we do not have documentary proof of this, we are almost certain that the song omitted on that occasion would have been 'The Swimmer'; which is undoubtedly the most orchestral in its nature.

The whole issue of what constitutes orchestrally conceived music or pianistically conceived music is quite a complex one; particularly in the 19th century, when many composers composed at the piano – it was the tool of their thoughts. That did not mean to say that as they produced ideas at the piano they were not imagining them on the oboe, the violins, whatever it happened to be. They could indeed be writing at the piano, but with a very strong – one imagines, in Elgar's case, an absolutely precise – image of the orchestral sounds. Nevertheless, the music is initially conceived with the aid of the piano and the orchestration process is a separate stage that comes afterwards. This may help to explain why the piano writing here is so effective.

'The Swimmer' can be described as the most orchestral in its feel, mainly because the piano has to execute many tremolandi – normally the preserve of the orchestral strings. On the other hand, the piano is very good at tremolandi as well and, if one were to start discriminating against piano works that used this effect, then Liszt's B minor Sonata would be one of the first casualties, which would be rather unfortunate.

It is a matter of record that Elgar played the piano for performances of *Sea Pictures* with a number of different singers so we can assume that he felt this version to be a valid concert work in its own right. The *Sea Pictures* give us Elgar's song writing in his prime and, certainly from our point of view, it gives us a wonderful recital work.

There is a further, very important, point to all this. When one hears *Sea Pictures* in this different format, with the piano accompaniment, it casts a new light on the songs that we thought we knew so well from their orchestral version.

No better illustration of that new light could be found than to play 'Where Corals Lie' on the piano at $\quarternote = 56$. This really does not work very well on the piano. In the intimate context of a recital hall, and with the immediate production of the notes on a piano, this tempo feels too slow. In recital, we perform this song at around $\quarternote = 70$ – more than ten beats a second faster than Elgar's metronome mark, which is designed for a symphony orchestra in a symphony hall where the whole sound is bigger and some of the instruments literally take longer to speak.

With all of the songs the voice and piano version of *Sea Pictures* is extremely effective in its own right and a very interesting foil to the form in which we normally hear the piece. The overriding difference between this and the orchestral version is, not surprisingly, a greater feeling of intimacy throughout the work as a whole.

The songs of Ralph Vaughan Williams

In the case of Vaughan Williams quite a number of songs are very well known, for example *Linden Lea* (1901); *The Vagabond* (1904); *The Water Mill* (1922–5). More of Vaughan Williams's songs are considered to be an important part of his output than is the case with Elgar and it is certainly true that Vaughan Williams did leave some more substantial song cycles than Elgar – if one did not perform the *Sea Pictures* with voice and piano one would not have anything comparable to *The House of Life* (1903) or *Songs of Travel* (1904).

Vaughan Williams's lifelong study of folk song is inevitably an influence on his own song writing. Folk songs tend not to have very wide pitch ranges and Vaughan Williams, no doubt as a result of his immersion in this music, tends likewise to write within a narrower pitch range than one finds in the late Romantic Lied, which is the background to Elgar's song writing technique.

Notwithstanding the popularity of certain songs within Vaughan Williams's output, there are some significant works that have been rather neglected. This applies particularly to the works in which Vaughan Williams is exploring sparser textures, such as *Along the Field* (1927) for voice and violin and the *Blake Songs* for voice and oboe (1957). This preoccupation with paring down the musical material to something absolutely minimal, but maximally eloquent, is also seen in the *Four Last Songs* (1954–8), wonderful settings of poems by Ursula Vaughan Williams, but again slightly more elusive, slightly less well known, less popular.

Even when Vaughan Williams is writing for the conventional combination of voice and piano some of his songs seem to have fallen by the wayside. For example, there are two songs from the *Four Poems of Fredegond Shove* (1925) that have been entirely eclipsed by their two more famous neighbours. The four Fredegond Shove settings are *Motion and Stillness, Four Nights, The New Ghost* and *The Water Mill*. The *Water Mill* is very well-known, having been extremely popular among amateur singers. Its companion piece, *The New Ghost*, an extraordinarily evocative piece of writing, is considered to be one of Vaughan Williams's finest songs, and yet the first two songs in the set, *Motion and Stillness* and *Four Nights*, are almost universally dismissed. Admittedly, they are short and they might seem, on paper, to be slighter works by comparison with the last two songs of the set but, whilst they are very different from the latter pair, each of these two songs is a miniature masterpiece. Furthermore, they act as a perfect foil to the others in the set.

Motion and Stillness is very short, very fleeting and elusive. This is a piece which, on the page, does not seem to do very much and yet it is a perfectly crafted example of one aspect of Vaughan Williams's musical language. Indeed this is the important thing about these two songs that, taken together with their more famous companions, they provide a complete snapshot of the mature Vaughan Williams's musical personality.

How is it that *Motion and Stillness* should appear to be so slight and yet actually be such an eloquent song? In answering this question one is reminded of Puccini's music, so often criticised in some quarters as clichéd. What Puccini does – and this is his particular genius – is to provide a vehicle for a great singer, for a great voice to display its full powers of expression. In just the same way *Motion and Stillness* simply does not come alive until a voice fills out the vocal line – no amount of playing it through on the piano can substitute for this.

Ex 2. Vaughan Williams: ***Four Poems of Fredegond Shove*** **–
'Motion and Stillness', opening**

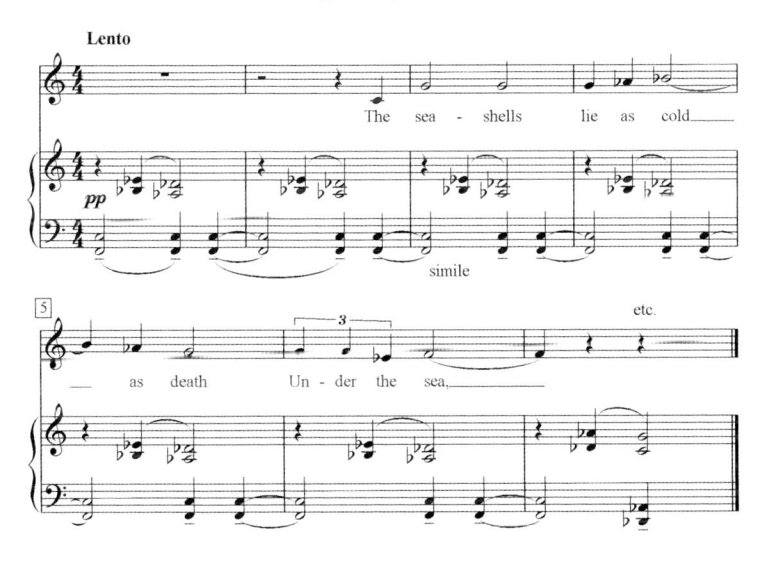

Furthermore, whilst it is a simple vocal line in its contours, it is far from simple to sing. At the required tempo, Lento, extraordinary control of breath and tone are demanded and without these the song will not 'come off'.

The other piece in the set which suffers an unjustified neglect is *Four Nights*. It sounds almost as though Vaughan Williams has simply taken a folk song and added a piano accompaniment. The vocal line is modal and the melody shapes are very characteristic of folk song, eg Ex.3.

Ex 3. Vaughan Williams: *Four Poems of Fredegond Shove* – 'Four Nights', bars 26–8

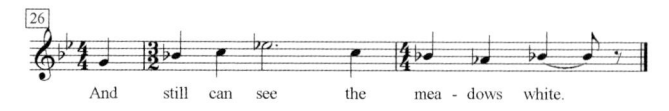

And still can see the mea-dows white.

This folk-like appearance, however, is very deceptive because this is not a folk song by any means. For one thing the song routinely modulates between modes – unthinkable in a genuine folk song – and then there are the professional demands that Vaughan Williams makes upon his singer's breath control.

Ex 4. Vaughan Williams: *Four Poems of Fredegond Shove* – 'Four Nights', bars 2–7

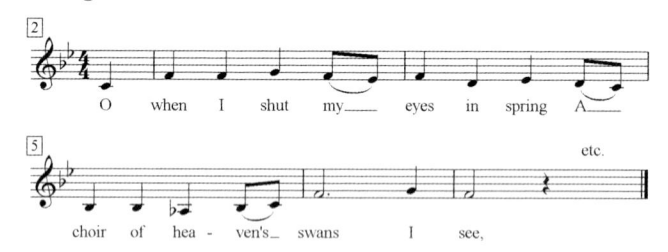

O when I shut my eyes in spring A choir of hea-ven's swans I see,

Ex. 4 is typical of the long phrases that Vaughan Williams asks of his singer throughout. Fredegond Shove's poem contains many two- and even three-line phrases and Vaughan Williams mirrors this in his setting. This opening phrase sets the first two lines of the poem and at this tempo – a flowing *andante* – the singer is given no opportunity to breathe until the comma at the end of line 2.

> O when I shut my eyes in spring
> A choir of heaven's swans I see,

Having set the first line as he has done, Vaughan Williams might perhaps have then used the same three-crotchet rhythm to end the phrase as a whole (Ex. 5).

Ex 5. Vaughan Williams: *Four Poems of Fredegond Shove* – 'Four Nights', opening phrase as it might have been set

[musical notation with lyrics: O when I shut my__ eyes in spring A__ choir of hea-ven's swans I see,]

In fact he extends the rhythm at this point (see Ex. 4) at the end of what is already a long phrase. The singer needs a lot of breath to perform this phrase but it should not show. On the contrary, the interpreter should make the whole song sound simple and artless even though it is anything but.

Vaughan Williams did, of course, work a great deal with amateur musicians, especially singers, and he was passionately committed to providing music which amateurs could perform. This has perhaps led to a misconception about his songs – that they are all intended to be within the scope of the amateur performer. Whilst Vaughan Williams's songs do tend to have a narrower pitch range than those of Elgar, that does not necessarily mean to say that every song he wrote is actually within the reach of the amateur singer. Both *Motion and Stillness* and *Four Nights* are cases in point, where the technical demands are not those of finding high notes or very low ones, but of sustaining and controlling very long breaths.

As one pursues Vaughan Williams into his more rarefied moments, for example the opening of *The New Ghost*; the opening of 'Procris' (from *Four Last Songs*, 1954–8); and, indeed, many of the *Blake Songs*, the singer has to have an almost instrumental control of tone. These are very much 'art' songs, written with highly trained voices in mind.

It is important to remember that both Elgar and Vaughan Williams wrote songs for amateurs and professionals and they both, in their different ways, can make significant technical demands on their performers.

Comparing Elgar's and Vaughan Williams's approaches to song writing

In comparing the songs of these two composers it is easy to draw distinctions between them. One contrast has already been made above, in respect of the pitch ranges of their songs. When they write specifically for amateurs they both restrict their pitch ranges accordingly, but in their songs for trained voices Elgar tends to explore wider extremes of pitch than does Vaughan Williams. The use of modal melodies and folk-like phrase shapes give the songs of Vaughan Williams significant differences in style from those of Elgar, whose musical language is so clearly rooted in the German

Romantic tradition. Nevertheless, in our comparison of their songs, we intend to emphasise the many important qualities that these composers have in common and we will start by discussing their 'Englishness'.

'Englishness' in music is a very elusive thing, and all the more so when we find two composers who are so quintessentially English, as we feel them to be, and yet who are so clearly very different in the sounds that they create. When one approaches this question from the point of view of song writing, there is perhaps an advantage because we see straight away the intimate connection between the language itself and a national character in the music. If one considers composers, such as Mussorgsky, Debussy and Janáček, who have striven to mould their music to their native language, we see that the rhythms and inflections of the language infiltrate the music and are a major factor in its distinctive character. Naturally, this is the case with the folk songs of any given area and if we look at composers who are influenced by their folk songs then we find a national flavour seeping in through that direction.

Even if we discount the influence of folk song, as we really have to do with Elgar, there is still the language itself. In the comparison which follows we examine several songs by the two composers and tease apart how they respond to the language, how they set it. Word setting is a great art, and a very difficult one, because the internal logic of a text is very often in conflict with the internal logic of the musical ideas that have been set up. One has only to think of all those hymn tunes where verses 2 to 7 do not fit the tune anything like as well as verse one. That simple example perfectly illustrates the way in which these two logics can pull apart.

Both Elgar and Vaughan Williams set the English language with great sensitivity and one might be tempted to ask why, if this is the case, their vocal lines are not more similar in shape. Whilst stylistic differences obviously play a part in this, the answer to this question lies, at least partly, in their choice of texts. To find a vocal line by Vaughan Williams that has soaring arches of quasi-Elgarian melody, one has to look, for example, at his early setting of Tennyson's *The Splendour Falls* (c.1896).

Ex 6. Vaughan Williams: *The Splendour Falls*, bars 20–23

3. Lucas & Darnborough – Dreamers of Dreams

Later in his career, however, Vaughan Williams does not set Tennyson, just as Elgar does not set Walt Whitman. On looking down the lists of their chosen poets one sees their different personalities and their different preoccupations perfectly reflected. So when they are setting those different poets – each composer with his own meticulous but personal approach to word setting – they arrive at vocal lines that are different because their starting points were different.

We will start our comparison of the two composers' approaches to word setting by looking, briefly, at their willingness, or otherwise, to make changes in their texts. It is quite common for composers to repeat or omit phrases, even whole verses, of a text to suit their musical purposes but, clearly, in doing so they may irrevocably upset the structure of the original text. Elgar more or less says as much in his oft-quoted remark:

> It is better to set the best second-rate poetry to music, for the most immortal verse is music already.

but this did not prevent him, in the song *In Moonlight* (1904), from taking a hatchet to the words of no less a poet than Shelley.

Perhaps he viewed the poem in question, *To Jane*, as a second rate offering and, as such, fair game for adaptation to his needs. He might well have held this view since he would probably have been aware that the poem was only partly written by Shelley, in 1832, and was completed by Mary Shelley in 1839.

In Moonlight is an unusual song for Elgar in that he wrote the melody first – as the *Canto Popolare* from the middle section of the overture *In the South* (1904) – and was then persuaded that he should put words to this melody. This was not a thing that he undertook lightly and he did so only because he found some words that really made a remarkably close fit to his melody. They are not a perfect fit, however, and that is what makes it such an interesting example because it teaches us a lot about Elgar's approach to word setting.

In Elgar's song the line at the end of the first verse reads:

> To the strings without soul **has** given its own.

Ex 7. Elgar: *In Moonlight*, bars 18–21

In the original poem, however, the line was,

> To the strings without soul **had then** given its own.

What is particularly interesting is that, had Elgar left the text as *had then* he could have written

Ex 8. Elgar: *In Moonlight*, bars 18–21, with Shelley's original text

[Musical notation: bars 18–21 with text "To the strings with-out soul had then giv-en Its own"]

which actually fits his melody better. So why has Elgar made this change?

The answer lies in the fact that Elgar is using only the second and fourth verses of the poem. The first verse of the poem describes how Jane's voice adds life and beauty to the strings of the guitar as she plucks them.

> The keen stars were twinkling,
> And the fair moon was rising among them,
> Dear Jane.
> The guitar was tinkling,
> But the notes were not sweet till you sung them
> Again.
>
> As the moon's soft splendour
> O'er the faint cold starlight of Heaven
> Is thrown,
> So your voice most tender
> To the strings without soul had then given
> Its own.
>
> The stars will awaken,
> Though the moon sleep a full hour later
> To-night;
> No leaf will be shaken
> Whilst the dews of your melody scatter
> Delight.
>
> Though the sound overpowers,
> Sing again, with your dear voice revealing
> A tone
> Of some world far from ours,
> Where music and moonlight and feeling
> Are one.

Without the context of verse one, quoted above, the poem's second verse (verse 1 of the song) makes more sense with *'has'* than *'had then'*. The liberty that Elgar takes with the text here is forced upon him by his initial liberty of setting only two of the four verses.

From Elgar's point of view four verses would perhaps have made the song longer than he wished it to be but his decision to omit verses one and three of the poem has another very straightforward explanation – they simply do not fit the pre-existing melody. The *Canto Popolare* melody from *In the South* starts on a downbeat and, therefore, requires a text with a stress on the first syllable. The poem's second and fourth verses start with syllables that can reasonably be stressed – although in each case the main stress of the first line lies on the third syllable. Verses one and three of the poem, however, both begin with the word *'The'* and have their first stress on the second syllable, eg

> The <u>keen</u> stars were twinkling,

from the first verse of the poem.

Simply to plug this text into the *Canto Popolare* would be unthinkable to someone with Elgar's sensitivity to text.

Ex 9. First line of Shelley's poem set to *Canto Popolare* with no upbeat

Elgar could only have set this text by adding an upbeat to his *Canto Popolare* melody, for example:

Ex 10: First line of Shelley's poem set to *Canto Popolare* with upbeat C

This apparently small modification changes the character of the melody significantly and if Elgar even considered this option he obviously rejected it.

Vaughan Williams, likewise, is selective when he is setting texts. He famously left out two verses of A E Housman's poem *Is my team ploughing?* in his setting from *On Wenlock Edge*, much to the chagrin of the poet himself. Housman's comment was, apparently, "How would he like it if I left out two bars of his music?"

It is quite possible, however, that Vaughan Williams did try to set these two verses but could not find appropriate music for their essentially mundane nature – the omitted verses deal with football. The main function of music, when setting words, is to intensify the emotions contained in those words and, from the songwriter's point of view, these two verses detract from the concentration of emotion on the dead man's work, his girl and his friend. Alternatively, Vaughan Williams's action may have been that of a critic. The two verses omitted are arguably weaker than the rest of the poem.

We now turn to the use of syllabic word setting and its alternatives in the songs of the two composers.

When words are set to music they are heard most clearly when set syllabically – that is to say with one note to each syllable. So, for example, recitative in opera is all syllabic because it is in the recitative that the narrative details are imparted to the audience. The greatest clarity of text will be achieved if the sung rhythm is closely modelled upon speech rhythms, as is also the case with recitative. There are, however, occasions when a composer will wish to depart from syllabic setting, speech rhythms or both, for expressive purposes.

There are two fundamentally different ways in which a syllable may acquire more than one note. The first way may be described as *incidental* and involves no change of the syllable's speech rhythm. In the second way, which may be described as *melismatic*, the syllable is lengthened relative to its natural speech rhythm.

An example of the *incidental* addition of extra notes to syllables may be seen in Ex. 18. The word *'thy'* in bar 16 is set to two semiquavers and *'soul'* in bar 19 to a dotted quaver and a semiquaver. These extra notes do not, however, alter the natural speech rhythm of the text which would make *'thy'* a quaver (= two semiquavers) and *'soul'* a crotchet (= a dotted quaver plus a semiquaver).

This device is a commonplace of song writing, to be found in centuries of word setting. It allows the composer greater melodic freedom whilst barely compromising the clarity of the text. We find it in the songs of both

Elgar and Vaughan Williams but, interestingly enough, Vaughan Williams is noticeably more restrained in its use. This generalisation holds good throughout his career – in fact *Linden Lea* (1901), his first popular success, is entirely syllabic. His restraint in this respect is certainly not an influence of folk song which frequently uses the device.

A syllable is usually described as *melismatic* if it is set to several notes. The effect of this is to extend the syllable beyond its natural length, as measured in terms of speech rhythm. This device is employed to highlight or illustrate particular words in a text.

Ex 11. Vaughan Williams: *On Wenlock Edge* **– 'Bredon Hill', bars 28–32**

Round both the shires they ring them In stee-ples far and near,

In Ex. 11, from 'Bredon Hill', the third song in Vaughan Williams's song cycle *On Wenlock Edge* (1908–9), the word *'ring'* is set to notes that mimic a peal of bells.

Whereas Vaughan Williams is reluctant to add notes to a syllable *incidentally*, he regularly uses *melisma* as an expressive device in his word setting. By contrast *melisma* is almost completely unused by Elgar. When he wishes to lengthen the speech rhythm of a syllable he invariably does so with a single long note.

What is the explanation for these differences? Elgar's use of *incidental* extra notes is so much a part of the tradition from which he springs that it requires no explanation, but why does Vaughan Williams avoid using them? It is interesting to note that, in this one respect, Vaughan Williams is closer than Elgar to the aesthetic of Wagner and this may not be a coincidence. Vaughan Williams was passionately concerned with creating a true marriage of words and music in his work and he may well have believed, as Wagner did, that to use this device was, in some way, 'cheating' – a means of shoe-horning text into a melody that it did not really quite fit.

As for *melisma*, Vaughan Williams's use of this almost certainly derives from his studies of Renaissance music. *Melisma* was one of the most important expressive devices throughout the Renaissance and Baroque periods but fell gradually into disuse thereafter. For Elgar, whose style is essentially late Romantic, *melisma* perhaps felt anachronistic.

The next aspect for comparison is the two composers' willingness to depart from speech rhythms for the purposes of musical expression.

Mention has already been made of the potential conflict between the internal logic of a text and that of the musical ideas in a piece. In fact the balance of power between the words and the music can vary from bar to bar at times. Both Elgar and Vaughan Williams are prepared to allow slight distortions of speech rhythm at times when the musical logic is compelling. In 'Sabbath Morning at Sea' we find the passage:

Ex 12. Elgar: *Sea Pictures* – 'Sabbath Morning at Sea', bars 13–17

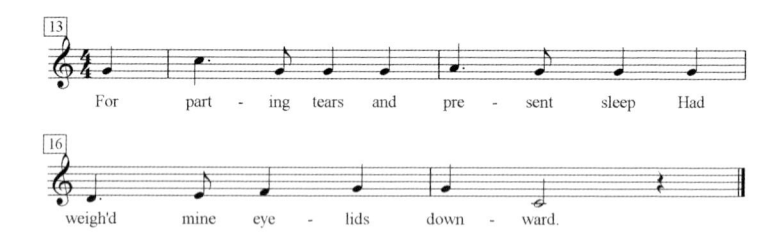

This passage is syllabic but it is also intensely lyrical. If one were to say these words then *'pre-sent'* would be two short syllables. In Elgar's setting, however, the musical logic is for each bar to have the same rhythm and, in this instance, Elgar allows the musical logic to override the speech rhythm.

In Vaughan Williams's *The Water Mill* we find something very similar in the opening verse. In this case Vaughan Williams is also allowing a rhythm to be repeated:

**Ex 13. Vaughan Williams: *Four Poems of Fredegond Shove* –
'The Water Mill', bars 6–9**

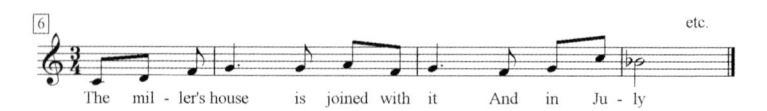

This rhythm fits *'the Miller's house'* and it fits *'and in July'* but it does not quite fit *'is joined with it'* because *'it'* receives undue stress, landing on the first beat of a bar. The singer has to be aware of these things and has *not* to come down heavily on beat one. This is just one example of the importance of the performer studying the text and knowing what is actually being set.

Part of the essential craft of any song writer, indeed of any composer, is the variation of phrase lengths. In a song this variation of phrase length is a key element in the musical expression of the text and may reflect analogous variations in the text itself. Not surprisingly both Elgar and Vaughan Williams show themselves to be masters of this aspect of their craft.

One can find examples of this in almost any of Elgar's songs, but a well-known example is 'In Haven', from the *Sea Pictures*.

Ex 14. Elgar: *Sea Pictures* – 'In Haven', bars 3–11

This song has a deceptive air of simplicity about it but the subtlety of Elgar's setting may be seen in the way that the phrases grow progressively in length through the verse. The first phrase is exactly two bars long, the second is two-and-a-half bars long and the third phrase lasts for three-and-a-half bars, extended by the two long notes that Elgar uses to set the word '*stand*'.

Looking, for comparison, to Vaughan Williams we can take the first verse of *The Water Mill*:

**Ex 15. Vaughan Williams: *Four Poems of Fredegond Shove* –
'The Water Mill', opening**

Vaughan Williams starts the melody with a straightforward four-bar phrase. The following phrase manages to extend to a fifth bar at which point it could finish but in fact Vaughan Williams continues to pay out the melodic line to the words *'to and fro, in and out, round the windows all about'*. After *'sun'* in bar 4, no further cadence point is reached until the end of this passage.

If one wished to set this verse using four-bar phrases throughout, it could be done as follows:

Ex16. Vaughan Williams: *Four Poems of Fredegond Shove* – 'The Water Mill', opening set to four bar phrases

[musical notation: three systems of four-bar phrases with lyrics: "There is a mill, an an-cient one, Brown with rain, and dry with sun, The mil-ler's house is joined with it And in Ju-ly the swal-lows flit To and fro, in and out, Round the win-dows, all a-bout;"]

This example sets every syllable to the same notes as Vaughan Williams uses, so the only difference is in the phrase structure. The result is not so satisfactory. There is quite clearly a slight distortion of the word *'windows'* – one would not naturally linger on the *'win'* of *'windows'* – but the main objection to this setting is its banality. It is simply too predictable.

As we saw in the opening of *The Water Mill* (Ex.15), Vaughan Williams uses a change of metre (the bar of 4/4) to help capture the speech rhythm of his text. The technique of changing metre allows a composer much greater flexibility in the placing of rhythmic stresses. On the face of it, this appears to be one technique that Elgar does not use, except perhaps occasionally at the ends of phrases, where the stresses within phrases are not affected – for example in *Speak Music*.

3. Lucas & Darnborough – *Dreamers of Dreams*

Ex 17. Elgar: *Speak Music*, bars 16–19

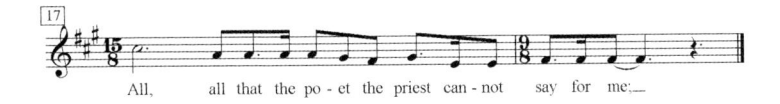

All, all that the po-et the priest can-not say for me:—

On closer inspection, however, we find that Elgar is by no means a hostage to the regularity of stress implied by an unchanging metre. Take, for example, the following passage from *In Moonlight*. Of interest here is the way that Elgar handles the word *'tender'* in bars 17–18. In his setting the second syllable lands on the downbeat of bar 18 which would appear to stress the wrong syllable.

Ex 18. Elgar: *In Moonlight*, bars 16–21

So thy voice most ten-der To the strings with-out soul has giv-en Its own

Can Elgar's sensitivity to language have deserted him? Certainly, if one were placing strong stresses on the first beats of bars then this passage would seem very clumsy. On closer inspection, however, we find no fewer than five special markings in the score that Elgar has added in order to ensure that the singer will perform this passage with stresses appropriate to the text.

Elgar's measures for ensuring that the tyranny of the beat does not upset the expression of the word are as follows:

- an *espressivo* marking in bar 17
- an accent on the B♭ of 'ten-' in bar 17
- an *ad lib* marking over the vocal line at the beginning of bar 18
- *colla parte* marked in the piano part in bar 18
- a crescendo over the vocal line from 'To' to 'strings' in bar 18, in effect displacing the stress in this bar to the second half of the bar

What this passage teaches us is that Elgar is clearly not a slave to the stress of the first beat and this is a useful thing to know about him because it can inform our interpretation of his music in other contexts.

There is another way in which this passage could be set, as shown in the following example. Here *'So thy voice...'* is now the start of a 9/8 bar and on *'soul'* the music reverts to 6/8.

Ex. 19. Elgar: *In Moonlight*, bars 16–21 notated using metre change

Had Vaughan Williams been setting this passage he might have adopted this approach. Such changes of metre are meat and drink to the composers of the 20th century – but rather less conventional for the composers of the 19th century tradition, from whom Elgar learnt his compositional craft. Elgar has simply told the singer very clearly how to sing this passage and, specifically, not to place too much emphasis on the first beat of the bar. The difference between the two composers on this point is purely a matter of notation.

Conclusion

In conclusion we have found that Elgar and Vaughan Williams have an enormous amount in common as writers of English song. This common ground is undoubtedly concealed by their differences in both musical style and choice of texts. Such differences between the two composers need come as no surprise when we consider their contrasting temperaments and backgrounds but in the final analysis they both approach their texts with similar sensitivity and craftsmanship. As a result, their songs are beautifully moulded to the natural speech rhythms and inflections of the poetry that they set, producing some of the most beautiful songs in the English repertoire.

Battle Songs & Elegies
Elgar, Vaughan Williams and British Music 1914–18

Lewis Foreman

My subject[1] is the musical imagery of the First World War and how it changed during and after the war, and how it was reflected in the music of British composers of different generations and idioms. Our featured composers are of interest because Elgar composed throughout the war, including works, often very emotional works, responding to the demands of the moment. Vaughan Williams, on the other hand, did not compose during the war, or at least he did not produce any new scores. Yet he was gestating music, and my focus is on the scores he wrote before and after the conflict, and in particular how his wartime experience on the Western Front was later distilled in a lifetime's music.

At the present time the resonance of these issues of nearly ninety years ago are, unfortunately, all the more vivid for us here in 2003–4. *Then* the war cast a long shadow and many works paid conscious tribute, many more unconscious memorials, to those who had not returned. The generally accepted imagery of war at the outset was in terms of duty and honour and, for want of a better word, of chivalry. Artistically this resulted in an initial inclination to represent conflict in terms of knights in shining armour, of St George and the Dragon, imagery as true for Belgium as for England. After the German invasion of Belgium, artists and cartoonists tended to personify France and Belgium as oppressed women.

The old order, music of chivalry, duty and honour, can best be represented for us in this context by Sir Hubert Parry's Scena for baritone and orchestra *The Soldier's Tent*, written at the time of the Boer War and first performed at the same Birmingham Festival in 1900 that also first heard Elgar's *The Dream of Gerontius*. Setting words by the then fashionable Carmen Sylva from her folk poetry (or was it folk-style poetry) collections *The Bard of the Dimbovitza*, it was very much the last of the old order in terms of sentiment and imagery. Carmen Sylva was the

---

1 – Notes for this chapter appear on pages 163–4.

pseudonym of Queen Elizabeth of Rumania, a well-known writer of the day in English and German translations:

THE SOLDIER'S TENT.

Across the mountains the mist hath drawn
  A cov'ring of bridal white;
The plains afar make lament, and mourn
That the flutt'ring veil of the mist-wreaths born
  Hath hidden the mountains from sight.

The soldier lay smiling peacefully
  Asleep in his tent on the sward,
The moon crept in and said: "Look at me,
A glance from thy sweetheart am I, for thee!"
  But he answered: "I have my sword."

Then the rustling wind drew softly near,
  Played round him with whispers light;
"I am the sighs of thy mother dear,
The sighs of thy mother am I, dost hear?"
  But he answered: "I have the fight."

Then night sank down from the dark'ning sky,
  Round the sleeper, and murmured: "Rest,
Thy sweetheart's veil o'er thy face doth lie!"
But he answered: "No need of it have I,
  For the banner doth cover me best."

By his tent the river, clear and wide,
  Rolled onward its silver flood,
And said: "I am water, the cleansing tide
More blessèd than aught in the world beside."
  But he answered: "I have my blood."

Then Sleep drew near to his tent, and low
  She whispered with soothing breath:
"I am Sleep, the healer of ev'ry woe,
The dearest treasure of man below."
  But the soldier replied: "I have Death."

Across the mountains the mist hath drawn
  A cov'ring of bridal white,
The plains afar make lament, and mourn
That the flutt'ring veil of the mist-wreaths born
  Hath hidden the mountains from sight.[2]

Before considering the music of the First World War and how it developed at the time, it is worth jumping ahead to the end of the 20th century from where we can look back at 1914–1918. It seems to me we can put the issues of that time into context, as far as this paper is concerned, by considering an extract from an orchestral song cycle written much later, which reflected Austro-German attitudes. It is by Patrick Piggott, composer, pianist, writer and one-time BBC Head of Music in Birmingham, who died in 1990.[3] His last work was *Rosanes Lieder*, a vivid orchestral song cycle setting of *Austrian* First World War anti-war poems by the Viennese author Flora Rosanes, in German, which provides us with a useful context for a discussion of musical responses to the First World War. Flora Rosanes is believed to be the person who first sent Mahler the German translations of Chinese poems by Hans Bethge published in *Die chinesische Flöte*, and later used by him in *Das Lied von der Erde*. She was the wife of a leading Viennese doctor and was one of Freud's first patients. She died at the age of 78 in Auschwitz. Here (Ex.1) is the scherzando second song 'Verklingende Regimentsmusik beim Ausmarsch' ('Regimental music dying away as the troops march off').

> The odd loud sound still passes through the air,
> But that is a long way from a 'blare',
> It remains suspended in grey mists
> And swells into a nameless lament
>
> It murmurs like a vagrant sound
> Through the dry downtrodden heather;
> It dwells so painfully in your ear
> And whispers at night in the dark marshes.
>
> It comes to rest upon your heart,
> It echoes heavily in all you do:
> From far away it beckoned to Autumn,
> And suddenly takes all our breath away!
>
> It makes the girls grow silent.
> And if one of them tries to hum the tune,
> Then it turns into something
> Which strangely resembles weeping.[4]

An Austrian family's worries and concerns as the troops march away from Vienna in 1915 are not too different to those experienced in London: weeping is the same in German and English. And here is the end of the story from the perspective of November 1920, as the coffin of the Unknown Warrior is brought back to London, and placed in Westminster

Ex.1: Patrick Piggott: The closing bars of 'Verklingende Regimentsmusik beim Ausmarsch'

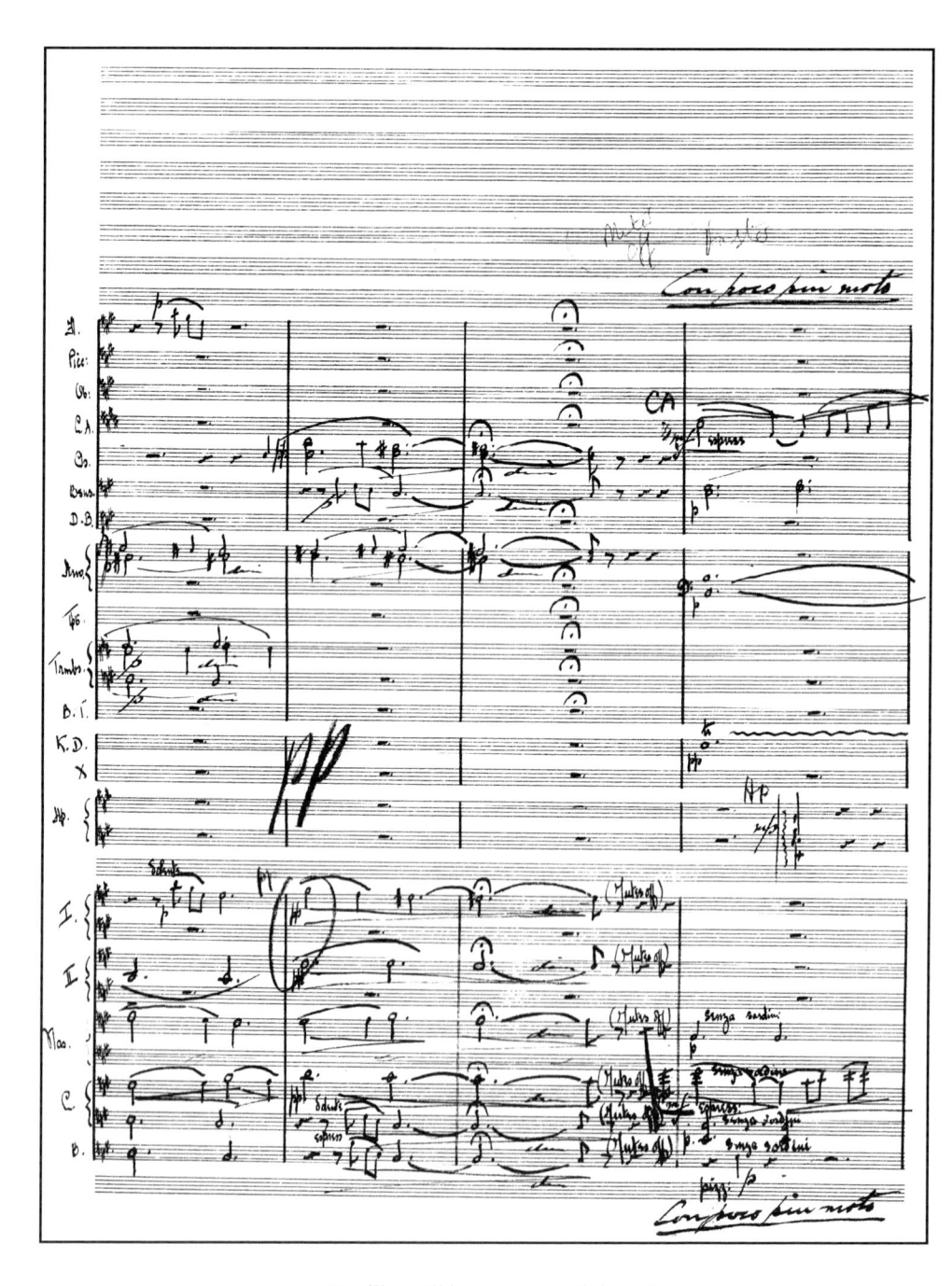

Ex.2: Lilian Elkington: Out of the Mist

4. Foreman – Battle Songs and Elegies

Abbey. At least two composers tried to mark this very emotional event: the elderly Stanford in his short choral work *At the Abbey Gate*, and Lilian Elkington, a young student of Bantock, whose short orchestral tone-poem *Out of the Mist* (Ex.2) was first heard in 1921. Stanford takes words by C J Darling – Judge Darling – and sets them in the context of a passionately felt funeral march which envisages the Unknown Warrior (baritone) seeking admission at the gates of Westminster Abbey:

> Stay —Who goes there?
> A Friend —
> What friend — Whence come you?
> From a dark cave beneath a ruined street.
> Oh friend, where fare you;
> Why would'st thou pass further?
> To lay my heart down at our Mother's feet.
>
> Whom call you Mother?
> England — Nelson's; thine;
> Her whom we proudly serve, in life, in death —
> Her do I guard, friend —
> Can'st thou also serve her?
> Aye, when they fail her who do yet draw breath.
>
> Who art thou, friend, then?
> I was — and am No One —
> No name is ours — An unknown host are we.
> Pass on, brave spirit.
> Oh, 'tis Christ that passes
> In thee, poor soldier, who didst die for me.[5]

Why it was not a success is difficult to judge; perhaps it was too short and specific to one occasion; perhaps people had moved on and did not want to be reminded so vividly of the recent war.

My other example, Lilian Elkington's *Out of the Mist*, also vividly evoked the event, but without words, and might have been expected to have lasted better. Here the problem was more that it was not only by an unknown composer, but a young woman who soon abandoned composition. Indeed, when it was revived in 1988, a BBC interview by Joanne Watson with the composer's daughter[6] revealed that even the composer's family was unaware of its existence. She did not know that her mother had not only composed it, but had also produced so timely a score. The composer wrote in the programme note for the first performance:

... when the Unknown Warrior was brought home to his last resting place there was a thick mist over the Channel, out of which the warship slowly emerged as she drew near to Dover. This explanation of the title will give some clue to the understanding of the music. The opening is quiet, with muted lower strings, as the ship feels her way through the murk . . . After a pause mutes are removed, the air grows brighter, and the deep gloom upon men's spirits is somewhat relieved . . . Gradually the style enlarges and becomes more elevated as larger views of the meaning of sacrifice calm the spirit . . . [in] the final section, *Largamente appassionata fortissimo*, as with a burst of sad exaltation the representative of the nameless thousands who have died in the common cause is brought out of the darkness to his own.[7]

Before August 1914, music in all its manifestations was a Europe-wide industry. Music printing had long been big business, with London a very active centre, but the finest work, such as complex orchestral scores of the latest music, came from Germany. The German engraving and printing industry near Leipzig was embedded in an international structure. Many British composers chose to publish with firms such as Breitkopf & Härtel or Schott of Mainz, through their London offices, as these companies were more likely to market their work outside the UK, through an international network of local offices. Even if it was published by a British company, such as Novello, it was highly likely that the score would be engraved and even printed in Germany where prices were very competitive and quality of work unsurpassed. Readers may remember the accounts of the frantic preparation for the first performances of Elgar's major works between 1900 and 1914 as proofs sped back and forth from England to Germany via the extremely efficient postal service of those days. In August 1914 all was severed, never to be restored.

The piano industry, too, saw the removal of German firms after war broke out. Firms that had been very widely established, and which had had the incidental effect of maintaining manufacturing standards, were suddenly no longer there and leading musicians were targeted if they performed on German instruments. Unfortunately, without German competition, as Cyril Ehrlich has noted, "prices rose almost as rapidly as quality deteriorated".

Perhaps the record industry was hardest hit by the war, for this was an industry that regarded *Europe* as the home market. Thus all the Gramophone Company's masters were held in Hanover and were lost on the outbreak of war. The market for such a luxury product evaporated, and had to be reinvented very quickly for a mass audience. This was done particularly by promoting patriotic songs. Later the press reported:

4. Foreman – Battle Songs and Elegies

Six weeks after the outbreak of war one London publisher had already received for approval three thousand patriotic songs. 'Tipperary' was the soldier's criticism of the efforts of his countrymen to find a voice for national feeling. Rather than sing the stuff that was offered him, the soldier sang a music-hall song without the remotest reference to the war. Perhaps it is a sign of the nation's good sense that the great stream of war songs has now become a mere trickle. The discovery that song writing and empty crowing are not the same thing is at least something. Even the most serious composer might hesitate before touching his harp to the tragedy of war.[8]

The establishment of 'Tipperary' as a song associated with the war effort was a real publishing coup. In December 1914, *The Musical Times* told the story of what by then was already the army's pre-eminent marching song, including a facsimile of the manuscript and a music-type version of the tune, noting that "sales have now passed the second million". It was probably the music publishing coup of all time, and indeed may have been said to have saved the record industry, with its biggest hit since the invention of disc recording. There were many recorded versions, though possibly that by John McCormack has proved most enduring.

It is surprising how quickly stability was achieved. The Promenade Concerts carried on much against expectations and, noted *The Musical Times* in its September 1914 issue, "the success that has so far attended the Queen's Hall Promenade Concerts is one of the most encouraging signs of the times".

Inevitably a variety of patriotic songs appeared in the first days and weeks of the war. In the early stages recruiting songs were promoted by the national press and they appeared in concerts, in the music hall and were popular on record. The leading singers of the day took them up, and recorded them. What had been premium price artists were suddenly available to all at moderate prices in these songs. One of these was Maggie Teyte who was perhaps most characteristic and affecting (to her contemporaries) in Paul Rubens's *Your King and Country Want You*[9] described as a "woman's recruiting song":

> We've watched you playing cricket and every kind of game . . .
> But now your country calls you to play your part in war . . .
> We don't want to lose you but we think you ought to go.

The leading composers, especially those of the senior generation, also wrote patriotic songs, though it's difficult to decide how far their hearts were in it. Sir Frederic Hymen Cowen, five years Elgar's senior, wrote several of these, and he seems to have done very well from them during the war. With its notably exploitative lyrics, Cowen's recruitment song *Fall In* was on the Winner label, Edison Bell's popular label of the time.[10] You might have bought this in Woolworths:

> What will you lack sonny . . .
> What will you lack
> When your mates go by
> With the girl who cuts you dead

It was possibly Clara Butt, celebrated for her recordings of *Land of Hope and Glory*, who achieved the greatest celebrity in such material, though when Sir Hubert Parry produced his *A Hymn for Aviators* (Ex.3) for her he satisfied neither himself nor his audience, and it was not recorded until the end of the war.[11]

Ex.3: Parry: A Hymn for Aviators *(words by Mary C D Hamilton)*

However, Parry's music was soon to become ubiquitous for *Jerusalem*, certainly the most widely disseminated and longest lasting popular piece by a serious composer from the First World War, now had almost the status of a second national anthem.

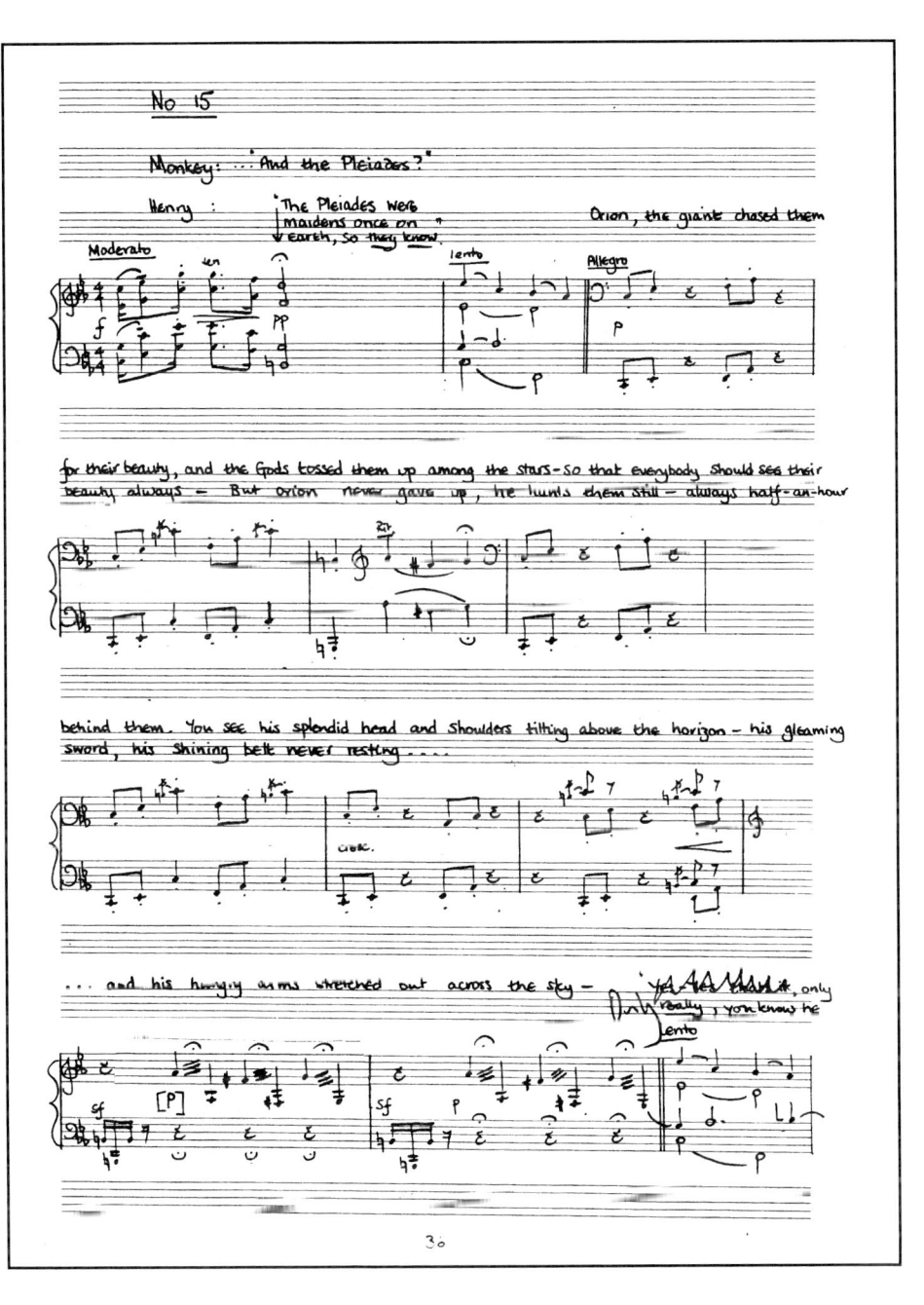

Ex.4: Elgar: Starlight Express *(vocal score by Robert Walker)*
[Reproduced by kind permission of Novello & Co]

Elgar was not able to repeat the success of *Pomp and Circumstance* no.1 and its setting as *Land of Hope and Glory*, and he certainly was not immune from blatant tub-thumping. For example, his unison song for boys' voices with bugles and drums published in 1914, *The Birthright*, is surely Elgar's worst single work! Given a larger canvas what might have been all too similar assumed a wider dimension when he produced the recitation *Carillon*. Written in November 1914 and first performed on 7 December, Elgar found he had exactly divined the nation's mood and had an enormous success, with the words being given both in French and in English. Elgar's wartime works are listed in table 1 (page 54).

There followed a second recitation, *Une Voix dans le Désert* (*A Voice in the Desert*), written in July 1915 but not heard until 29 January 1916 when it appeared on stage – and in *costume* – as a patriotic curtain raiser between 'Cav' and 'Pag'.

For me the incidental music Elgar wrote for *The Starlight Express* (Ex.4, previous page) during November and December 1915 is among his most cherishable work. Possibly taking his cue from the success of the children's patriotic play *Where the Rainbow Ends* with music by Roger Quilter (a West End hit since 1912), it was an ill-fated exercise; opening on 29 December 1915, it only lasted for a month. Here Elgar's response to the conflict was music of childhood and innocence. The 1969 BBC production by Raymond Raikes caught the mood perfectly and it needs to be remembered, for it gave voice to Elgar's wistful reminiscent mood to perfection, using music to underpin voices to create a magical effect.

It is remarkable how, from total paralysis in the first half of August 1914, the music industry responded and serious works from serious composers were soon in evidence, as well as an active participation from more popular publishers with songs and piano music. At the beginning of the war existing music was pressed into service if it had even a hint of a patriotic aura. Examples include Elgar's *The Banner of St George*, Stanford's *The Revenge* and Bax's *Fatherland*. *The Banner of St George* was probably Elgar's most successful work with orchestra at the time, at least if we take sales as our measure, and by 1915 Elgar's vocal score had sold 73,500 copies.[12] Another good seller as far as Novello was concerned was Stanford's setting of Tennyson's death and glory poem *The Revenge*, which had sold in similar substantial quantities. Tuneful patriotism seems to be the order of the day, though honour is lauded at the price of everything. Here (Ex.5) is Sir Richard Grenville:

Ex.5: *Stanford:* The Revenge

Table 1

Music by Elgar composed 1914–1918

1914
The Birthright: unison song with bugles and drums
Carillon, Op 75, for orator and orchestra

1915
Polonia: Symphonic Prelude
Rosemary ("That's for remembrance"), for small orchestra
Une Voix dans le Désert, Op 77 (*A Voice in the Desert*),
        for orator, soprano & orchestra
The Starlight Express, Op 78: incidental music

1916
The Spirit of England, for soloist, chorus and orchestra.
    'The Fourth of August'
    'To Women'
    'For the Fallen'
Le Drapeau Belge, Op 79 (*The Belgian Flag*),
        for orator and orchestra
Fight for Right, for voices and piano

1917
The Sanguine Fan, Op 81: ballet music
The Fringes of the Fleet,
    for baritone, 3 obligato baritones, orchestra
    'The Lowestoft Boat'
    'Fate's Discourtesy'
    'Submarines'
    'The Sweepers'
Inside the Bar: a sailor's song for 4 baritones and orchestra

1918
Violin Sonata in E minor, Op 82
String Quartet in E minor, Op 83
Big Steamers: unison song
Piano Quintet, Op 84

Table 2
Music and the First World War
(some examples excluding Elgar and Vaughan Williams)

PRE-WAR WORKS

Bax: *Fatherland*
Butterworth: *A Shropshire Lad*
Sir Frederick Bridge: *The Flag of England*
Somervell: 'Killed in Action' (slow movement of *Thalassa*)
Stanford: 'Farewell' (from *Songs of the Fleet*); *The Revenge*
Walford Davies: *Solemn Melody*

WARTIME WORKS REFLECTING THE WAR

Marion Arkwright: *Requiem*
Bridge: *A Lament*
Howard Carr: *Three Heroes*
Cecil Coles: *Behind the Lines*
German: *Have You News of my Boy Jack?*
Gurney orch Howells: *In Flanders*
Howells: *Elegy for Bunny Warren*
F S Kelly: *Elegy for Rupert Brooke*
Parry: *From Death to Life*; *Jerusalem*; *The Chivalry of the Sea*
Rootham: *For the Fallen*
Stanford: *Verdun* (orch from Organ Sonata no.2)
Walford Davies: *A Short Requiem*

POST-WAR WORKS SUBLIMATING OR MEMORIALISING THE WAR

Armstrong: *Friends Departed*
Bridge: *A Prayer*
Bliss: *Storm*; *Morning Heroes*
Bridge: *Oration*; Piano Sonata
Delius: *Requiem*
Lilian Elkington: *Out of the Mist*
Finzi: *A Short Requiem*
Foulds: *A World Requiem*
Gurney: *War Elegy*; *Lights Out*
Holst: *Ode to Death*
Stanford: Mass *Via Victrix*; Piano Trio no.3

Many composers responded to events or tried to capitalise on the spirit of the time – often for perfectly legitimate and usually personally tragic reasons. After 1918 the wound was so deep the war must have been the unspoken source for many artistic undertakings – in the case of music often with remarkable eloquence.

Vaughan Williams and Elgar were actually very complex in their response to the reality of conflict. Others tried to distance themselves from it, with greater or lesser effect. One pre-war work pressed into patriotic service, much against its composer's better judgement, was Arnold Bax's *Fatherland*, in fact a setting of what became the Finnish national anthem.

Many composers wrote patriotic music and a host of marches, hymns and other works appeared which would need a longer study to illustrate. A prime example is the celebrated legend of the 'Angel of Mons', a happening widely reported and believed, whereby a manifestation was reported in the sky which caused the German advance in 1914 to check, allowing the British to complete their withdrawal. Two examples of topical popular music from that time are Sydney Baldock's piano solo *Angels of Mons (Rêve Mystique)*[13] (see illustration on page 65) and Paul Paree's[14] valse *Angel of Mons*.

During the war, music that lasted was often a response to a specific event, typically a catastrophic or tragic one. Examples include Elgar's three recitations with orchestra, Frank Bridge's *Lament* for strings, F S Kelly's *Elegy for Rupert Brooke*, Herbert Howells' *Elegy* (for his friend Bunny Warren), and Parry's *The Chivalry of the Sea*. While we have no way of sharing the impact these must have had at the time, especially to those who knew those being remembered, at their best these composers created a body of work only some of which held a place in the repertoire but is well worth exploration today. Typical is the Parry choral work,[15] written to remember those who died at the Battle of Jutland when the battle-cruiser HMS Invincible exploded with the loss of over a thousand lives. Here the inexorable ocean swell of Parry's introduction underlines the ambivalence of his response (Ex.6).

Then there was music to be called on for all too necessary practical use. Stanford's 'Farewell', the last of the *Songs of the Fleet*, was often heard in the concert hall, and Henry Walford Davies wrote his *Short Requiem* for widespread church use. I think it is worth taking note of the Walford Davies, for it reminds us that great events were set in a domestic scale. This was music for all too practical purposes in 1915. The printed copies are written without organ accompaniment, the organ instead doubling the

Ex.6: Parry: The opening orchestral evocation of The Chivalry of the Sea

Ex.7: Marion Arkwright: The final movement of her Requiem Mass

voices when required. With its solos in the first, fifth, sixth and ninth movements, natural chant, the hymn 'No more to sigh', and ending with 'Vox Ultima Crucis', setting John Lydgate's emotive words 'Tarry no longer', its impact must have been devastating when used during the war.

> Tarry no longer toward thine heritage
> Haste on thy way and be of right good cheer.
> Go each day onward on thy Pilgrimage . . .
> Come on, my friend, brother most dear!

Finally there was the larger-scale, quasi-philosophical work, often vocal or choral, reflecting on loss and viewing things in universal terms. These were requiems in effect though not necessarily in name. However, several substantial works were written, of which Marion Arkwright's *Requiem Mass* for soprano and baritone soli, chorus and orchestra (Ex.7), published in 1914,[16] was probably the first. This substantial score did not disclose its composer was a woman, the composer giving her name as 'M U Arkwright'. Her pre-war perspective and her intention is immediately apparent from the expansive opening funeral march and the superscription:

> No matter where or when
> Or how we die, the while you say of us —
> "O, nobly died! O glorious Englishmen!"

We may gather the not unsuccessful flavour from the opening of the concluding Agnus Dei when the opening funeral march returns:

Very much of its time, it was little performed, and now the orchestral full score has proved impossible to trace. Yet for an audience that responds to the Brahms *German Requiem* (as it is clear Arkwright did), it would be worth exploring in a local performance.

The first large-scale work to find a place as a widely played work of memorial and consolation was Elgar's *The Dream of Gerontius*. During the war a variety of special concerts took place, almost always to raise money for war charities, usually under aristocratic or royal patronage. Notable among these was a variety of Red Cross concerts, a typical example of which was Clara Butt's season of performances of *The Dream of Gerontius* at Queen's Hall programmed with the premières of the two then completed parts of Elgar's *The Spirit of England*. *Gerontius* was given for a week; the concerts were attended by royalty and were packed. From our perspective the most important part of the fund raising effort is the extracts recorded by Clara Butt.

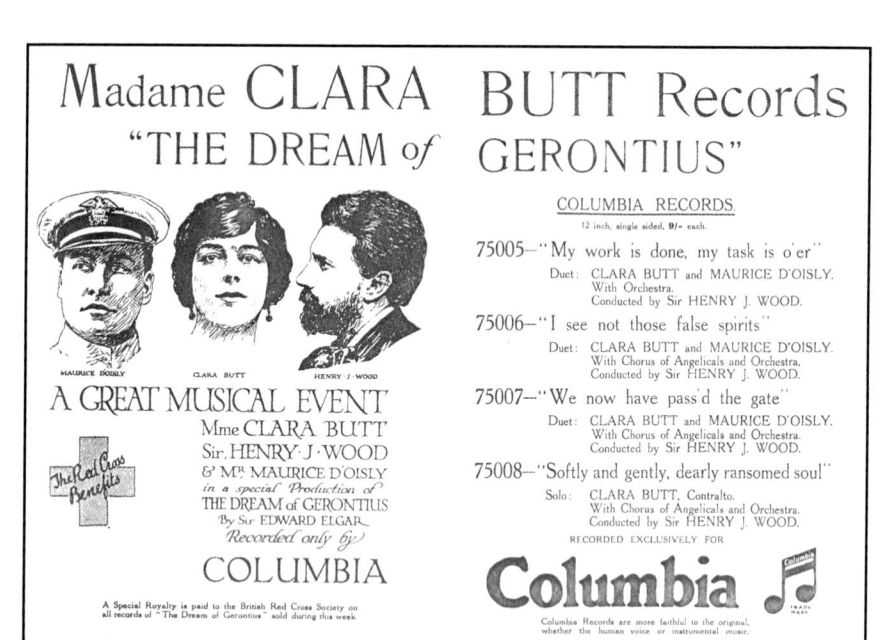

Madame CLARA BUTT Records "THE DREAM of GERONTIUS"

A GREAT MUSICAL EVENT
Mme CLARA BUTT
Sir HENRY J WOOD
& Mr MAURICE D'OISLY
in a special Production of
THE DREAM of GERONTIUS
By Sir EDWARD ELGAR
Recorded only by
COLUMBIA

The Red Cross Benefits

A Special Royalty is paid to the British Red Cross Society on all records of "The Dream of Gerontius" sold during this week.

COLUMBIA RECORDS
12 inch, single sided, 9/- each.

75005—"My work is done, my task is o'er"
Duet: CLARA BUTT and MAURICE D'OISLY.
With Orchestra.
Conducted by Sir HENRY J. WOOD.

75006—"I see not those false spirits"
Duet: CLARA BUTT and MAURICE D'OISLY.
With Chorus of Angelicals and Orchestra.
Conducted by Sir HENRY J. WOOD.

75007—"We now have pass'd the gate"
Duet: CLARA BUTT and MAURICE D'OISLY.
With Chorus of Angelicals and Orchestra.
Conducted by Sir HENRY J. WOOD.

75008—"Softly and gently, dearly ransomed soul"
Solo: CLARA BUTT, Contralto.
With Chorus of Angelicals and Orchestra.
Conducted by Sir HENRY J. WOOD.

RECORDED EXCLUSIVELY FOR

Columbia

Columbia Records are more faithful to the original, whether the human voice or instrumental music.

Elgar's *Carillon* when it first appeared in December 1914 was a heartfelt instinctive response to a deeply felt current event. Elgar sets topical and emotional words responding to the brutal invasion of Belgium, which generated an enormous following in its day. When Elgar attempted a sequel with the much shorter 'marche militaire' *Le Drapeau Belge*, he attracted a much smaller response: the moment had passed. Between these two, his second recitation, *A Voice in the Desert* was more reflective and for a modern audience can still be found touching. It included the poignant song of the peasant girl whose home has been destroyed 'When spring comes round again' beginning to touch wider sensibilities than its somewhat crude companions. Elgar's copy of the words was given him by the poet Cammaerts himself and was inscribed 'Après Anvers'. The fall of Antwerp (Anvers) was one of those key turning points in the breaking of inhibitions and was also the point at which the Allied depiction of the 'Huns' as savages took root. The peasant girl's song in *A Voice in the Desert* is littered with such names, all of them once of great emotional significance in the fall of Belgium – Antwerp, Ypres, Nieuport, Ramscapelle – and an appreciation of them adds immeasurably to the emotional impact of the music.

C'ÉTAIT sur le front,
A cent pas des tranchées,
Une petite maison
Morne et désolée.

Pas un homme, pas une poule,
        pas un chien, pas un chat,
Rien qu'un vol de corbeaux
        le long du chemin de fer,
Le bruit de nos bottes sur le pavé gras,
Et la ligne des feux clignotant sur l'Yser.

    Une chaumine restée là,
    Porte fermée volets clos,
    Un trou d'obus dans le toit,
    Plantée dans l'eau comme un îlot.

Pas un cri, pas un bruit,
        pas une vie, pas un chat,
Rien que le silence des grands cimetières
Et le signe monotone des croix,
        des croix de bois,
Par la plaine solitaire . . .

Puis, tout à coup, chaude, grave et douce
Comme le soleil sur la mousse,
Tendre et fière, forte et claire
Comme une prière
Une voix de femme sortit du toit
Et la maison chanta!

A HUNDRED yards from the trenches,
Close to the battle front,
There stands a little house
Lonely and desolate.

Not a man, not a bird,
        not a dog, not a cat,
Only a flight of crows
        along the railway line,
The sound of our boots on the muddy road
And, along the Yser, the twinkling fires.

    A low thatched cottage
    With doors and shutters closed,
    The roof torn by a shell,
    Standing out of the floods alone.

Not a cry, not a sound,
        not a life, not a mouse,
Only the stillness of the great graveyards,
Only the crosses —
        the crooked wooden crosses —
On the wide lonely plain . . .

Suddenly, on the silent air,
Warm and clear, pure and sweet
As sunshine upon golden moss,
Strong and tender as a prayer,
Through the roof a girl's voice rang
And the cottage sang!

Nevertheless *Carillon* was the hit and it attracted many very favourable reviews. Elgar had certainly responded to the need of the moment. "The poem . . . is an inspiring subject for a musician, and it has nerved Elgar to one of his happiest and strongest achievements", wrote one critic. "The music moves irresistably on a broad full stream of manly emotion to a series of noble climaxes. It is sonorous without clamour, and euphonious without weakness . . . The words were spoken with extraordinary emphasis (in French) by Mme Tita Brand."

Here is another. "Perhaps one of the most impressive features of it all was the wonderful way in which Mme Tita Brand flung the splendid lines at the audience. The music, however, has caught the exact spirit of the poem . . . Poem and music together produce a thrilling effect, and there were numerous recalls for poet, composer, and reciter."

The reception was so vigorous that it was programmed again on 17 December, when *The Daily Telegraph* noticed: "Yet, again, Elgar's *Carillon* aroused a storm of approval and appreciation on its second public performance." Performances quickly multiplied and the work was widely performed, not least by the celebrated actor Henry Ainley, then well-known as a romantic lead, who recorded a slightly abridged version with Elgar in January 1915 and then toured it with him. Listening to a work whose opening depends on the ringing of bells, via the medium of an acoustic 78, has always seemed a rather doubtful proposition. However, I have to say that Mike Dutton of Dutton Laboratories, by using mint originals and his own brand of technical magic, achieved the seemingly impossible. He made an acoustic recording of bells *ring*![17]

I have already mentioned Elgar's *The Spirit of England* consisting of the three choral settings of Laurence Binyon's 'The Fourth of August', 'To Women' and 'For the Fallen'. This appeared during 1916 and 1917 and thus stands astride the conflict, an eloquent and uniquely Elgarian vision in its ambivalence, and Elgar's most expansive musical response to it. John Norris has remarked[18] that "this is the spirit of Elgar, not of England". Yet when we consider the music which was written in the years that followed, notably that of Vaughan Williams, *The Spirit of England* seems very much of its time, underlined by the fact that it was little heard during the Second World War and, on one occasion at least, a choir of music students are reported as refusing to sing it, owing to the words.

In 1921 Arthur Bliss lectured to the Society of Women Musicians on 'What Modern Composition is Aiming At', and in celebrating the music of Stravinsky, Bartók, de Falla and the younger British composers declared "I take my hat off to [Stravinsky] and the others . . . not only for what they have created, but also for what they have killed", and among a varied selection of the pre-war musical world he celebrates the demise of "the symphonic poem à la Strauss", the "pseudo-intellectuality of the Brahms camp followers" and "frothing Wotans and stupid King Marks".[19] Another curious reminiscence of the war is one not designated as such by its composer. We all know Bliss's later salute to his brother and the fallen of the First World War, in *Morning Heroes*, but I have long thought it strange that a composer newly returned from the Western Front should write a storm as incidental music for *The Tempest* in terms that suggest the sound of an artillery barrage. Scoring it for a battery of percussion as well as piano, trumpet and trombone it generates a prodigious volume of sound, a remarkable tour de force of drumming surely informed by Bliss's

4. Foreman – Battle Songs and Elegies

nightmare of the trenches. Although there is a modern recording on Hyperion in which the sound has been contained remarkably successfully, I am not sure that is what Bliss was aiming at. Its first modern revival was given by Leslie Head in a Kensington Symphony Orchestra concert, when the drumming was so loud in the hall as to be quite overwhelming, suggestive I feel of what Bliss really imagined.[20]

All too soon the roll-call of those who fell included promising young musicians who had started to make their name before the outbreak of war. One of the first was Lieutenant Edward Mason, cellist and conductor of the choir that bore his name, who was killed on active service on 9 May 1915 in his 37th year. Soon he was followed by William Denis Browne, who was killed at the Dardanelles on 7 June. Denis Browne was a friend and student of Dent at Cambridge and is remembered for two songs (out of some ten songs), *Diaphenia* and *To Gratiana Dancing and Singing*, a ballet and a few short choral pieces that survive. He was present when Rupert Brooke died on Skyros, as was his composer-friend, the brilliant Australian pianist F S Kelly who wrote:

> We reached the grove at 10.45pm, where, in the light of a clouded half-moon, the burial service was read . . . It was a most moving experience. The wild sage gave a strong classical tone, which was so in harmony with the poet we were burying that to some of us the Christian ceremony seemed out of keeping. . . . . The body lies looking down the valley towards the harbour, and, from behind, an olive-tree bends itself over the grave as though sheltering it from the sun and rain. No more fitting resting-place for a poet could be found than this small grove, and it seems as though the gods had jealously snatched him away to enrich this scented island.[21]

Kelly survived Gallipoli long enough to produce an atmospheric *Elegy for Rupert Brooke* for harp and strings, in which he evokes the rustling of the olive tree over the grave, a piece that deserves recording and wider dissemination. Kelly himself was killed on the Western Front in November 1916.

1916 was the year which also saw the death of George Butterworth, perhaps the best-remembered of the British composers who died in the war. Yet curiously, while Butterworth wrote no overtly war works, his is an important name in the creation of the imagery of the war, and it has been the association of his music with the poetry of A E Housman that gives it so powerful a feeling for us, one redolent with loss. Specifically we think of the orchestral rhapsody *A Shropshire Lad*. "We understand, as we listen to it", wrote Sir Thomas Armstrong "why Butterworth's death on the

Somme in 1916 seemed to be a disaster for English music: and we wonder, as his friends did at the time, what his final achievement might have been if he'd lived".[22] Butterworth's death gives an added piquancy to his two sets of Housman songs – *A Shropshire Lad* and *Bredon Hill* – and in the latter the song 'On the idle hill of summer' seems to gain enormous significance from our knowledge of Butterworth's fate, as it also does in Ivor Gurney's[23] even more haunting setting. The dreamer enjoys his reverie on the sunlit hillside and, while feeling war to be all foolishness, lightly joins the soldiers who pass by. Both Butterworth and Gurney draw great effect from a subtle presentation of "the steady drummer drumming like a noise in dreams".

Other composers killed before the conflict ceased included Ernest Farrar, teacher of Gerald Finzi, who died in the closing weeks of the war, and the Scottish composer, Cecil Coles. Recently, the conductor Martyn Brabbins has championed his music,[24] which had been completely forgotten, and some of whose music was actually written in the trenches. Coles was one of those commemorated by Holst's *Ode to Death*. It's piquant to remember he was long associated with Germany and lived and studied in Stuttgart for several years, where he worked under von Schillings. Others, such as E J Moeran and Ivor Gurney, were damaged when wounded or gassed. Recently the shambolic manuscript of Gurney's *War Elegy* has been heard again,[25] and while not a great work it worked in performance. Hearing Gurney's trudging funeral march given added voice by the clumsy second climax followed by its all-too-expressive fade out, one could not help but feel that we were hearing an authentic account of the hardships and sorrows of an eloquent poet whose terrible experience it encapsulates. We must hope that, suitably edited, it will join the repertoire of first-hand memorials written by soldier-musicians who were writing from personal experience.

In brief, we should also note the Australian Arthur Benjamin, later a successful pianist and composer, who, as a First War airman, was shot down and taken prisoner but who returned to an active musical career. The conductor and composer Eugene Goossens lost his brother (who is named on the Royal College of Music war memorial), and the composer Gordon Jacob who was taken prisoner in April 1917, was long affected by the death on the Somme of his brother, Anstey, to whom he dedicated his First Symphony some ten years later. These were musical examples of emotions and experiences that must have been very widespread in the 1920s.

Angels of Mons, *cover illustration of the score of Sydney Baldock's piano solo*

As time passed various works appeared which may have been informed by the war. Arnold Bax's aggressive First Symphony in 1922, with its searing funereal slow movement, was ascribed to the war by many in the 1920s, though we now know it is far more likely to have actually recalled the events in Dublin over Easter 1916. This is probably the most deeply felt elegy of all, and certainly uses the most advanced language of any British work of its date.

Vaughan Williams's *Pastoral Symphony* has been widely interpreted as an elegy for his companions on the Western Front, and particularly for what he witnessed whilst toiling as an orderly with the field ambulance. After the war a new generation of composers flourished, and Vaughan Williams was briefly its epitome. Even Stanford and Parry were soon forgotten, while former leading figures such as Mackenzie and Cowen, both of whom lived until the mid-1930s, now seemed like fish out of water. Elgar survived but, although he was still treated as an honoured name, his following began to wane and the first performance of the Cello Concerto in October 1919, later for many the ultimate requiem for the lost, played to a disappointingly small audience.

Vaughan Williams did not compose during the war, but it is arguable that his service on the Western Front generated a lifetime's musical imagery, and during this time he clearly thought about revisions to *A London Symphony*, as well as gestating his *Pastoral Symphony*. His works which straddle 1914–1918 include the opera *Hugh the Drover* and *The Lark Ascending*. We might talk of *Sancta Civitas*, of the Piano Concerto, of *Job*, of the Fourth Symphony and *Dona Nobis Pacem*. Certainly a close examination of many of the texts RVW set would give us a wealth of resonances of his wartime experience. Musically speaking the Great War cast a long shadow, and when Vaughan Williams conducted the London Philharmonic Orchestra in the first performance of his Fifth Symphony at the Royal Albert Hall on 24 June 1943, during the dark days of the Second World War, his vision of heaven is surely informed by the hell he had shared twenty five years before.

The period 1914–1918 saw the death of a musical culture in a quite remarkably sudden and dramatic way. This was a very real change, and in many ways it was a generational thing. It prompts one to ask how far the music imagery we have come to associate with the war was pre-figured in the music from the pre-war period. It has long seemed to me that the turning point came with Vaughan Williams's *A London Symphony*, first performed at Queen's Hall on 27 March 1914. At that date RVW had no clue as to the way world events would turn, nor how soon. At much the same time his friend Gustav Holst was writing his suite *The Planets*, the other big work of the time whose imagery has been related to the war and re-visited by later composers. Now Vaughan Williams very much heralded the new, and in many ways the post-war brave new world dates from that time in the summer of 1914. Also, now that we have a recording[26] of the earlier version of *A London Symphony*, we find various passages which seem to anticipate the later world. For example, that "bad hymn tune" as Vaughan Williams later referred to it, which is completely cut in the later version. In his notes to the Chandos CD, Stephen Connock draws our attention to it as "remarkable and memorable . . . of such tender sadness". Seen with the aid of our longer view ninety years on, here RVW had already written music which, had it come even a year later, would now be viewed in the context of the conflict.

Vaughan Williams did not respond musically to specific wartime events during the war. Yet if, when again at peace, Vaughan Williams could, in his *Pastoral Symphony*, sing an eloquent and universal elegy for what had been lost, Elgar's last remembrance was more traditional but no less deeply felt for that. This came in his music for *The Pageant of Empire* at Wembley, where in 'The Immortal Legions', words by Alfred Noyes, he celebrates the lost armies of the Western Front in a language familiar from the earlier memorials of the Empire.

> Now, in silence, muster round her
> All the legions of her dead.
> Grieving for the grief that crowned her,
> England bows her glorious head.
> Round the ever-living Mother,
> Out of the forgetful grave,
> Rise the legions that have saved her
> Though themselves they could not save.
> Now the living Power remembers,
> Now the deeper trumpets roll —

Viewed superficially from this distance, the musical activity which quickly developed after the war tended to highlight the new, and certainly a composer such as Bliss, fresh back from war service and with a private income to facilitate his musical curiosity, was quickly seen as a harbinger of the new. Whether the average music-lover saw things in quite the way Bliss did is more difficult to assess. Yet there was a constant stream of new music which in one way or another memorialised the war, often without

Ex.8: Stanford: Via Victrix

contemporary audiences realising its significance, a notable omission in the case of Vaughan Williams's *Pastoral Symphony*. *The Lark Ascending*, a work first written with piano accompaniment in 1914, now appeared with orchestral accompaniment, newly celebrating England in a poetic and oblique way. My short list (see page 55) of works sublimating or memorialising the war is very varied, and overt celebrations were curiously unsuccessful, indicating that there had been a very real change of sensibilities. Thus Stanford's grandiose victory mass which he called *Via Victrix*, although published in vocal score (Ex.8), may well never have been produced; while his *Merlin and the Gleam*, a half-hour cantata for baritone and orchestra which celebrated the passing of an age in the symbolism of the death of Merlin in Tennyson's difficult poem of the same title, had a few provincial performances before being completely forgotten.[27] Before Bliss's *Morning Heroes*, first heard in 1930, only John Foulds's *A World Requiem* enjoyed a wide popular following, having a tremendous success at the Royal Albert Hall on Armistice Night 1923. Malcolm MacDonald tells us "the audience was ecstatic, many of them in tears: the ovation lasted ten minutes".[28] Although it was repeated for the three succeeding years it did not last, and was dropped after a campaign to discredit it by many of the leading music critics. Quite why is difficult to say. It is a difficult work to assess from the vocal score, but a performance of some extracts at a concert in London in 1983 suggested that it may yet surprise us.

But let us give the last word to Arnold Bax, from his autobiographical talk broadcast in 1949:

> The catastrophe of 1914 certainly threw a cloud upon the imaginations of men and bundled away dreams such as those in which I had hitherto indulged. Yet despite the restless and sombre mood of the world, or perhaps because of it, many creative artists managed to continue with their work and even gained in strength. The demon of the time seized upon us and forced us to his will.[29]

"What Have We Learnt from Elgar?"
Vaughan Williams and the Ambivalence of Inheritance

Byron Adams

"The one question we have to ask is, has Elgar achieved beauty?" Ralph Vaughan Williams strategically positioned this query at the heart of an essay published in a 1935 issue of *Music & Letters* designed as a memorial tribute to Elgar.[1] The forcefulness of this question is startling enough, but even more surprising is that Vaughan Williams avoided providing an immediate answer. For the rest of the paragraph in which this question appears, Vaughan Williams uses the programmatic elements inherent in Elgar's *Falstaff* as a pretext to deride a "certain class of critics" that prefer "literary" composers, such as Berlioz, to purely "musical" creators such as Dvořák.

After this digression, Vaughan Williams finally answers with eloquence: "Elgar has the one thing needful", he writes, "and all his philosophical, literary and technical excellences fall into their proper place: they are a means to an end". Vaughan Williams then continues, "But to say that he has beauty is only half the truth: he has that peculiar kind of beauty which gives us, his fellow countrymen, a sense of something familiar – the intimate and personal beauty of our own fields and lanes; not the aloof and unsympathetic beauty of glaciers and coral reefs and tropical forests".[2] Aside from the irony that Vaughan Williams would himself portray the "aloof and unsympathetic beauty of glaciers" in his *Sinfonia Antartica* of 1952, the alert reader cannot help but relish the author's sly rhetorical sleight-of-hand, for Vaughan Williams deftly removes Elgar from the realm of the literary and moves him into that of the pastoral. In other words, Vaughan Williams recasts Elgar as a pastoral nationalist, a veritable Dvořák of Albion – and thus a suitable precursor of his own musical idiom and nationalist preoccupations. Later in this essay, Vaughan Williams states his reasons for awarding Elgar such a prominent niche in the pantheon of English musical history: "It falls the lot of very few composers, and to them not often, to achieve this bond of unity with their countrymen. Elgar has achieved this more often than most and, be it

1 – Notes for this chapter appear on pages 164–5.

noted, not when he is being deliberately 'popular', as in *Land of Hope and Glory* or *Cockaigne*, but at those moments when he seems to have retired into the solitude of his own sanctuary." [3]

Vaughan Williams articulated his own aspirations while eulogizing his departed colleague, for he clearly aspired, like Elgar, to forge a "bond of unity" with his countrymen. But for Vaughan Williams the creation of such a bond must be on his own terms: the eulogist tellingly dismisses two of Elgar's most popular scores: *Land of Hope and Glory*, which may have seemed too jingoistic for the younger composer; and the *Cockaigne* Overture, which was perhaps too extroverted and urban for Vaughan Williams's taste by 1935.

By repositioning Elgar in this manner, Vaughan Williams may have sought to lighten somewhat the burden of the traditions that he had inherited from his musical elders. Vaughan Williams was fond of paraphrasing a dictum of the classicist Gilbert Murray to the effect that "original genius is at once the child of tradition and a rebel against it".[4] Unlike America, where the cultural productions of preceding generations are simply thrown upon what Marx has termed the "ash heap of history", in England the relation of composers to their past is quite different.

In a controversial tome entitled *The Anxiety of Influence: A Theory of Poetry*, the noted literary critic Harold Bloom adapted Freud's hypothesis concerning the Oedipal struggle that he insists occurs between all heterosexual fathers and their sons. Bloom finds in Freud a congenial explanation for the struggle he posits between strong poets against their predecessors. According to Bloom's theories, a weak poet succumbs to imitation, idealization and allusion, while a strong poet assimilates and then annihilates the work of poets of previous generations. Bloom goes so far as to assert that "weaker talents idealize; figures of capable imagination appropriate for themselves". He is concerned "only with strong poets, major figures with the persistence to wrestle with their strong precursors, even to the death".

Aside from the bleak social Darwinism evinced by this theory, not to mention a crude misappropriation of Freud's already rather literal hypotheses, Bloom's vision is one of, as Raymond Knapp aptly states, "underlying ungenerosity".[5] Contemplating Bloom's theory, it is useful to recall Richard Taruskin's searching critique: "At its core is bleakness – a view of human nature founded on jealousy, territoriality, resentment." [6] As Knapp observes, Bloom implies that "idealizing – which is to say, respecting and valuing the work of others – is a mark of weakness and failure". [7]

Were he to read Vaughan Williams's essay, Bloom would surely dismiss him as a "weak poet" on the basis of his admission of how much he 'cribbed' from Elgar. Vaughan Williams declares forthrightly, "I suppose one may say that when one has cribbed from a composer once has learnt from him . . . I am astonished, if I may be allowed a personal explanation, to find on looking back on my own earlier works, how much I cribbed from him". Bloom might be slightly more tolerant of this assertion: "Real cribbing takes place when one composer thinks with the mind of another even when there is no mechanical similarity of phrase . . . In that case one is so impressed by a certain passage in another composer that it becomes part of oneself." In a later passage, Vaughan Williams notes how deeply he was influenced by a phrase from *The Dream of Gerontius*, set to the words sung by Elgar's eponymous protagonist, "Thou art calling me". To prove his case, Vaughan Williams cites irrefutable evidence: "For proof of this see *Sea Symphony* (vocal score, p.84, nine bars before letter B) and *London Symphony* (full score, p.16, letter H)."

Vaughan Williams may well have considered such 'cribbing' part of a process by which each generation learned and evolved from their precursors. Vaughan Williams was an heir to the Victorian faith in evolutionary progress, however much he may have later questioned the validity of this ideology – and he did question it searchingly during the Second World War and its atomic aftermath – he never wholly eschewed its promise for humanity. Although the writings of his great uncle Charles Darwin may have played a part in the development of such convictions, Vaughan Williams saw music history through the prism of ideas developed by his teacher Hubert Parry. Parry's formulation was influenced by the 'scientific' evolutionary philosophy of Herbert Spenser, as he articulated in his suggestively titled *The Evolution of the Art of Music*.[8] Vaughan Williams maintained that each generation evolved inexorably towards higher accomplishment, and that such musical evolution culminated in the flourishing of a supremely gifted composer. Furthermore, he believed that each generation must honour the standards bequeathed to them by the achievement of their predecessors, and yet must distinguish their thinking by challenging the assumptions of generations that they have succeeded; in other words, composers must be simultaneously the heirs of tradition and rebels from it.

Living in an ironic postmodern era, we may smile at the confident faith in 'progress' evinced by the Victorians. Interpreted as an historical metaphor, however, Vaughan Williams's evolutionary progressivism can become a remarkably accurate way to account for the changes that occur in musical taste, a paradigm that is by the way more humane than that of Harold Bloom. In fact, Vaughan Williams's evolutionary ideology was remarkably flexible. He virtually reinvented all of the traditions that he selected from the past: he thought nothing of making an idealized version of a folksong to suit his own taste, and he absorbed only such aspects of Tudor music as appealed to him.[9]

Although innocent of a ravening need to devour his precursors after the example of Bloom's "strong poet", Vaughan Williams certainly regarded the previous generation of English composers with ambivalence. Vaughan Williams's admiration for Parry was tempered by his recognition that his teacher's puritanical abhorrence of luscious sonorities had circumscribed his expressive range. Vaughan Williams also observed that Stanford's formidable technical acumen led the older composer to accept facility as an end in itself, thus diluting the expressive force of his music.

Of all of his older contemporaries, Elgar posed the greatest challenge to Vaughan Williams's powers of assimilation. Unlike Parry and Stanford, Elgar was an autodidact who sprang forth virtually *sui generis* without benefit of public school, university or academic musical training. Vaughan Williams acknowledged that Elgar's music outpaced that of Parry and Stanford in skill, intensity and formal assurance. This must have been a hard, even bitter, admission for the younger composer, as he admired Parry and his other teachers at the Royal College of Music, most of whom viewed Elgar with suspicion if not – as in the case of Stanford – corrosive envy. Vaughan Williams's statements concerning Elgar are a conflation of qualified admiration and brusque assertion.

Exacerbating Vaughan Williams's ambivalence concerning Elgar were the acute disparities between their respective social status, education and personalities. One cannot imagine two men more dissimilar, with the possible exception of Vaughan Williams and Britten. Vaughan Williams, the scion of intellectual Anglican gentry, carefully crafted a public persona that was forthright and utterly British. He was a leftist radical whose vision of England chimed with that of such progressives as William Morris, Gilbert Murray and E M Forster.

What must have Vaughan Williams, a radical agnostic with a Cambridge degree, thought of Elgar? What did he make of the Elgar who appeared in flamboyant court dress to conduct at the Three Choirs; the Elgar who hungered after the kinds of official honours that he disdained; the Elgar who wrote an overtly Roman Catholic masterpiece, *The Dream of Gerontius*; the Elgar who was a true-blue Tory; the Elgar who, with his adoring wife, was such a social climber that many, such as Osbert Sitwell, considered him little better than a parvenu? All of these factors, added to Elgar's constant nervous blinking and habit of weeping when conducting his music, must have made Vaughan Williams acutely uncomfortable.

What, then, did Elgar think of Vaughan Williams? How could he not have reflexively distrusted the younger man? Vaughan Williams was a pupil of his great enemy Stanford and an associate of such convinced anti-Elgarians as Hugh Allen, Cyril Rootham and, worst of all, Edward Dent. For a man who famously declared, "I write the folk-songs of this country" [10] and who had little interest in early music, Elgar must have found Vaughan Williams's obsession with folk song and Tudor music an incomprehensible fad. And finally, the touchy Elgar may have resented the younger composer's social status and modest inherited income.

And yet, despite these unpromising impediments, the two composers seem to have maintained a professional *entente cordiale*. For his part, Vaughan Williams realized the limitations of his training at the Royal College, and sought to broaden his horizons by studying with the older man. Politely rebuffed by Alice Elgar when he attempted to secure some lessons with her husband, Vaughan Williams testifies that he spent hours in the British Library studying the 'Enigma' Variations and *The Dream of Gerontius*.

And, despite the caveat in his essay on Elgar, Vaughan Williams must have attentively studied the *Cockaigne* Overture as well. For all of his vaunted downrightness, Vaughan Williams was – like many composers, including Elgar – often quite cagey when discussing the influence of other composers upon his music. He downplayed the decisive impact of his studies with both Bruch and Ravel upon the development of his mature style. As Roland John Wiley shrewdly notes, "Surely we should not accept at face value composers' statements about composers including themselves . . . we should not be inclined to agree with them but rather be suspicious of their motives if one disclaims the influence of another".[11] (Especially when the composer in question succumbed to the temptation of retrospectively revising the history of their stylistic evolution, a habit to which Vaughan Williams became prone as he grew older, most spectacularly in his *Musical Autobiography* of 1950.)

Evidence that Vaughan Williams was fascinated with Elgar's *Cockaigne* Overture is reflected by two sources: an article from 1912 entitled 'Who Wants the English Composer?' and the opening movement of *A London*

Symphony (Second Symphony, 1914; revised 1918, 1920 and 1934), composed at the same time as the essay was written.

By 1912, the *Cockaigne* Overture, op.40, which was premièred in 1901, was established as one of Elgar's most popular orchestral scores; its ubiquity on concert programmes guaranteed that Vaughan Williams would have heard it often. With his omnivorous curiosity, it is unimaginable that Vaughan Williams did not study this popular work.

With its cheeky cockneys, Salvation Army bands and military processions, Elgar's *Cockaigne* Overture presents a vivid musical portrait of a teeming city. While Elgar was characteristically elusive about the existence of a programme for the overture, his letters confirm that he was thinking in terms of a work "cheerful and London – 'stout and steaky'" and he admitted that "certainly a military band passes".[12] Two critics who knew Elgar well, Edwin Evans, who wrote the introductory analysis for the Boosey and Hawkes Pocket Score, and Ernest Newman both use synoptic language that draws upon this imagery to describe the music. The coruscating vitality of *Cockaigne* derives from its engagement with urban vernacular music: the military band, the music hall, and what Ernest Newman identified as the whistle of "the perky, self-confident unabashable London street boy".[13]

Some eleven years after the première of the *Cockaigne* Overture, Vaughan Williams wrote his essay 'Who Wants the English Composer?' and, amazingly, published this incendiary polemic in the 1912 Christmas Term issue of *The Royal College of Music Magazine*. If Vaughan Williams's ambition with this essay was to differentiate himself from the aesthetic assumptions of his teachers, he succeeded brilliantly: Stanford was predictably furious, and even the broadminded Parry dismissed his pupil's essay as "chaff".[14] What in this essay prompted Stanford's ire and Parry's dismay?

Although 'Who Wants the English Composer?' is often described as propaganda in a campaign to establish folk-song the cornerstone of British composition, in fact Vaughan Williams barely alludes to rural traditions. Instead, he writes an extended encomium to urban vernacular music: "the lilt of the chorus at a music hall joining in a popular song, the children dancing to a barrel organ, the rousing fervour of a Salvation Army hymn, St Paul's and a great choir singing in one of its festivals, the Welshmen striking up one of their hymns whenever they win a goal at the international football match, the cries of the street pedlars, the factory girls singing their sentimental songs".

Such proletarian music meant a great deal to at least one English composer, for Vaughan Williams's celebration of urban music echoes the programmatic descriptions associated with the *Cockaigne* Overture. Vaughan Williams's familiarity with *Cockaigne* becomes even more apparent if Elgar's overture is juxtaposed with the younger composer's *A London Symphony*. While a full comparison of the two works is beyond the scope of this investigation, several broad connections can be mentioned briefly. Aside from the obvious – that both scores are celebrations of the same city – the *Cockaigne* Overture and *A London Symphony* are filled with strikingly similar musical imagery: evocations of Cockney music making with barrel organs and concertinas; reminiscences of music halls; and martial hymns from Salvation Army bands. Like *Cockaigne*, the first movement of *A London Symphony* has an extended subdued interruption whose poignancy offsets lively music that portrays, in Vaughan Williams's words, the "noise and scurry" of the city. Both of these quiet interruptions have evoked vaguely ecclesiastical descriptions: in his analysis of *Cockaigne*, Edwin Evans envisions two lovers entering a hushed London church, while Michael Kennedy characterizes the analogous section in the first movement of the symphony as "a quiet reverie which seems to suggest London's green places, or the inside of a church". [15]

But few would describe *A London Symphony* as a mere homage to *Cockaigne* as is for example John Ireland's *London Overture* (1936). While assimilating elements from Elgar's score, Vaughan Williams filters these through the prism of his peculiar musical preferences, achieving thereby an aesthetic distance from both *Cockaigne* and Elgar's style in general. As early critics correctly surmised,[16] Elgar's overture owes a formal and expressive debt to Wagner's Overture to *Die Meistersinger*. Vaughan Williams's symphony would have been unthinkable without a prolonged study of the orchestral music of Ravel and Debussy. In his essay on Elgar, Vaughan Williams makes a telling distinction: "I do not consider that the opening of my *London Symphony* is a crib from the beginning of *Gerontius* Part 2; indeed, my friends assure me that it is, as a matter of fact, a compound of Debussy's *La Mer* and Charpentier's *Louise*." [17] Vaughan Williams's rejection – or, at least, substantial modification – of the Teutonic tradition upon which Elgar predicated much of his work could not have been stated more explicitly.

While Vaughan Williams declined to acknowledge the influence of *Cockaigne* upon *A London Symphony*, he did willingly admit to a 'crib' from one of Elgar's other works, the 'Thou Art Calling Me' phrase from

The Dream of Gerontius. This phrase appears as a prominent thematic element of *A London Symphony*, but reoccurs throughout the earlier *A Sea Symphony* like an *idée fixe*. Unlike his friend Edward Dent, who mockingly referred to Elgar's oratorio as "Gerry's Nightmare",[18] Vaughan Williams commended the skill evinced in *Gerontius*, was moved by a great deal of the music (if, in all probability, slightly repelled by the text), and conducted an acclaimed broadcast performance of the score during the 1934 Leith Hill Festival. By a sad synchronicity, the final rehearsals for this performance of *Gerontius* occurred while its composer himself lay dying.

This coincidence prompts a crucial question: why did Vaughan Williams so deeply love this phrase of music from *Gerontius* that he felt impelled to make it his own? An agnostic, Vaughan Williams would hardly have prized the words "Jesu, Maria, I am near to death, And Thou art calling me" as an expression of Roman Catholic belief. Dogma aside, these words, set to this phrase, are not merely the plaint of a dying man or the letter of a specific creed. They express a call to spiritual adventure in an unknown region. Vaughan Williams wrote that the "object of art is to stretch out to the ultimate realities through the medium of beauty". Furthermore, he opined that "the human, visible, audible and intelligible media which artists (of all kinds) use, are symbols not of other visible and audible things but of what lies beyond sense and knowledge . . . the symbols of the musical composer are those of the ear".[19] The phrase from *Gerontius* that appears in both *A Sea Symphony* and *A London Symphony* is not merely a 'crib' but also a musical symbol representing a transcendent quest, undertaken by the Soul of Gerontius in the second part of Elgar's oratorio. In his own way Vaughan Williams expresses a similar desire for spiritual adventure in the finale of *A Sea Symphony* through his setting of Walt Whitman's exhortation: "Away, O Soul! hoist instantly the anchor!"

While Vaughan Williams's official tribute to Elgar, the essay in *Music & Letters*, was necessarily conditioned by his almost filial need to assert his independence from his great predecessor, he sent a more spontaneous tribute in the form of a letter that was posted just three days before Elgar's death. Vaughan Williams wrote of *Gerontius* that "I had been longing to do it for years, but had thought it too dangerous an experiment as I could not bear to do it badly . . . it will be one of the great moments of my life when I stand with trembling baton to conduct it". And, in heartfelt lines that recall the passing of generations as well as the poignant silence of those who have vanished from this world, Vaughan Williams concluded, "we shall think of you – please give us your blessing. Of course, this wants no answer".

Stanford, Elgar and Vaughan Williams
Influences and Reflections

Michael Pope

The 150th anniversary of the birth of Stanford last September prompts various questions relevant to the theme of this symposium. How much did Elgar and Vaughan Williams owe to Stanford? What influence did Elgar have on Vaughan Williams? What is the relation between their music and the works of Stanford's maturity? What reflections can be drawn from their artistic philosophies?

In October 1885 Edward Elgar played with the first violins in the Birmingham Festival Choral Society's performance of Stanford's new oratorio *The Three Holy Children*, under the direction of William Stockley. This experience evidently made an impression.[1] In *Elgar in Manuscript*, published by the British Library in 1990, Dr Robert Anderson pointed out that Elgar had jotted down a reference to "C.V.S. 3 Children" on one of the sketches for *The Dream of Gerontius*.[2]

In 1896 Stanford spent his summer holiday in Malvern, staying at Tintern House in Abbey Road. At the beginning of September he completed his *Requiem* for the Birmingham Festival of 1897, and wrote to Elgar to ask how he could best meet the new chorus master of the Festival, Charles Swinnerton Heap, the dedicatee of *The Light of Life*. Elgar was then living a mile or so away, at Forli in Alexandra Road. He had just finished the full score of his cantata *King Olaf*, and he arranged a meeting at Forli on 15 September, at which Stanford went through his *Requiem* with Dr Heap. Stanford and his wife Jennie visited the Elgars again three days later, and the following day the two composers walked to Birchwood. No doubt Stanford heard parts of *King Olaf* during these visits, and he certainly grew to admire the work.[3] A few days before the first performance, at the end of October, he sent a friendly letter to Elgar from 50 Holland Street, Kensington, ending with the words: "Good luck to yr. Norseman".[4] As Dr Percy Young has said, it was the first evidence of his generous attitude to a brother composer.[5]

1 – Notes for this chapter appear on pages 166–7.

6. Pope – Stanford, Elgar and Vaughan Williams

The warmly lyrical qualities of the cantata are demonstrated by the love duet in Scene 7, between Olaf, the King of Norway, and his recently-wedded wife, Thyri, sister of Svend, King of Denmark. The scene is set at Trondheim in early Spring of the year 1000. Thyri is urging Olaf to redeem her domains from Burislaf of Vendland, but their underlying love is manifest in Elgar's ardent setting.

Example 1 [§]

Stanford's pioneering support of Elgar and his music is vividly conveyed to us by Sir Alexander Mackenzie, then Principal of the Royal Academy of Music, in his autobiography, *A Musician's Narrative*: "The publication of *King Olaf* brought Edward Elgar's name into sudden prominence by immediately stamping him as an exceedingly accomplished musician .... It was Stanford who enthusiastically drew my attention to the almost unknown new-comer's splendid gifts..." [6]

At the Royal College of Music and the Leeds Festival Stanford continued to champion Elgar's works, especially *Sea Pictures* and the 'Enigma' Variations. Nor did he forget *King Olaf*, which he conducted at a Leeds Philharmonic Society concert in November 1905.[7] In 1900, as Professor of Music at Cambridge, he recommended that the University should confer on Elgar the honorary degree of Doctor of Music.[8] This was the first honour which Elgar was to receive.

In 1903 Stanford asked Elgar if he could put his name down for membership of The Athenaeum. With the support of Parry, who was on the Committee, Elgar was elected a member of the Club in April 1904, under Rule II relating to "persons of distinguished eminence in science, literature or the arts, or for their public service..." [9]

In addition to these and other signs of appreciation, the trail which Stanford had blazed in every branch of composition was one which might encourage and inspire his younger contemporaries, even subconsciously: symphonies and concertos; cantatas and oratorios; operas and incidental music; motets, anthems and services; partsongs and keyboard works; songs and chamber music. To all these Stanford made a notable contribution.

Dr Thomas Dunhill, who admired the work of both composers, pointed out that Stanford and his senior contemporaries belonged to "a previous school of musical thought" to that of Elgar.[10] Further, Stanford

[§] – See page 84 for a list of the musical examples accompanying this lecture.

tended towards the Apollonian means of expression characteristic of Brahms, whereas Elgar tended more towards the Apollonian embodiment of the Dionysiac spirit. It should however be stressed that Stanford described Wagner, in his book on *Musical Composition* of 1911, as "one of the greatest masters of our day".[11]

Elgar held that "the Symphony without a programme is the highest development of art".[12] Stanford believed that while a picture may suggest musical ideas to a composer, no detailed explanations can be given without narrowing the effect of the composition.[13] In June 1905 he completed his Sixth Symphony, in E flat, in memory of the great painter and sculptor George Frederick Watts, who had died the previous year. It was inspired by several works of Watts on the general theme of Life, Love, and Death, and its eloquence of expression may be illustrated by the fine melodic line of the Adagio.

Example 2

To hear the whole symphony is to understand more completely John Porte's comment that "The creative spirit of Stanford in its maturity has much that is akin to Elgar".[14] The Sixth Symphony is perhaps the greatest of Stanford's seven symphonies, and it is a matter of real concern that, unlike Nos.3, 4, 5 and 7, it has not yet been published. Since today is the 79th anniversary of the composer's death, it seems appropriate to suggest that strenuous efforts should be made to bring about publication of this work – one of the outstanding symphonies to appear in Britain before Elgar's A flat some three years later – in time, if possible, to mark the Watts Centenary in July 2004.

Let us turn now to Ralph Vaughan Williams, who was a composition pupil of Stanford at the Royal College of Music between 1895 and 1897. He later wrote an account of that period which sheds valuable light on his teacher: "When all is said and done, what one really gets out of lessons with a great man cannot be computed in terms of what he said to you or what you did for him, but in terms of the intangible contact with his mind and character. With Stanford I always felt I was in the presence of a lovable, powerful, and enthralling mind."[15]

Stanford's influence was much in evidence during the years to come. It was owing to his strong recommendation that Vaughan Williams's song 'Linden Lea' became his first published composition in 1902;[16] and it was under his auspices that the Leeds Festival promoted the first performances of *Toward the Unknown Region* in 1907 and *A Sea Symphony* in 1910.

6. Pope – Stanford, Elgar and Vaughan Williams

Vaughan Williams was in the audience at the Birmingham Town Hall on 3 October 1900 when Elgar's *Dream of Gerontius* received its first performance.[17] He later described how he spent several hours at the British Museum, studying the full scores of the *Enigma* Variations and *Gerontius*. "The results", he said, "are obvious in the opening pages of the finale of my *Sea Symphony*..." After Elgar's death he wrote: "I find that the Elgar phrase which influenced me most was 'Thou art calling me' in *Gerontius* ... not so much perhaps in its original form as when it comes later on in combination with another theme."[18] This motive, named by Jaeger "Christ's Peace",[19] appears as a counter-subject at Fig.37, where it is played by flutes, clarinets, and violas. It is then taken up by the first violins, followed by the basses singing 'By Thy birth'.

Example 3

The figure of an ascending fifth, followed by a descending triplet, was a potent influence on Vaughan Williams. In the introduction to the fourth movement of *A Sea Symphony*, 'The Explorers', it undergoes what we may well call a 'sea-change', with the triplet on the fifth beat, lower in the scale, and the tempo marked *Grave e molto Adagio*. The words by Whitman, for whose poetry Vaughan Williams retained a lifelong admiration, were included in 1917 in the *Oxford Book of English Mystical Verse*:

> O vast Rondure, swimming in space,
> Covered all over with visible power and beauty ...

Example 4

Dr Ernest Walker, in the 1924 edition of his *History of Music in England*, described *A Sea Symphony* as a great choral landmark, and placed it in Vaughan Williams's second period.[20] It seems to me that the visionary mastery of that music gives cogent support to such a view.

Stanford, who admired *A Sea Symphony*, may well have encouraged Vaughan Williams's interest in Whitman's poetry. His own *Elegiac Ode*, which had come out in 1884, was a pioneering setting of Whitman, and, as Dr Jeremy Dibble points out in his new biography of Stanford, was arguably the first substantial musical interpretation of his verse.[21]

Stanford's ode is one of many works which deserve revival, along with other fine choral works by Mackenzie and Parry; and it is a matter for regret that the art-forms of the oratorio and the cantata were subjected to such blasts of adverse comment by 'Corno di Bassetto', alias G.B.S. That

Shaw was a brilliant and amusing writer, who became an outstanding playwright and a stimulating philosopher, could not be denied; but his destructive sallies as, in his own words, a "constitutional scoffer" need no longer be taken seriously. It may be of interest to add that some years ago, in a conversation with Maurice Jacobson, who was a pupil of Stanford at the Royal College of Music, our discussion turned to the dramatic oratorio *Eden*, op.40, which has a libretto by Bridges and is dedicated to Parry. He told me that this work, which had been performed at the Birmingham Festival in 1891, meant a great deal to Stanford; and when I was later able to arrange a broadcast of the *madrigale spirituale*, 'Flames of pure love', I began to understand why.[22]

It was Dunhill who described Stanford as "the first considerable British composer to write Chamber music of importance..." [23] His major contribution in this field included eight string quartets, composed between 1891 and 1919. It seemed to me strange that they were so unfamiliar, and that the last three had not yet been published. In 1968, after perusing the manuscript of one of these, I became convinced that it should be broadcast.

Example 5

Stanford's Eighth Quartet, in E minor, was completed in June 1919, and illustrates the ripe mastery of his later chamber music. It was given its first performance by the London String Quartet on BBC Radio 3 in March 1968. The first concert performance took place the following November at the Savile Club, where Stanford was a member for forty years from 1884 until his death. It is worth mentioning that after Sir Sidney Colvin proposed Elgar for membership of the Savile on 14 November 1918, the signatures of members who signed in support included that of C.V. Stanford; and Elgar was duly elected on 24 January 1919.

Stanford displayed what Professor Edward Dent described as "a more than Handelian courage" in writing operas for most of his life, from *The Veiled Prophet of Khorassan* of 1879 to *The Travelling Companion* of 1916.[24] Fuller-Maitland summed up their claims to be made known to the public with these words: "Stanford's vivacity in humorous situations, expressiveness in tragic, easy mastery of all the resources of music, and readiness to accept any challenge offered him by dramatic situation or problems, are merits that cannot be ignored for ever." [25] Seven of his nine completed operas are published, and their neglect is hard to understand.

6. Pope – Stanford, Elgar and Vaughan Williams

One might have thought that the trail he blazed, including his reasoned advocacy for an English National Opera as long ago as 1908,[26] would have made the situation better for his successors. Unfortunately there are many cases where this is not so. Three of the most important English operas since 1945 had problematic productions followed by greater or lesser neglect thereafter: *The Olympians* by Bliss (1949); *The Pilgrim's Progress* by Vaughan Williams (1951); and *Troilus and Cressida* by Walton (1954). Of course many of the problems have arisen through lack of adequate funding; and it is clearly essential that a proper level of financial support should be available to assist the staging of operas which are of importance to the artistic heritage of Britain.

There are those who regard *The Pilgrim's Progress* as one of Vaughan Williams's supreme achievements.[27] When I was lucky enough to hear a fine performance of the work at the Royal Northern College of Music in 1992, I felt that it represented the quintessence of his art, and threw fresh light on his music. Its character and quality are well represented by the Second Scene of Act II. Doleful Creatures are wandering about howling in the Valley of Humiliation. Apollyon, the Destroyer, confronts the Pilgrim. There is a hard struggle, but Pilgrim wins.

Example 6

Last August one of our daily newspapers asked if there were still compelling reasons for English National Opera to exist. I would suggest that *The Pilgrim's Progress*, *The Olympians*, and *Troilus* provide excellent reasons, quite apart from exploring Stanford and the other neglected composers of English opera.

What final reflections can we draw from these three great musicians? Stanford wrote in his *Studies and Memories* that "we are in danger, and imminent danger, of a set-back of the clock, of losing touch with the most ennobling, the most civilising ... of all the arts..." [28]

Let us now hear Elgar: "changes are in the air and all around us; now is the time to divert the stream of money ... into the pure river of art and give English music the refreshing support it so much needs." [29]

And now Vaughan Williams: "May we take it that the object of an art is to obtain a partial revelation of that which is beyond human senses and human faculties – of that, in fact, which is spiritual?" [30]

Each of these illustrious composers enriched immeasurably the Fine Art of Music. Let us resolve that the flames they lit, each a special flame, shall continue to burn brightly in the years ahead.

Acknowledgements

The lecturer wishes to acknowledge with gratitude the help of Mr Timothy Day, Mr Simon Rooks, Miss Catherine Sloan, and the staff of the Guildhall Library.

List of Musical Examples Played

1. Elgar: *King Olaf* – Love duet from Scene 7: 'I fear not, doubt not',
   Teresa Cahill (soprano), Philip Langridge (tenor),
   London Philharmonic Orchestra conducted by Vernon Handley
   (E 2705541).

2. Stanford: Symphony no.6 in E flat, op.94 – part of slow movement
   Ulster Orchestra conducted by Vernon Handley
   (CHAN 8267).

3. Elgar: *The Dream of Gerontius* – 'By Thy birth'
   Combined Hallé Choir & Sheffield Philharmonic Chorus,
   Ambrosian Singers, Hallé Orchestra, conducted by Sir John Barbirolli
   (ASD 648).

4. Vaughan Williams: *A Sea Symphony* – 4th movement: 'O vast Rondure'
   London Philharmonic Choir & Orchestra conducted by Sir Adrian Boult
   (CDM7 64016–2).

5. Stanford: String Quartet no.8 in E minor, op.167 – part of 1st movement
   London String Quartet (Carl Pini (violin), Ray Gillard (violin),
   Christopher Martin (viola), and Anthony Pini (cello))
   (Recording made available by courtesy of BBC Sound Archives).

6. Vaughan Williams: *The Pilgrim's Progress* –
   Act II, Scene 2: Pilgrim's encounter with Apollyon
   John Noble (baritone), Robert Lloyd (bass),
   London Philharmonic Choir & Orchestra conducted by Sir Adrian Boult
   (CMS7 64212–2).

"My dear Elgar"
The Letters of Elgar and Vaughan Williams

Hugh Cobbe

The title of this article reflects more the intentions of the piece than the reality. As it stands it might be taken to imply that a long and friendly correspondence between Elgar and Vaughan Williams survives, giving us insights into both men and their music – but this is not the case. There appear to be only two letters extant written by Vaughan Williams (hereafter 'VW') to Elgar (neither incidentally beginning with the familiarity of "My dear Elgar"), both published in Jerrold Northrop Moore's *Letters of a Lifetime* (and just one brief postcard in the other direction). Both these letters were written towards or, in the case of the second, right at, the end of Elgar's life. Furthermore a brief examination of the indexes of the various published collections of Elgar's letters reveals that Elgar appears never to have mentioned Vaughan Williams in his letters to anyone else (though this of course is open to correction). However there are interesting insights to be found by comparing the two corpuses of letters as a whole, the two actual letters from VW to Elgar themselves raising interesting questions which will emerge later, and even if Elgar did not refer to VW in his correspondence, VW did refer to Elgar on a number of occasions and these references together help delineate the relationship between the two men. In the paper that follows the topic is largely considered from the perspective of Vaughan Williams since the paper emanates from a VW-based project rather than an Elgar-based one.

According to Jerrold Northrop Moore[1] more than 10,000 letters from and to Elgar are preserved in public collections, many at the Elgar Birthplace; in contrast, the number of extant letters in the VW database is at present only about 3,250, almost entirely outgoing letters. That is not to say that the one composer actually *wrote* fewer letters than the other it is probably more to do with personal habits in paper management. Elgar's papers were clearly kept in good order, almost certainly by Alice

1 – Notes for this chapter appear on pages 167–8.

(though also aided, in the case of the music manuscripts, by a wide variety of rubber stamps now arrayed in the birthplace) and his incoming correspondence was filed away carefully; VW on the other hand discarded incoming letters into a large wastepaper basket once they had been dealt with. It is not clear how many of Moore's 10,000 letters are incoming rather than outgoing, but if say 50% of Moore's figure is taken as the number of incoming letters, the figures for outgoing letters become more comparable – 5,000 Elgar as opposed to 3,250 VW survivors. The remaining discrepancy cannot be explained by length of life: since Elgar died at the age of nearly 77 and VW at the age of nearly 86, one would expect to find more VW than Elgar letters. Factors in the matter probably include the advent of the telephone whose use became widespread at an earlier stage in VW's life than in Elgar's. However the most likely reason for the discrepancy probably comes down to the accident of survival – I have calculated that the 3,250 letters collected so far in my database represent only about 20% of the number of letters one might expect VW to have written over his lifetime. The survival rate of Elgar letters seems to be rather higher – does this mean that overall they were more treasured by their original recipients? The existence of the Birthplace Museum as an obvious repository may also have been crucial in ensuring survival – experience indicates that similarly the Britten-Pears Library's existence in Aldeburgh has played a key role in concentrating Britten letters. The fact that, for good reasons, no institution devoted to VW has ever been established may therefore have something to do with the rate of survival of his letters, though it is good that, as a result of the letters project, the number of VW letters held by the British Library has grown considerably.

As has been said, only two letters between the composers have survived (and there is no indication that there were ever any others); and the indexes to the published collections of Elgar's letters reveal no glancing references to VW in other letters. Writing in 1944, declining to provide a reminiscence for the tenth anniversary of Elgar's death, VW said:

> I had very little acquaintance with Elgar — I used to meet him for a few minutes once a year at the 3 choir [sic] festivals — he was always very kind & friendly — but we were never intimates.[2]

From the point of view of Elgar, is it the case that VW and his music simply were of little interest? They met briefly at the Three Choirs and even shared concerts such as that in 1910 at Gloucester when VW conducted the first performance of the *Fantasia on a theme by Thomas Tallis* and Elgar

7. Cobbe – "My dear Elgar"

The Dream of Gerontius. But Elgar was inherently unsympathetic to the underlying spirit, based in part on folk-song, of the music of VW and his circle. VW himself explained this in understanding terms in *National Music*[3] pointing out that folk-songs were simply not "in the air" at the time Elgar was forming his musical style.

Turning to VW's view of Elgar, one is reminded of the amusing image recorded by Benjamin Britten in his diary for July 1937 (quoted in Humphrey Carpenter's biography[4]). Speaking of William Walton, Britten remarks:

> He is so obviously the head-prefect of English music, whereas I'm the promising new boy. Soon of course he'll leave and return as a member of the staff — Vaughan Williams being of course the Headmaster. Elgar was never that but a member of the governing Board.[5]

If the image is taken back a generation, it seems clear that VW in his early years regarded Elgar as the Headmaster of English music (with perhaps Parry as Deputy Head?). Indeed VW at one point sought lessons with the 'Headmaster', as he recalled in his musical autobiography, but was turned down in a letter from Alice Elgar, who said Elgar was too busy and suggested he approach Granville Bantock.[6] He had to be content with simply studying the Headmaster's published works. In his public references he always treated Elgar with due deference, such as in this passage from *National Music*:

> I have some hesitation in discussing in public or venturing to appraise the music of one whom we, in England, all revere as our leader.[7]

However it is worth noting that, with the exception of that remark which dates from 1932, the others in his published writing all postdate Elgar's death in 1934. The significance of that will become clearer.

Considering the references to Elgar in VW's private letters over the years will perhaps give us a more personal picture of VW's attitude to his senior colleague. The earliest mention of Elgar in the database is not in fact in a letter of VW but in one written by Gustav Holst to VW while on holiday in Germany in 1903.

> Seeing foreigners is a mistake as a rule. Don't you think we ought to victimise Elgar? Write to him first and then bicycle to Worcester and see him a lot? I wish we could do that together. Or else make a list of musicians in London whom we think worthy of the honour of being bothered by us and who have time and inclination to be bothered and then bother them.[8]

I include this because there is something of the air of the schoolboy about it – 'let's go and tease the Headmaster' as it were, to pursue the Britten simile. It is not quite clear what Holst was suggesting they would do as they appeared regularly on Elgar's doorstep – the plan would in all likelihood have been doomed to failure at the hands of Alice Elgar.

Moving on to less familiar territory, VW wrote in March 1910 to Ruth Charrington, the daughter of Mrs W Hadley who was the organiser of the dramatization of *The Pilgrim's Progress* at Reigate Priory in 1906 which sowed the seeds for VW's great opera of nearly 50 years later. Ruth Charrington was then secretary of an amateur orchestra called the St Valentine String Orchestra of which VW was the conductor. For a concert, probably in March 1910, alongside the Suite in B minor and two choral preludes by Bach, folk-songs sung by Clive Carey (including Greek folk-songs arranged by Ravel), songs of his own and finally music by Grieg, VW programmed Elgar's *Serenade for Strings* which had received its first professional performance in London only five years before. Sadly the orchestra ceased to exist in November of that year.[9]

In the following year, 1911, VW wrote to Cecil Sharp to congratulate him on being awarded a Civil List pension of £100 pa in recognition of his work on folk-song and dance. VW had, characteristically, taken a leading role in the efforts to bring this about. In particular he had sought support from leading figures, both literary and musical, and, as he tells Sharp:

> I wish you cd have seen the document we sent in to the prime minister — it was the most remarkable collection of distinguished names I have ever seen — about 30 in all — and I am certain many more wd have signed if they had been asked only we were advised that with such a list we need go no further. I cannot remember them all but here are a few of them: Lord Alverstone, Baring-Gould, Thomas Hardy, Frazer, E.V. Lucas, Gilbert Murray, C.V. Stanford, Edward Elgar, Plunket Greene, Henry J. Wood, J. Masefield etc. (By the way this is private because they do not know that you know they have signed). You see you have admirers in all sorts of unexpected quarters![10]

I would be surprised if Elgar was quite as enthusiastic about this proposal as VW, though he was a founding member, by invitation, of the Folk Song Society.[11]

It was Cecil Sharp who gave Fox-Strangways the idea of founding the quarterly *Music & Letters*[12] (which remains to this day as one of the two major journals in British musicology): the first issue in January 1920 included an article by G B Shaw on Elgar while the second in April of that year included an article by Fox-Strangways himself on VW. VW referred to Shaw's Elgar article years later in a 1952 talk on Stanford:

> The belittling of Stanford's work was encouraged by one who ought to have known better. The late Mr. Bernard Shaw in the first number of "Music and Letters" used Elgar as a stick to beat what he called "the Academic Clique" forgetting, or pretending to forget, that it was the acknowledged head of this "clique", Hubert Parry who was instrumental in obtaining the first performance of Elgar's variations.[13]

The direct juxtaposition in *Music & Letters* makes clear that Elgar and VW were, for the musical public of the time, the two figureheads of English music. Further, we know from *Letters of a Lifetime* that when the filling of the position of Master of the King's Musick was under discussion in the Royal Household in April 1924 the choice lay between Elgar and VW; VW was thought "to be the most representative of British music" but Elgar, already an OM, was the senior figure and indeed had expressed interest in the post (VW would almost certainly have politely declined).[14]

In 1928 VW wrote to Holst about the Gloucester Three Choirs Festival:

> I enjoyed Gloucester v. much ... I also shared bottles of beer with Elgar but, I fear, rather pained him by saying that in my opinion the Reformation was indirectly responsible for the 3 choirs festival, since if we had kept the celibacy of the clergy we shd not have to have provided for their widows, but only their orphans.[15]

There is a slight reprise of the mischievous schoolboy here but in fact this is the first time there is, in the letters, a report by VW of a direct contact – though, as we know, they encountered each other regularly at the Three Choirs.

About August in the following year (1929) VW advises Diana Awdrey (one of his many honorary 'nieces' who had established a Festival at Stinchcombe in Gloucestershire in 1922, modelled on the Leith Hill Musical Festival) about partsongs for her festival's choral competition: he recommends Elgar's *Evening scene* (along with Ireland's *Cradle Song*, Stanford's *O breathe not his name* and Parry's *Since thou O fondest and truest*) but warns her it is difficult. Later in October he repents of his recommendation, advising her: "*Don't* do the Elgar its *awful* (this in confidence)." He recommends a Handel chorus instead.[16]

In 1930 VW was advising his young cousin, Peter Montgomery, who had asked about a career in music and whether he should go and study abroad. VW discourages him on this, producing one of his hobby-horses:

> If we are to do any good in England for music we must find out the kind & style of music which is best for us — & not make our music a weak imitation of foreign models. Of course if your ambition in life is to write like Hindemith or Webern you must go to the source to find out how to do it — But is that the best basis for one's own self-expression? ... After all nearly all the musicians of note in England have done most of their study at home — the people who study abroad seem to come to nothing.

And he goes on to quote the examples of Parry, Elgar, Holst, and Bax, admitting that Sullivan and Stanford are exceptions to his generalisation. He does relent too in admitting that if one has had one's groundwork at the RCM, six months abroad to "get new ideas and broaden one's mind" is a good idea.[17]

At last in 1931 we come to the first of the two letters VW sent to Elgar, which are both preserved at the Elgar Birthplace Museum. It was a joint letter, though the text is in VW's hand, from a light-hearted group at the house of Herbert and Alice Sumsion in Gloucester on, Jerrold Northrop Moore suggests, 9 September following a gathering the previous evening after the concert at which Elgar conducted his *Nursery Suite*:

> Millers Green,
> Gloucester
> [9th September 1931]
>
> Dear Sir Edward Elgar
>
> You said last night that owing to the badness of the Woolworth pencils you could no longer write music. We all want that new symphony & the 3rd part of The Apostles.
>
> Will these pencils of varying softness help?
>
> Yrs affectionately
>
> R. Vaughan Williams
> W.H. Reed
> R.O. Morris
> Alice Sumsion
> Emmeline Morris
> E. Reed
> J. Bailey
> Herbert Sumsion[18]

The group was a very typical 'Three Choirs' one: VW was there to conduct *Job* and *The Lark Ascending* (*On Wenlock Edge* was also given); while R.O. Morris and his wife were there for the first performance of Morris's Sinfonia in C major. The Reeds of course were regulars; J. Bailey (not H Bailey as transcribed by Moore[19]) was a member of the Festival chorus, possibly its superintendent, given his presence in such an august gathering.[20]

Returning to the letter: the literature by and large ascribes the beginnings of serious talk of the Third Symphony to mid 1932, though Shaw had written to him as early as January that year urging him to "make the BBC order a new symphony" and then again in June ("Why not a financial symphony?"); this time Elgar responded by forwarding the card to Fred Gaisberg at HMV asking him what he thought of the idea.[21] Discussion about the symphony became more general then, culminating in the BBC's commission in December. It would be a mistake to place too much emphasis on this rather earlier reference to a new symphony. Shaw had been on at Elgar in a general way for some time about writing another symphony, but was not a signatory to the letter, presumably because he wasn't there when it was written (VW seems to have always felt ambivalent about Shaw, largely because of his negative views on Stanford). However he was certainly at Gloucester and would have been present at the gathering the evening before the letter was written. One can imagine him pressing Elgar about completing the oratorio trilogy and writing another symphony and Elgar flippantly turning away the topic with a defensive remark about the poor quality of Woolworth's pencils making it impossible for him to write music.

Nonetheless, this letter, joke as it may have been, is a further sign of how the relationship of the two composers, which had been, on VW's own admission, acquaintance rather than friendship, had changed. Perhaps the turning point had come with Elgar's enthusiasm for *Sancta Civitas* in 1930.[22] Certainly from now on there is a much more positive inter-action. For example in 1933, at the Three Choirs at Worcester, Elgar made a fruitful suggestion, as VW later recalled in a reminiscence broadcast on the BBC:

> Not long before his death I met him at the Three Choirs, and he talked to me about Skelton, of whom I knew little then, except through the Anthologies. He said "You should make an oratorio out of Elinor Rumming". He went on to point out how the metre of Skelton was often pure jazz. I remembered this when following his advice I attempted a setting.[23]

Thus were born the *Five Tudor Portraits*.

On 27 December 1933 Elgar sent VW a postcard from the nursing home where he then was which shows clearly how familiarity between the two had increased:

> My dear Ralph
>
> Many thanks for your card. I send you all good wishes for the New Year. My love to you.
> Edward Elgar[24]

This warmth fits well into the picture of the growing friendship but slightly conflicts with a statement further on in VW's BBC reminiscence:

> He wished us to be on Christian name terms, and even invited me to call him Teddy. This I could not do. He was at least ten years older than me, and was already famous, so I compromised, agreeing to drop Sir, and Dr.

On VW's side the warmth was reciprocated in a practical way: he had overcome his hesitation about the difficulties of *Gerontius* and decided that the work should be performed on 20 April at the 1934 Leith Hill Musical Festival (it was to be the first time a work of Elgar was done at the festival). Rehearsals progressed to the point that on 19 February 1934 VW wrote the other extant letter from him to the composer:[25]

> Dear Elgar
>
> I want to tell you how my choirs of the Dorking Festival are loving preparing "Gerontius" — Greatly daring I suggested it for this year's festival — I had been longing to do it for years, but had thought it too dangerous an experiment as I could not bear to do it badly — Whether we shall do it well I do not know — But if enthusiasm and hard work can achieve anything be sure that it will not lack those.
>
> And it will be one of the great moments in my life when I stand with trembling baton to conduct it — we have good soloists — Astra Desmond, Steuart Wilson and Harold Williams — and we shall think of you — please give us your blessing.
>
> Of course this wants no answer.
>
> Yours affectionately
> R. Vaughan Williams

As we know, no answer was possible since Elgar died three days after receiving this letter – as Jerrold Northrop Moore puts it in *Letters of a Lifetime*: "With this performance [Elgar's] masterpiece had reached the hands of the greatest English composer of the next generation." [26]

7. Cobbe – "My dear Elgar"

The story of the relationship between Elgar and VW does not end with the performance of *Gerontius* at Dorking; in a sense that is when it began. Elgar's death just under two months before clearly placed an enormous emotional burden on the *Gerontius* performance at Dorking of which VW was very conscious: on 4 March he wrote rather cautiously to the regular leader of the orchestra, Isidore Schwiller, asking him to agree to vacate his place for that occasion so that he could invite Willie Reed:

> I feel sure that you will see the point of inviting W.H. Reed to lead the orchestra on that occasion. He has the whole Gerontius tradition at his fingers ends and therefore will be of great help to me. And I think he would be complimented at being asked. If you agree and if Reed accepts my invitation I ... should also much esteem it if you would consent to sit at the 1st desk with Reed on Friday. But if you would rather not do this I shall quite understand.[27]

VW brought to the performance everything which he brought to his annual performances of the Bach Passions and by all accounts it was an extremely moving occasion. Elgar's daughter, Carice, was naturally there and wrote afterwards on 25 April:

> But I do want you to know what a wonderful performance I thought it — & to thank you for all the love & care & the tremendous amount of work you put into it. The choir sang marvellously, & the whole atmosphere was so beautiful & what my father would have loved I feel. It means so much to know you are teaching this generation to know & love his works and above all teaching them in such a splendid way.[28]

On the same day VW himself wrote to Diana Awdrey:

> The Dream I think surpassed all my expectations — the choir were superb & the orchestra played up splendidly. There were about 2 tiny hesitations in the choir. I made one silly mistake — but the orchestra pulled me through that. Steuart & Astra were magnificent & H[arry] Williams also v[ery] good.[29]

Finally, a few days later, Willie Reed himself wrote:

> I feel I must write to you to express my feelings about the splendid performance of "The Dream of Gerontius" at The Leith Hill Festival.
>
> I thought it was truly remarkable that a choir, composed as it is of separate units from the various towns, should produce such a marvellous ensemble when massed as they were for the Festival.
>
> ...
>
> I feel too that I must congratulate you personally —, if I may presume so to do, upon getting such a sensitive & well-balanced rendering, & for imbuing

it with that spirituality one always felt when Sir Edward himself conducted. I must say I was completely uplifted from beginning to end & I felt that as long as his works are handled & given in the way that you and your splendid choir gave "The Dream" so sure I am that those works will live.

This letter is printed in full in *RVW*.[30]

Moving forward to 1938, VW wrote to Ernest Newman about Newman's proposal for a letter to the press to deplore the general neglect of Bloch's music, especially by the BBC. It was to be signed by Newman and others whom he had invited to join in. VW declined to sign:

> I am a great admirer of Bloch's music — but I cannot find that he is unduly neglected in this country in comparison with other composers — one could, I believe, make out a similar case for every contemporary composer (except Sibelius) — and even include Elgar in the list if it were not for the three Choirs festival.
>
> I always feel, when I see the public declaration that a composer is "unduly neglected" that there is something suspect about him. Such a declaration, I believe, creates distrust, e.g. the strong prejudice created against Van Dieren by the unwise propaganda of some youthful enthusiasts [Philip Heseltine and Cecil Gray].
>
> I believe much more can be done by private work than by letters to the press.[31]

Is it a reasonable assessment that Elgar was neglected in the later 30s by all except the Three Choirs Festival?

The following year Ursula Wood typed out the libretto for *The Pilgrim's Progress* for which VW wrote and thanked her on 7 November. She had made suggestions about masks for the Vanity Fair scene and appears to have suggested some words from the Wisdom of Solomon for incorporation. VW responded:

> I know the passage in Wisdom — it is very wonderful — some of it has been used by Elgar in "The Kingdom".[32]

The passage in question was Wisdom of Solomon, II 5–8:

> (5) For our time is a very shadow that passeth away: and after an end there is no returning; for it is fast sealed, so that no man cometh again.
> (6) Come on therefore, let us enjoy the good things that are present and let us speedily use the creatures as in youth.
> (7) Let us fill ourselves with costly wine & ointments; & let no flower of the spring pass by us.
> (8) Let us crown ourselves with rosebuds, before they be withered.

In fact v.7 is used by Elgar not in *The Kingdom* but in *The Apostles* – it is given to the fantasy chorus in the Tower of Magdala scene. The words were not used in the *Pilgrim's Progress* libretto but were echoed eventually in Ursula's own words for Lord Lechery: "nothing endures so choose while you can."

In May 1941, VW sent his well-known essay of advice to Lord Kennet on his son's wish to pursue a musical career – which is printed in full in *RVW*. In it, as in his earlier advice to Peter Montgomery, VW again discourages study abroad (Leipzig had been suggested) since:

> creative work must grow out of its native soil ... almost all the British composers who have achieved anything have studies at home and only gone abroad when they were mature — Elgar, Holst, Parry, Bax, Walton. Stanford is an exception, but he was by no means a beginner when he went to study abroad and as a matter of fact never quite recovered from Leipzig.[33]

Later the same year he was writing to John Ireland thanking him for a copy of his piano suite *Sarnia*:

> I think No 1 is beautiful and I liked the simplicity of No 2 so much — I hope you don't think it cheeky of me to say all this. No 3 I did not make so much of first time — partly because the pianistic brilliancy of it prevented my seeing the wood for the trees. I used to feel the same with Elgar's Symphonies — the actual orchestral virtuosity prevented me seeing the music behind it — all my own fault as I realise now.[34]

Here again we see the evidence of possibly a fuller understanding of Elgar and his music. I believe this was engendered primarily by the 1934 *Gerontius* performance. Indeed in 1942 he was considering putting forward *Gerontius* again for 1943, despite wartime constraints. He wrote to Adrian Boult in July:

> Do you think it wd be possible to do Gerontius with strings & organ only (with possible pfte & timpani) — I want to suggest it to my L H M F Ctee on July 25th and the above in present circumstances (performance in church with high pitch, very little room & no names) are the only available means.[35]

Boult's reply (which I don't think has survived) appears to have sensibly discouraged this notion for *Gerontius* was not performed at Dorking again until 1957.

In 1948 VW was incensed by an article on Parry in the *Musical Times* and wrote to say that he found it "inept, inaccurate and impertinent". In the course of this long letter in defence of his teacher we find the first version of the story about Elgar on Parry's orchestration which he also recounted in his *Musical Autobiography* of 1950 and later on in his talk on Parry and Stanford broadcast in 1956:

> I was once sitting next to Elgar at a rehearsal of Parry's "Symphonic Variations". I commented on the curious spiky sound of the orchestra which fascinates me though it may repel others. I said to Elgar, "I suppose this would be called bad scoring though personally I do not think so." He turned on me almost fiercely and said, "Of course it's not bad scoring; that music could not have been scored anyhow else." Elgar probably recognised this profound truth when he tried, at the request I believe of Sir Hugh Allen, to smarten up the orchestration of "Jerusalem" with the result that the music seemed to lose much of its character.[36]

In his paper at this symposium Byron Adams discussed the distinction between 'cribbing' and 'absorbance' – one paragraph in a letter of VW to Cedric Thorpe Davie from 1949 is apposite. VW, in response to Davie's asking if he might include a quotation from one of VW's symphonies in a composition, replied:

> Please quote the whole Symphony if you feel inclined to, but whatever you do, do not make acknowledgments. Dear Robin Milford is always plastering his printed works with notes such as "This C natural is taken from Vaughan Williams' Symphony", or "The D flat in the third bar is a quotation from Elgar's Gerontius", or "I wish to acknowledge my indebtedness to Dr. R.O. Morris for the bar's rest on Page 27".[37]

We now come to the final years of VW's life when his and Ursula's friendship with Michael Kennedy, whose keen interest in both composers elicited, in the course of a rich correspondence (Kennedy wrote him letters which, as VW put it, made him "sit up and think"), a number of observations on Elgar.[38] Writing on 26 May 1953 VW said he did not enjoy the new edition of Dora Powell's *Edward Elgar: Memories of a Variation*: "She seems to think that hers is the only variation, and to my mind it is the weakest of the lot"; in October 1955 he regretted that Percy Young's book on Elgar omitted "the great story of Parry rushing out on a stormy night to make Richter play the Enigma", a story shown by Kennedy to be unfounded.[39] In March 1957 VW confessed that he had never liked *The Apostles* except for the final alleluias which were beautiful:

> I always feel that he was oppressed by the fact that he was writing for the Church of England and could not get rid of the bombazine and bonnets of the Anglican Sunday morning service. On the whole I like the Kingdom better, though of course there is nothing so bad in the Apostles as the "Lord's prayer".[40]

7. Cobbe – "My dear Elgar"

In May, at the time of the Elgar centenary, Kennedy asked VW for his memories of Richter and Elgar:

> I think I only heard him conduct Elgar twice, first the Variations, when I was absorbed by the music, and naturally being the first time I heard it, did not know if it was being done well or badly. And then came that extraordinarily bad first performance of Gerontius, which nearly killed the work. But it was not Richter's fault that the semi-chorus consisted of second rate professionals from Birmingham and district, that the choir got hopelessly flat at the end of Part 1, that Plunkett Greene lost his voice, that Marie Brema had none to lose, and that Edward Lloyd sang it like a Stainer Anthem in the correct tenor attitude with one foot slightly withdrawn.[41]

As part of the centenary VW, initially reluctantly, agreed to give a radio talk on Elgar the transcript of which survives.[42] In it he recalled some of the encounters with Elgar already mentioned. He also described how the 'Enigma' Variations on first hearing had been for him "something new, yet old; strange, yet familiar; universal, yet typically English"; how he had not enjoyed *Gerontius* on first hearing (as we have just heard) adding "but I know better now"; how Elgar had come to a performance of *Sancta Civitas* and had praised it generously, saying that he had had some thought of setting the words himself, but added "I shall never do that now", to which VW said that that made him sorry that he had attempted a setting himself. His final paragraph:

> I should like to finish off with a small technical point: in the introduction to Elgar's first Symphony the melody is given to fairly heavy woodwind. The bass violoncellos and double basses playing détachées, while the inner harmony is left to two muted horns. This looks all wrong but sounds all right. Here indeed we have a mystery and a miracle.

As VW explained it in a note to Kennedy: "By all the rules those horns ought to be inaudible, but they sound all right and that is the mystery and the miracle."[43]

In conclusion, the references scattered through the letters of VW taken as a whole bear out the picture of a distant relationship which draws a little closer towards friendship in the very final years of Elgar's life, to the point where Elgar even suggested that VW had, with *Sancta Civitas*, completed his great Oratorio trilogy for him.[44] For VW in his turn the circumstance of the Dorking *Gerontius* performance coming so soon after Elgar's death led to a deeper engagement in Elgar's music – he now appreciated more fully the true significance of his predecessor as Headmaster of English music.

Acknowledgements

I should like to thank warmly those who have provided information and other assistance in the course of the preparation of this paper: Anthony Boden (whose *Three Choirs: a history of the Festival* [Stroud, 1992] has been of particular use), Stephen Connock, Chris Grogan (Britten-Pears Library, Aldeburgh), Michael Kennedy, Diana McVeagh, Donald Mitchell, Oliver Neighbour, Andrew Neill and Cathy Sloan (Elgar Birthplace Museum).

From *The Apostles* to *Sancta Civitas*
The Oratorios of Elgar and Vaughan Williams

Charles McGuire

In 1902, before the public and critical success of Edward Elgar's *The Dream of Gerontius*, popular writer Annie W Patterson openly wished for "a native Handel with Wagnerian ideas of Modernity"[1] to create a new kind of oratorio. Such an oratorio would lead the community to praise God in no uncertain terms while adopting new ideas, including leitmotivs, into a genre many critics considered moribund. Within *The Apostles* and *The Kingdom*, Elgar met this challenge – but the ideal community Elgar's characters called to prayer was less like England as a whole and more like Elgar as an individual. Indeed, Elgar's compositions include portraits of a series of flawed but extremely human individuals, from Gerontius to Falstaff. For Elgar that individual became the symbol for universal issues of suffering and redemption. Ralph Vaughan Williams's portraits, while no less interesting, take a different approach, often presenting individuals as symbols of the community within a frame of nationalism. This is certainly the case in *Sancta Civitas*, wherein he promoted a series of community prayers that are effective, but almost impersonal.

Why do these oratorios differ so much in method, intent, and use, and why did the ideal oratorio change so much over such a limited time? The key is the two divergent methods of portraiture used by Elgar and Vaughan Williams, and the issues of reception history this divergence engenders. Although Wagnerism seems a natural comparison by which to discuss these two compositions it too often becomes the only method. Elgar's works were popularly received as Wagnerian while *Sancta Civitas* was largely positioned as anti-Wagnerian. Such a construction uses an anti-Wagner stance to convey ideas about nationalism, compositional technique, and even modernity. These Wagnerian transformations, as well as the countervailing influence of J S Bach, shroud the actual portrait of *Sancta Civitas* until it appears the polar opposite of Elgar's oratorios. This

1 – Notes for this chapter appear on page 168–75.

'Wagner vs. Bach' (or 'Elgar vs. Vaughan Williams') interpretation obscures the larger issue at hand when considering these works: that because of each composer's use of portraiture, the basic theological or philosophical intent of these oratorios is at odds. Ultimately, *Sancta Civitas* is the more traditional English oratorio: it draws together the community in the name of religious ritual rather than focusing on the individual's need for redemption.

Examining their immediate and secondary reception histories, their intersections with Wagnerism, and their use of portraiture can elucidate the differences within these oratorios. Great differences are already apparent when one considers reception history. Given the premières of these oratorios, the dichotomy of Elgar's individual versus Vaughan Williams's community might initially seem misplaced. The premières of *The Apostles* and *The Kingdom* were treated as triumphant public successes, while the reception of *Sancta Civitas* was a tepid critical failure. The Birmingham Festival, a popular affair, premièred *The Apostles* and *The Kingdom* to a middle-class, Anglican audience.[2] Building on the recent success of *Gerontius* in Düsseldorf, Elgar ensured the premières of both would be a Wagnerian spectacle of the highest order: they were the central part of their festivals, and he demanded (and received) publication of August Jaeger's leitmotivic guides for both oratorios, much like the pamphlets by Hans von Wolzogen and many others that accompanied the middle classes to Wagner's operas.[3] Libretto text analyses, completed by Canon Charles Vincent Gorton and available shortly after the compositions' premières, lent the oratorios an instant theological weight. The strategy worked. Both première concerts for *The Apostles* and *The Kingdom* were oversubscribed.

In contrast, the première of Vaughan Williams's *Sancta Civitas* neither occurred at an established festival, nor elicited a popular celebration. Discounting the increasing passivity of music appreciation that the post-World War I population engendered by the phonograph, radio, and film, even the secondary literature reflects a phenomenal shift in the perceived 'worth' of an oratorio première. Elgar's biographers lavish great detail on all aspects of *The Apostles* and *The Kingdom*, including their commissions; difficulties with the publishing company; their compositional process; and the place of the music festival in Elgar's life.[4] *Sancta Civitas*'s secondary sources are virtually silent on the première performance, relating that Vaughan Williams began working on the oratorio in 1923, apparently without a commission,[5] and it premièred on

7 May 1926 at the Heather Festival, a multi-day celebration commemorating the 300th anniversary of the establishment of a chair in music at Oxford University.[6] The opening quotation of the work is in Greek, from Plato's *Phaedo*, and some of the compositional material was drawn from earlier abandoned settings of Walt Whitman. This is a paltry amount indeed when compared to the 75 pages Jerrold Northrop Moore alone devotes to *The Apostles* and *The Kingdom* in his Elgar biography.

Nonetheless, a Moore-style exegesis of *Sancta Civitas* is possible from a lengthy article by Frank Howes in the June 1926 issue of the *Musical Times*; Table 1 (pages 102–3) is a reconstructed programme.[7] The Heather Festival had an academic air about it, concentrating mainly on works either by J S Bach or English composers trained at Oxford or Cambridge. The major focus of the Bach Choir, brought to Oxford to perform at the festival, was the music of Bach; it also premièred Vaughan Williams's oratorio. The Heather Festival was viewed as an academic, nationalistic affair. Howes's article is even bookended with two large photographs of English folk dancing in the New College Gardens (the only photographs in the article), and a small description of this event ends the review.[8]

The oppositions between these première histories speak to a broader trope within English music during the first few decades of the 20th century: the value of Wagnerism. Vaughan Williams's Heather Festival was Bach-oriented and of an elite, academic character; Elgar's Birmingham Festival was Wagnerian and targeted a popular, middle-class audience. The change over these years might indicate that in the 1920s there was a reaction against Wagner. In fact, this is one of the central arguments put forth by Robert Stradling and Merion Hughes in their book *The English Musical Renaissance, 1840–1940: Constructing a National Music*. In the argument of Stradling and Hughes, English musicians and critics of the time disavowed Wagner as a "bad German" because of his perceived connection to "German militarism" and celebrated Bach as a "good German" for his ostensible connection to Protestant religion and values.[9] Further supporting this shift, Elgar's contemporaries viewed his last two oratorios as Wagnerian in origin, composition, and execution;[10] while Vaughan Williams associated himself with Bach throughout his career, as in the yearly concerts of the *St Matthew Passion* at the Leith Hill Festival.

But such a binary 'Vaughan Williams versus Elgar' or 'Bach versus Wagner' opposition does not adequately capture the complexity in critical and public responses to Wagner. While many in the Elgar generation idolized Wagner, they did not unquestioningly accept his place within the

Table 1

Programme of the Heather Festival, Oxford, 2–8 May 1926

(All information taken from Frank Howes, 'The Heather Festival at Oxford' in *The Musical Times* (1 June 1926), pp. 537–541)

Concert 1 : 2 May, afternoon
organ recital in the Cathedral given by Dr. H G Ley

This concert's programme included unidentified "works by four Oxford men": John Stainer, Hubert Parry, Basil Harwood, and W H Harris.

Concert 2 : 2 May, evening
a cappella choir concert in the Cathedral

This concert featured the "combined choirs of New College, Magdalen, and Christ Church, conducted in turn by their respective organists, Drs W H Harris, H C Stewart, and H G Ley"; included "a little Bach. . . Motets by [Charles] Stanford and Charles Wood, and then followed by anthems and motets by [Frederick] Ouseley, Croft, Crotch, Lloyd, and the three conductors "[Harris's motet 'Faire is the Heaven']. The concert also included organ compositions by S.S. Wesley (Introduction and Fugue in C# minor), Harwood and Ley.

Concert 3 : 3 May, Evening
City of Birmingham Orchestra, conducted by Adrian Boult

R O Morris: Toccata and Fugue;
Ernest Walker: 'Sleep Song' and 'Summer Rain'
George Butterworth: *The Banks of the Green Willow*
Balfour Gardiner: *Overture to a Comedy*
Guy Warrack: *Variations on an Original Theme*
H. M. Strickland Constable: Symphony (Finale)
Franz Joseph Haydn: 'Oxford' Symphony.

Concert 4 : 4 May, afternoon
Bach Choir, conducted by Hugh Allen, Sheldonian Theatre

J S Bach: 'The Spirit also helpeth us', 'Sing Ye to the Lord',
'Latin Magnificat', Second Orchestral Overture in D
Silk: unidentified songs

Concert 5 : 5 May
Oxford Orchestral Society, conducted by Maurice Besly

Franck: Symphony
Besly: *Phaedra*
Dohnányi: Concertstück in D for cello and orchestra
"other works in the ordinary repertory"

Concert 6 : 6 May, evening
Playhouse, conducted by Guy Warrack

Ralph Vaughan Williams: *The Shepherds of the Delectable Mountains*
J S Bach: *Coffee and Cupid*
Henry Purcell: *The Gentleman Dancing Master*

Concert 7 : 7 May
Bach Choir, conducted by Vaughan Williams

Vaughan Williams: *Sancta Civitas*
Hubert Parry: *L'Allegro ed Il Pensieroso*
J S Bach: Brandenburg Concerto no 5

8 May, afternoon
New College Gardens

"a display of folk dancing"

music world in general and the oratorio in particular. For example, in *The Story of the Oratorio*, Annie W Patterson felt obliged to defend against the supposed Wagnerian characteristics of George Macfarren's *St John the Baptist*.[11] The attribution of influence is not at question here – only the fact that someone who admired Wagner so much within her text would still feel it necessary in 1902 to defend a composer from charges of being Wagnerian.

Certainly the critics and the audience for Elgar's oratorios, the most successful of the decade, viewed them as being steeped in Wagner. A list of Wagnerian contexts and methods for Elgar's work is lengthy. These include the Baedeker-like analyses Jaeger supplied for the first performances of Elgar's last three oratorios.[12] Elgar often stated that their leitmotivic structure would make them coherent to the listener.[13] This interpretation continues into the present. Secondary-source descriptions of Elgar's oratorio contexts focus on their Wagnerian influences, including long comparisons of *Parsifal*'s prelude to that of *Gerontius*,[14] as well as Elgar's acquisition of W A Ellis's *Richard Wagner's Prose Works* as he began composing *The Apostles* in earnest. Statements such as "Wagner had shown the way; Elgar followed with comparable skill" abound in the Elgar literature.[15] Assumptions that *The Apostles* and *The Kingdom* comprised an English *Gesamtkunstwerk* existed at the 1906 première of *The Kingdom*, when both oratorios in this cycle were performed together at the festival, and continue into the present with frequent critical announcements that they were an attempt "to Assail the Castles of the Ring".[16] Their popular interpretation as ardently Wagnerian is solid.[17]

In apparent contrast, the secondary-literature descriptions of *Sancta Civitas* divorce the oratorio from anything remotely Wagnerian to the extent that it almost becomes a mantra. As early as 1928, A E F Dickinson removed immediately any Wagnerian association, stating "there are no leading themes in this Oratorio [sic]... *Sancta Civitas* is held together, not by the interweaving into the general design of one or two notable lines of melody, but rather by the continual predominance of certain flashes of colour".[18] Similar is Hubert Foss's comparison of Vaughan Williams's oratorio with the usual festival fare:

> In print the work is labelled "oratorio." Anything less like Handel's oratorios, or that long list of 'festival' works that led to the popular decadence of Penitence, Pardon and Peace, could be imaginable only by another Vaughan Williams. Sancta Civitas bears much the same

relationship to the traditional Three Choirs, Birmingham-Festival oratorios as do the paintings of El Greco to those of Angelica Kauffmann, or the ceilings of Michelangelo to a well-designed Christmas card. There is, in truth, more than a little of El Greco in this choral work, though the composer may not be aware of it – an angularity of draughtsmanship and design, a dramatic use of unexpected colour. We do not find here the warm, smooth curves of Raphael, the bountiful glow of Andrea del Sarto. Instead there is a stark squareness of pattern, though the music itself is as fluid as speech.[19]

As Byron Adams and others have pointed out, 'decadence', besides being a code for the perceived excesses of Wagnerism from the turn of the century forward, was also frequently applied to Elgar's *Gerontius*.[20] The comparison of Kauffman to El Greco, with its attendant associations of feminine versus masculine – and opposing the work of a painter considered at the time to be minor to an important artist – further contrasts Vaughan Williams's strong, masculine oratorio with the work of the Wagnerian-influenced and feminine Elgar. In a similar vein, Simona Pakenham fills her description of *Sancta Civitas* with masculine descriptions (including "white-hot climaxes" and "jewel-hard dissonances"), and explicitly compares Vaughan Williams's composition of *Sancta Civitas* with that most masculine of 19th-century composers, Ludwig van Beethoven.[21]

Later criticism of the composition is more veiled, and cloaking the work as anti-Wagnerian usually means distancing it from Elgar while mentioning something about Elgar's Wagnerism in the process. Frank Howes, in his discussion of *Sancta Civitas* from 1954, notes that it avoids "the newer dramatic form used by Elgar in *The Dream of Gerontius*".[22] Michael Kennedy's 1964 *The Works of Ralph Vaughan Williams* states that "Vaughan Williams's incandescent work is an approach to a vision of the after-life quite different than the expansiveness of Elgar ... Its conciseness, concentration, and complexities of texture are the very reasons why it is a masterpiece".[23] Kennedy's descriptions of Elgar are firmly Wagnerian; those of *Sancta Civitas* are the opposite.

The secondary literature, then, strongly characterizes *Sancta Civitas* into an anti-Wagnerian vein – even by 1928.[24] Yet hunting for a larger anti-Wagnerian context during the decade of *Sancta Civitas*'s première yields only mixed results. Indeed, many anti-Wagnerian examples are either humorous (such as Francesco Berger's 'More Wagner', wherein the composer claims "Music was reared by me"[25]) or based almost entirely on objections to Wagner's personal moral fibre. A typical example is found in

R W S Mendl's 'Confession of an Anti-Wagnerian', from the June 1924 issue of *The Chesterian*. Working through a number of examples from *Tristan und Isolde*, *Die Meistersinger* and *Parsifal*, Mendl concludes that there is "a vulgar streak in Wagner's mentality, which is frequently revealed in his music" and compares a God-like Beethoven to a satyr-like Wagner.[26] A similar example occurred in 1926 – a minor controversy about the inclusion of Wagner at the Three Choirs Festival. Ivor Atkins's attempt to programme the prelude to *Parsifal* in that year engendered an angry response from Dr Lacey, one of the Worcester Cathedral canons. In a letter to the *Worcester Daily Times*, he referred to Wagner as a "sensualist", finding within his music dramas that "the sensuality of pietism matching the sensuality of his erotics . . . in my work as a priest I have had acquaintance with both kinds of sensuality, and I know what kind is the more dangerous".[27]

Strong as Lacey's critical voice seems, it was in the minority. Even discounting the continuing Wagner celebrations of George Bernard Shaw, a cursory glance through the major journals and periodicals of the 1920s reveals a great deal of Wagner-worship still extant within the English musical critical establishment. For instance, throughout the 1920s the periodical *Music and Letters* printed a number of articles contextualizing the work of Wagner, noting his indebtedness to other composers, his aesthetic likes and dislikes, and numerous production reviews.[28] In one long article Agnes Savill even boastfully posited that British audiences were better receptors than some Germans for Wagner's *Parsifal*:

> In Munich the audience remain throughout the spectators of a ceremony; however absorbed, they never forget that they are onlookers, watching a beautiful and dignified service, where strange knights, dreamlike figures, are seen in a remarkable temple carved out of stone in the heart of a primeval forest. In Covent Garden the audience forget that they are merely spectators; carried away, they become worshippers in the Temple; they too, take part in the religious ceremony. They are scarcely conscious that the scene is beautiful, because they are dwelling in another and more sacred region of thought. When the music dies away they come back to earth with a shock; it is with difficulty that they realise they have only been witnessing an opera in a theatre.[29]

Whereas Munich Germans could never become one with *Parsifal*'s story, the English audience submersed themselves within it to a point where they became a community of believers in the Wagnerian religion. To Savill, the only audience more receptive than the English to Wagner's works was that at Bayreuth.

Increasingly, however, even Wagner's best allies felt it necessary to apologize for his character. Within the 1920s, Lacey's comments regarding the degeneracy of Wagner's morals were often repeated, leading to suspicion of his absolute value as an artist. A review of Jean Bartholini's *Wagner et le recul du temps* in *The Chesterian* rejects the author's assertion that "It is therefore established that Wagner is a classic and with Beethoven the greatest classic" with the phrase "We cannot forget that fortunately Bach lived before them" – this in an article by a self-described Wagnerian.[30] Other articles from the time do chip away at Wagner's monolithic presence within the dramatic world.[31] But for every criticism of Wagner, there were his strong defenders, including George Ainslie Hight. Hight's celebratory *Richard Wagner: A Critical Biography* [32] was a self-described attempt to refute assaults "by the English press" on Wagner's character.[33] The critical activities of the 1920s were not so much a repudiation of Wagner for Bach, as Stradling and Hughes would have us believe, as a retrenchment and expansion of earlier thinking about Wagner's character, but not his music.

Supporting this, Vaughan Williams's own writings reflect the ambiguous position Wagner held in English society. They present a genuine appreciation for Wagner's music with certain criticisms about passages he found ineffective.[34] More often Vaughan Williams criticized not Wagner but Wagnerism, because it was too persuasive a language for younger composers, and consequently a threat to native English music. In these cases, Vaughan Williams links Wagner to a series of Continental figures, whose influence Vaughan Williams hoped to dispel. Such arguments occur even as early as 1912, within 'Who Wants the English Composer?':

> The desire to "do it too" whenever the newest thing comes over from abroad is very strong with us all. So long then as our composers are content to write operas which only equal Wagner in length, symphonies made up of scraps of Brahms at his dullest, or pianoforte pieces which are merely crumbs from Debussy's table, we can hardly blame the amateur for preferring the genuine article to the shoddy imitation.[35]

Vaughan Williams is not negative about Wagner's music *per se*, just copies of it by aspiring English composers – rejecting derivative Brahms and Debussy as well. Like many of his contemporaries, Vaughan Williams's writings abound with references to Wagner, as he was easy to use as an example of both compositional technique and the success or failure of a composer. In short, he was valuable to Vaughan Williams because Wagner was an instantly identifiable and understandable link to his ideal reader.

Vaughan Williams's continual reference to Wagner becomes somewhat curious by its absence when we consider his article 'What Have We Learnt from Elgar?' published in *Music and Letters* shortly after Elgar's death.[36] Early in the article, Vaughan Williams links Elgar's choral technique to both Handel and Wagner, with the qualifier that it had "never . . . been used so consistently or successfully" as it was by Elgar.[37] But when Vaughan Williams begins to detail Elgar's own musical "derivation" from past composers, he mentions only Henry Smart and John Goss.[38] In the previous paragraph he distances Elgar entirely from a compositional succession:

> No composer appears absolutely new out of the welkin; indeed when, like Schoenberg, he is said to do so he is to my mind at once suspect. But it is a mistake to suppose that there is an unbroken line of great composers, one handing on the torch to the next; that Mozart comes from Bach, Beethoven from Mozart, Wagner from Beethoven, and so on.[39]

Acknowledging that Elgar used similar choral techniques to Wagner – only better – and then not acknowledging Wagner in a run-down of inheritance on Elgar and even dismissing the idea that there could be a positivistic Continental succession might have been a way for Vaughan Williams to keep Elgar within the English tradition, presenting a native and unified front against other composers – be they German or otherwise.

How does the music bear out these Wagnerian interpretations? *The Apostles*, *The Kingdom* and *Sancta Civitas* do differ greatly – but not so much around precepts of Wagnerism as around how they each express community. Elgar's oratorio choruses ('The Spirit of the Lord', 'O Ye Priests,' etc.) can be read to include the community into the oratorio experience, but all essentially react to individual characters. And even the most basic of Elgar's scenes from *The Apostles* and *The Kingdom* point to a strong vision of individual character – especially when the characters themselves are weak, controlled as they might be by jealousy, fear, or even a depressed sense of self-esteem. Peter is a typical example. Before he begins his climactic third-movement sermon in *The Kingdom*, drawn largely from Acts 2:14 and following, Elgar presents him as a vulnerable individual. The sermon's direct result was that the crowd of people gathered at the Temple in Jerusalem converted to Christianity.[40] But Elgar tempered this statement of strength, because his vision of Peter's character was of the failed man making amends. Before he begins his sermon, Peter must textually and musically apologize for his earlier weaknesses. He states: "I have prayed for thee, that thy faith fail not; and thou, when thou are converted, strengthen thy brethren." [41] Elgar sets these words to a complex of leitmotivs; prominent among these is what Jaeger called "Prayer". As I have discussed elsewhere, this theme took on great significance in the last movement of *The Apostles*, being the representation of a grand orchestral sunrise in scene I and part of the climactic merging of themes in scene VII when Christ ascends into Heaven.[42] Our first introduction to the theme in *The Apostles* occurs at the beginning of scene I (see Example 1). Here, Elgar bookends the entire structure within repetitions of what Jaeger calls the "Pastoral" theme; "Prayer" is further introduced directly by a small motif designated "Christ the Man of Sorrows".[43] (These are marked in the example.) Elgar's Christ at this moment has ascended the mountain to pray to God for guidance; when he returns, he chooses the twelve Apostles. At the parallel point in *The Kingdom*, Elgar begins to repeat this musical structure (Example 2). The last measure of the previous chorus ends on "Christ, the Man of Sorrows" (mm.1 and 2 of the example), and Peter continues with a quiet version of the "Prayer" theme. But Elgar's Peter is human and fallible, manifested through an interruption of "Prayer" by a poignant, two measure theme (mm.6–7 of your example) which Jaeger called "Peter" and described in an earlier iteration as "a soul-picture of Peter as he reflects on his denial of Christ".[44] This theme of doubt occurs immediately after Peter sings the words "that thy faith fail not". The complex of themes is a reminder of the presence of Christ and the importance of the Apostles' mission on earth, but also a statement that Peter is fallible as an individual. Elgar's complex of interrupted themes to show the human side of the characters occurs in a number of other places in both *The Apostles* and *The Kingdom*, including Judas's soliloquy of despair in scene IV and the initial response of the Apostles to their calling in scene I.[45]

The text, too, reminds us of Peter's place within this spiritual hierarchy. Within Peter's initial prayer, he recalls a statement of Christ, which seemingly comforts him. But this interpolated passage has a double-edged meaning. When placed within its full context, we note that these were the words with which Christ upbraided Peter at the Last Supper, directly before Christ predicted the famous denial, taken from Luke 22:31–34:

> 31 And the Lord said, Simon, Simon, behold, Satan hath desired to have you, that he may sift you as wheat.
>
> 32 But I have prayed for thee, that thy faith fail not: and when thou art converted, strengthen thy brethren.

Music Example 1: Edward Elgar, The Apostles *(1903), scene I, cues 14–16*

Music Example 2: Elgar, The Kingdom (1906), scene III, cues 94–95

33 And he said unto him, Lord, I am ready to go with thee, both into prison, and to death.

34 And he said, I tell thee, Peter, the cock shall not crow this day before thou shalt thrice deny that thou knowest me.

With but a single textual interpolation to this scene, Elgar presents his audience with a complex, vulnerable, and all too human character – and a character who ultimately shows Elgar's own interpretation of the individual's place within Christian fellowship: continually asking forgiveness.[46]

In stark contrast, Vaughan Williams's *Sancta Civitas* negates character. He refuses even to keep a single model of consistent text presentation within his oratorio. At first, he presents the narrative texts within the baritone solo and response texts in the choir, but soon this two-part model of narration breaks down, and Vaughan Williams begins to set the narrative revelation in the voice of the chorus as well. For the remainder of *Sancta Civitas*, Vaughan Williams splits the voice of the apocalyptic envisioner between the baritone and tenor solos and various choirs. The absence of character is absolute; as an audience, Vaughan Williams demands that we feel no sympathy for or identification with the individual, instead relegating us solely to the text itself.[47] The communal aspect of this text always outweighs any individual characterization.

Vaughan Williams complicates this communal aspect with a specific but obscure reference to national pride and tradition. The announcement on the title page of *Sancta Civitas* states that Vaughan Williams drew the "Words from the Authorized Version [of the Bible] (with additions from 'Taverner's Bible' and other Sources)".[48] These "other sources" have been identified as the Sanctus from the contemporary *Book of Common Prayer's* Communion Service.[49] Within the secondary literature regarding *Sancta Civitas*, the title-page description of texts has been mostly accepted; Michael Kennedy's strong assertion of this is typical.[50] Perhaps the closest anyone has come in print to doubting the statement on the title page was Dickinson; his wry statement on the matter "Where the additions from Taverner's Bible can be found, would be hard to say" is exactly to the point. A careful comparison of the text as set by Vaughan Williams in *Sancta Civitas* with both the Authorized Version and Taverner's Bible of 1539 reveals that there is little difference between the two versions, and often Vaughan Williams's text differs from both.[51] Indeed, Vaughan Williams seems to have often simply shortened the Authorized Version, and tightened up the language as he saw fit, in some cases radically changing words and phrases to create a new context.

Table 2

Comparison of Rev. 7:17, as found in *Sancta Civitas*, the Authorized King James Version of the Bible, and John Taverner's Bible

Authorized Version

For the Lamb which is in the midst of the throne shall feed them, and shall lead them unto living fountains of waters: and God shall wipe away all tears from their eyes.

Taverner's Bible

For ye Lambe whiche is in the myddes of the seate, shal fede them, and shall leade them unto the fountaynes of lyuynge water, and God shall wype away all teares from their eyes.

Sancta Civitas

For he that sitteth on the throne shall feed them and shall lead them unto living fountains of waters.

A case in point is the setting of Revelation 7:17 (see Table 2). The Authorized Version of the passage reads: "For the Lamb which is in the midst of the throne shall feed them, and shall lead them unto living fountains of waters: and God shall wipe away all tears from their eyes." The same verse from Taverner is a close match: "For ye Lambe whiche is in the myddes of the seate, shal fede them, and shall leade them unto the fountaynes of lyuynge water, and God shall wype away all teares from their eyes." [52] Besides the rearrangement of "fountaynes of lyuynge water" to "living fountains of waters", the only real difference is the use of the word "seate" in the Taverner instead of "throne". [53]

Vaughan Williams's text alters this passage considerably: "For he that sitteth on the throne shall feed them and shall lead them unto living fountains of waters." [54] This is a radical departure from either base-text. Vaughan Williams has dispensed with the metaphor of the Lamb (changing the subject to the nondescript pronoun "he"), deleted entirely the salve of despair present in the other two versions, and further condensed the poetic "in midst of the throne/seat" to the simple "sitting." The words are direct, and work well for the homophonic piano dynamic with which Vaughan Williams composed this passage. But the curtailment loses some of the poetry of the original. Many similar examples exist in Vaughan Williams's libretto. But the point is clear: Vaughan Williams's text is no more influenced or derived from the Taverner Bible than from any other biblical source. Why, then, include this ascription on *Sancta Civitas*'s title page? Vaughan Williams was obviously not concerned with instant recognition of his texts, but did want his audience to associate the text with an idealized English tradition – which would go a long way towards building a strong community.

In the end, despite some attempts to construct both Vaughan Williams's and Elgar's oratorios as anti-Wagnerian versus Wagnerian, the difference in the musical portraiture presented within is less about a wider context and more about interior personality and beliefs of each composer. Elgar used his oratorios to present a highly idiosyncratic interpretation of religion, including a focus on sin and its forgiveness; the redemption or despair of the individual; and a quiet celebration of the individual becoming a hero. All of these tenets work well in both *The Apostles* and *The Kingdom* because Elgar grants his listeners a way through his interpolated texts into the minds and ideas of each major character of both works, either via the longer soliloquies of Mary Magdalene, Judas, and the Virgin Mary, or simple momentary flashes of thought, such as Peter asking God for strength before his sermon. Elgar's use of leitmotivic structure granted him a way of presenting the plots of both works in a kind of shorthand so that he could pass quickly and fluidly to his real concentration – that of the individual's reaction.[55]

Vaughan Williams's approach in *Sancta Civitas* is much more co-operative, avoiding character as it does for a smaller amalgamation of sacred texts presented by the community for the community. Its preface, from *Phaedo* invites those present "to have a song in . . . heart and sing about it" instead of monolithically proclaiming the dedication of the work "Ad Majorem dei Gloriam" ("To the Greater Glory of God"), as Elgar positions his oratorios. Even the subject of *Sancta Civitas* itself, while apocalyptic, is unthreatening: instead of pictorially interpreting the great mysteries of the church for the audience as Elgar does, Vaughan Williams simply presents his listeners with a small narration of the coming glory of heaven. There can be no doubt of the final outcome, for he sweeps away the limited presentation of tribulation with a climactic use of the Sanctus from the *Book of Common Prayer* – a text his audience would have associated with tradition, stability, and the church community, all values Vaughan Williams forwarded himself in other aspects of his life, including editing *The English Hymnal*. The only personal spin Vaughan Williams places on the work is his reference to the use of Taverner's Bible as the source for part of *Sancta Civitas*'s text. Yet even this positions the oratorio within the English community, because coupled with the use of the 'Sanctus' text, Taverner's Bible links the oratorio to a national tradition of Protestantism focusing on the organization of the nation as a unit against the outside religious or compositional aggressor. Ultimately through this subtlety *Sancta Civitas* is the more traditional English oratorio: it draws together the community in the name of religion rather than focusing on the autobiographical individual's need for redemption.

"Sheer early morning loveliness"
Ralph Vaughan Williams and *The Poisoned Kiss*

Stephen Connock

"You're in for a good time", wrote Richard Capell on the opening of *The Poisoned Kiss* in May 1936:

> The songs and ensembles, all are charming as they are skilful, seem to formulate the right of music still to be what it naturally was of old — namely, good and at the same time popular.[1]

This review in the *Daily Telegraph* captured early reactions to the opera: beguiling music with Vaughan Williams providing an inexhaustible supply of good tunes. As for Evelyn Sharp's libretto, it was "frankly nonsense" (*The Musical Times*),[2] "babyish" (*Daily Telegraph*),[3] "arch wistfulness" (*The Listener*).[4] As Scott Goddard said in 1941:

> Vaughan Williams's music seems to have waltzed away with half the plot and run away from the remainder.[5]

The music is the thing – "sheer early-morning loveliness" was Frank Howes's description.[6] How did this come about by the composer of the Fourth Symphony who was also writing *Job* and the percussive Piano Concerto at the same time as *The Poisoned Kiss*?

Background to the opera

At first glance, *The Poisoned Kiss* seems to stand alone in Vaughan Williams's music. It is a comic opera, with songs, duets, trios and ensembles interspersed with spoken dialogue. Furthermore, there are waltzes and tangos which raise a smile mainly because they are unexpected. Yet Vaughan Williams was fully aware of an English light operatic tradition through Gilbert & Sullivan to John Gay's *The Beggar's Opera* and *Polly*. Within this tradition we have comic operas, 'ballad-operas' and musical comedies using sung numbers interspersed with

1 – Notes for this chapter appear on pages 175–6.

spoken dialogue, in English and often – especially in the period before Gilbert and Sullivan – using old English airs and folk melodies.

Vaughan Williams had written about these trends in *The Music Student* just before the First World War:

> The history of English music has been one continual struggle between the natural musical proclivities of the English people and the social and artistic conditions which have prevented these national tendencies from pursuing their natural course.
>
> There could be no more striking example of this than the history of English opera from 1720 to 1860. For it is a fact that, all through this period of Italian opera and fashionable Italian singers ... there flowed a thin but very distinguishable stream of English opera. We can date this period of English opera to the year 1727, when *The Beggar's Opera* was produced. *The Beggar's Opera* is what we should nowadays call a 'musical comedy', and what the Germans call 'sing-spiel'. That is a spoken comedy interspersed with songs.[7]

Vaughan Williams adds that the great success of *The Beggar's Opera* led to all successful English opera of later dates, even when the music was original and not adapted. As he put it "the principle remains the same – the slight texture and almost invariable spoken dialogue instead of recitative ..." He adds that "the famous comic operas of Arthur Sullivan were in the direct line of this English tradition".

With *The Poisoned Kiss*, a spoken comedy interspersed with songs, with its 'slight texture' and absence of recitative, Vaughan Williams was clearly writing an opera in an English tradition as he saw it. That this was very much on his mind is clear from the RVW-Evelyn Sharp correspondence. For example in his letter of early August 1927 he asks Evelyn Sharp for "a quiet lyrical quartet or quintet, with solo lines (eg Sullivan's 'Brightly dawns' or 'Tower Tomb' in *Yeoman of the Guard*)".[8] In his letter of 18 August 1927 he says "If you happen to be stuck up for metres I have been studying 'Polly' and he gets some very good metres from fitting words to tunes".[9]

Polly was what John Gay called the 'second part' of *The Beggar's Opera*. The score consisted of a number of short tunes, borrowed from traditional or contemporary sources, to which (as with *The Beggar's Opera*) an overture by Dr Pepusch had been added. For a revival at the Kingsway Theatre in London on 30 December 1922, conducted by Eugene Goossens, Clifford Bax had reconstructed the play itself and Frederic Austin had arranged and added to the additional music. This revival of *Polly* had been spurred by the success of the revival of *The*

Beggar's Opera at the Lyric Theatre in Hammersmith, which ran from 5 June 1920 for over 2,000 performances.

Both *Polly* and *The Beggar's Opera* are musical comedies, amusing with lovely melodies and songs. The lyrics are set to popular songs of the day. Both works are in three acts. As Vaughan Williams was studying *Polly*, it is interesting to note that this opera has 52 sections, split as follows:

>   Act 1 1–17
>   Act 2 18–36
>   Act 3 37–52

The Poisoned Kiss (1936 edition) has 46 sections, split along these lines:

>   Act 1 1–17
>   Act 2 18–32
>   Act 3 33–46

As in *The Poisoned Kiss*, *Polly*, in Frederic Austin's arrangement, has dances and interludes. The comparison need not be pressed too far – the point is that *The Poisoned Kiss* takes its place in a distinguished line of English comic opera, of which *Polly* was an early example.

And what of Gilbert and Sullivan? As noted above, Vaughan Williams draws Evelyn Sharp's attention to ensembles from both *The Mikado* and *Yeoman of the Guard*. *The Mikado* example is the quartet for Yum-Yum, Pitti-Sing, Nanki-Poo and Pish-Tush:

> Brightly dawns our wedding day;
> Joyous how we give thee greeting!
> Whither, whither art thou fleeting?
> Fickle moment, prithee stay!
> What though mortal joys be hollow?
> Pleasures come, if sorrows follow…

The *Yeoman of the Guard* example is another quartet, this time for Fairfax, Sergeant Meryll, Dame Carruthers and Kate:

> Strange adventure! Maiden wedded
> To a groom she's never seen —
> Never, never, never seen!
> Groom about to be beheaded
> In an hour on Tower Green!
> Tower, Tower, Tower Green!

Both quartets are high points in Sullivan's music, which is lyrical yet with beautiful solo lines emerging from the texture. In *The Poisoned Kiss*, the quartet 'Father, where are you?' comes closest to this model, led by Tormentilla who sings a sweet lullaby:

> Lullaby, sweet light of my eye,
> Zephyrs all laden with poisons draw nigh
> Sweet'ning your sleep as you languorously lie,
> Lullaby, lull-a-lullaby

Back in 1914 Vaughan Williams had written:

> Now that the Wagnerian boom is dying down, it is not impossible that English composers will once again take up the thread and develop to a much higher and nobler degree the tradition which has been handed down to them by the English opera composers from the time of Purcell.[10]

In 1927 Vaughan Williams seems to pick up his own challenge and to write an un-snobbish, English language, spoken dialogue-plus-sung-numbers comic opera. As he kept saying to Evelyn Sharp, he wanted the opera light-hearted, not too high-falutin', the reverse of Wagnerian opera. He must have been amused by Richard Garnett's title for his book of short stories – *The Twilight of the Gods* – published in 1888, since Garnett's light-hearted fables are the antithesis of Wagner.

It is likely that Mozart's 'sing-spiel' *The Magic Flute* was another useful model for Vaughan Williams. The composer was impressed by the pioneering staging of it at Cambridge, in 1911, in the English translation by his friend Edward Dent. We know from Edward Dent that Vaughan Williams was present at a staging of *The Magic Flute* by Clive Carey and Dent himself, in Cambridge in 1911. Vaughan Williams's reaction was described as "enthusiastic". In this opera, there is a succession of arias and ensembles with linking spoken dialogue (often omitted in recordings). The central figures of Sarastro (a magician comparable to Dipsacus) the Queen of the Night (Persicaria), Tamino (Amaryllus) and Pamina (Tormentilla), along with a pair of lower order characters in both operas, does tempt comparison with *The Poisoned Kiss*.

One final influence on Vaughan Williams's *The Poisoned Kiss* is much closer to home: his own incidental music for *The Wasps*. Written in 1909 for a Cambridge production of the play by Aristophanes, the complete score comprises 18 sections in three acts for tenor and baritone soloists, male chorus and orchestra. With its songs interspersing spoken dialogue, its wit, satire and contemporary feel, it is a clear precedent for *The*

Poisoned Kiss. Vaughan Williams had shown a liking for the spoken dialogue-plus-sung-numbers routine. *The Wasps* was quickly followed by his all-sung 'ballad opera' *Hugh the Drover* – Vaughan Williams knew exactly what he was saying by use of this historically important English opera sub-title – and *Hugh* was being worked on again in the years immediately preceding composition of *The Poisoned Kiss*. So, from *Polly* to *The Wasps*, the musical context is clear and revealing.

Evolution of the libretto

The story for *The Poisoned Kiss* begins in 1846 and ends in 1981 with the publication by OUP of the final revised edition. It is a complicated narrative and Vaughan Williams had a major hand, as we shall see, in both the shape and detail of the libretto. The evolution of the libretto begins with the American writer, Nathaniel Hawthorne (1804–1864).

Hawthorne's short story, 'Rappaccini's Daughter', was published in 1846 in his collection *Mosses from an Old Manse*.[11] Hawthorne was born in Salem, Massachusetts, and is best remembered today for his powerful story of adultery, guilt, secrecy and passion, *The Scarlet Letter* (1850). His use of allegory and symbolism influenced Emerson and Whitman and he was at the forefront of the development of the short story as a distinctive American genre.

'Rappaccini's Daughter' is a powerful tale which ends bleakly. It concerns Giovanni Guasconti, a handsome student newly enrolled at the University of Padua. He takes lodgings in an old mansion which overlooks a resplendent garden, cultivated by the old, sickly and thoughtworn Dr Rappaccini. The young man notices that the doctor tends to the garden in thick gloves and a face mask. He has a beautiful daughter, Beatrice, who can touch the gorgeous flowers without protection. All the young men of Padua are wild about this simple and sweet girl who "glowed amid the sunlight". Giovanni is captivated by Beatrice, and by the garden, and arranges to meet her. She in turn becomes spellbound by his looks and charm. In the garden, he goes to admire and touch a particularly beautiful plant, only to find Beatrice shrieking "Touch not! It is fatal!" She explains that her father has brought her up within this poisonous garden, such that for her "poison was an element of life". Although her rich beauty was a madness to him, he acknowledges she is as "poisonous as she is beautiful". Beatrice adds "though my body be nourished with poisons, my spirit is God's creature and craves love as its daily food".

Giovanni resolves to free Beatrice from her poisonous addiction by offering her an antidote. If this doesn't work, he adds "let us join our lips in one kiss ... and so die!" She takes the antidote whilst challenging her father, Dr Rappaccini: "why did you inflict this miserable doom upon thy child?" Rappaccini, it seems, has been indulging in a scientific experiment, one destined to empower his daughter with such strength that all would be quelled by her influence. Meanwhile the antidote was having a terrible effect: as poison had been her life, so the powerful antidote was her death. Beatrice dies as a result of her father's perverted attempt at wisdom.

Hawthorne's descriptive powers are considerable and the themes of *The Scarlet Letter* emerge – love, fate, troubled and feverish emotions, temptation, the force of passion. It is also a diatribe against intellectual zeal and academic vanity.

This powerful and moving short story contains many of the elements which would appear in Vaughan Williams's opera *The Poisoned Kiss* : the beautiful maiden who lives on poison, the role of antidotes, the obsessive and powerful father. Some of the language of Hawthorne, for example the use of the word 'evanesce', turns up in Evelyn Sharp's libretto. However, another short story has a more direct influence – this is Dr Richard Garnett's *The Poison Maid*.

Richard Garnett (1835–1906) was Keeper of Printed Books at the British Museum. He was a poet, critic and man of letters, whose best original work was a collection of short stories, *The Twilight of the Gods*.[12] There is a gentle irony and humour in these stories which is quite delightful.

'The Poison Maid' is the last story in the collection. A footnote says "The author wrote this tale in entire forgetfulness of Hawthorne's 'Rappaccini's Daughter', which nevertheless he had certainly read". Garnett's tale involves Mithridata who has been brought up by her father, the magician Locusto, on arsenic, opium and prussic acid. Her father tells her "thy kiss would be fatal to anyone not fortified by a course of antidotes". Her father plots the death of a young prince by this one kiss – revenge for an earlier act involving the prince's father, the King "whose father slew my father".

Mithridata rebels ; "I will not be the cause of his death." In a typical reflection of Garnett's humour, her father replies: "O, these daughters! We bring them up tenderly and when all is done they will not so much as commit a murder to please us!" Her father disinherits her. She finds herself rescued by a handsome young man who kisses her. It transpires that far from killing this young man, who is revealed as the prince, the

King had fathomed Locusto's vengeful plot and brought his son up on antidotes. All is well, for the "kiss of love is the remedy for every poison".

A third author, Evelyn Sharp, now enters the tale. Vaughan Williams knew the Garnett short story well and, as Ursula Vaughan Williams tells us, he had thought that the story "had the makings of a light opera".[13] His choice of Evelyn Sharp (1869–1955) as librettist was an interesting one. Why her? She had been a journalist on the *Manchester Guardian*, had contributed to the *Yellow Book* and was the writer of fairy tales and children's books. She had also written a short story in 1902 called *The Spell of the Magician's Daughter*, published in a book of Victorian fairytales, edited by Jack Zipes. This tale is full of 'Poisoned Kiss'-type allusions. This and her use of satire and symbolism in these tales and, in *The Loafer and the Loaf* of 1925, would have seemed to Vaughan Williams well suited to developing Garnett's gentle fable, with its humour and irony, into a full libretto. She was the sister of Cecil Sharp, a close friend and fellow folk-song collector, and therefore to be trusted. Shared sadness at Cecil Sharp's death in 1924 may have drawn composer and future librettist closer together. Finally, as a politician and suffragette, she could be relied upon to invest the libretto with contemporary wit and relevance.

So far, so good, and by July 1927 Evelyn Sharp had produced a libretto and Vaughan Williams was working on Act I. Interestingly Evelyn Sharp had opted for characters with botanical names, following Hawthorne's luxurious garden, and introduced a neat symmetry in the characters. As Frank Howes points out, each main character has an equal and an opposite:[14]

Tormentilla	— Amaryllus
Angelica	— Gallanthus
Empress	— Dipsacus
Three Hobgoblins	— Three Mediums

Evelyn Sharp and Vaughan Williams had decided from the outset to introduce spoken dialogue into the libretto. The outline of Garnett was there : revengeful magician father, young lovers, clever use of antidotes, the initial fear that the poisoned kiss would be the lovers' doom, happy reconciliation at the end as love unites. To this simple tale, Evelyn Sharp added many contemporary references, mainly in the spoken dialogue. Thus we find references to 'state control', to Freud and the Oedipus complex, to the 'Marconigram', to the cricketer Jack Hobbs (in a word play on 'Hob') who had hit his hundredth first class hundred in 1923 (and was specially featured in *Wisden* in 1926), to women MPs and the "distressing result of the higher education of women". When the Empress Persicaria summons Angelica to her side she says "Come hither by Underground". Gallanthus, in an aside, points out this is the quickest way – clearly the tube system in 1927 was in better shape than today!

Evelyn Sharp introduced humour, therefore, although of a kind that can sound dated and contrived. Occasionally, it still works:

> Angelica: Well, it's like this. Tormentilla's kiss is a poison kiss, see?
> Gallanthus: A poison kiss? What's that?
> Angelica: She's been trained to poison the first man she kisses
> Gallanthus: Lumme, what are modern girls coming to!

or, in Act III:

> Empress: Ah, Dipsacus, have you forgotten what you once said to me?
> Dipsacus: I hope so!
> Empress: I have not forgotten!
> Dipsacus: That's the worst of women. They never forget anything.

However, by early August 1927, Vaughan Williams was taking a stronger line regarding the libretto. Whilst insisting that "I don't believe in dictating to other people" he suggests what each character should say, how each character is to be delineated (for example, neologisms reserved for Angelica "in contrast to the purely romantic speeches of Tormentilla",[15] the order of events and the type of metre the composer wants. As Vaughan Williams puts it, "occasional short lines and mid-rhymes are useful to a composer – also 5 and 7 lines occasionally (not always 4 or 6). Then we want some pure and lyric romantic movements I think to give the poor sentimental old composer a chance".[16]

Subsequent correspondence between the composer and librettist shows Vaughan Williams making ever more detailed suggestions. He is sensitive to Evelyn Sharp's levels of patience at all this – he hopes she has "learnt to put up with me" [17] and that "You will have patience with me".[18] By 1931 he writes: "are you tired of the whole thing and would you prefer some arrangement by which you should hand all your work over to me and have no more to do with it …?" [19] In 1935 Vaughan Williams begins his letter to his librettist with "I need hardly say that I am writing about the opera which by this time you must be heartily tired of".[20]

The essence of the difficulty between composer and librettist is uncertainty over how serious the opera should be and whether *The Poisoned Kiss* was to be a musical comedy or real comic opera. In the surviving correspondence, Vaughan Williams says he likes the lyrics but has serious problems with the opera dramatically. In a letter of 12 September 1928 he says of Act II: "I feel it is rather too serious and grand opera-ish".[21] By December 1929 he is still trying "to prevent the thing from becoming too high-falutin' ".[22] As to the dilemma between musical comedy and real comic opera, Vaughan Williams says:

> In musical comedy (or ballad opera) the music is purely incidental, ie the music could be left out and the drama would remain intact. In comic opera at certain points (usually the finale) the drama is carried on through the music — the only difference this makes to the librettist is that in certain places the drama goes on in verse and not in prose — and usually in short sentences not long songs.[23]

Vaughan Williams then points out changes that are necessary if the work is to be a *comic opera*: strengthening the ensemble in Act I and introducing a choral set song at the end of Act III. All this is very confusing.

Evelyn Sharp laid out her difficulties in an extraordinary and revealing letter of 14 September 1928:

> I don't pretend to know what is effective on the stage; you have written operas and I haven't, and seeing that it is a fluke in any case you are much more likely to be right than I am. Besides, the music must decide finally because it is the more important of the two. So please go ahead if the spirit moves you, without waiting for consultation. I am sure it will work out all right in the end.

Evelyn Sharp is clearly, as early as Autumn of 1928, letting Vaughan Williams have the major say as "you are more likely to be right than I am". The RVW-Sharp correspondence in the British Library shows this influence extended beyond the music to the libretto in detail. Take this extract from the composer's letter to Evelyn Sharp written just two days before her candid outburst:

> Now I have the following suggestion which will keep all your lyrics (except one "He's broken all my bones" which I shd like to keep) & much of your dialogue.
>
> Hobgob opening song
>
> Alter dialogue to mean that the object of their visit is to let Amaryllus into the house & to tell him that the kiss is the only way of winning her — so as to ensure that the kissing business comes off all right.
>
> Then follows entry of Gallanthus, Angelica, mediums and journalists as in your script — journalists to hide entry of Tormentilla — dialogue about

9. Connock – "Sheer early morning loveliness"

chocolates first then song "There was a time" — followed by a very few lines of dialogue (spoken through music)

The duet "Wearily I go to rest"

Exit of Tormentilla

Then we want something new

Hobgobs creep out and let in Amaryllus — interrupted by entry of Angelica ("My work is done" etc)

Then Angelica must be got rid of so that she & Gallanthus do not appear till the end of the act — but how? But how?!!!!! (Though I think you are not v. convincing here) (I think all this should be sung — I think short even lines of the type of Angelica's entry is the best — plenty of give and take between the characters[)] (But the scene can be quite short)

Then follows Amaryllus serenade (I want from here all sung)

Entry of Tor:

Scene between these two leading to Tor: "If you touch me you die" at this moment chorus of spirits (unseen, or through transparencies) casting a spell over her so that she gradually yields to Am & she falls swooning in the arms as he kisses her.

The goblins then dance round the pair singing a mocking song — & retire

Amaryllus "I have kissed and I am willing to die like the prince I am"(all spoken!)

Tor: Who are you?
Am: I am the prince
Tor: O father you have won. My fate has been too much for me

Then short sung finale (slow) ending with unseen chorus.

Or (b) at climax of ensemble
a knocking heard at the door & a voice (all this spoken)

Herald's voice: "Open in the name of the empress" (enter Herald and guards)

Herald: Hear the proclamation of our sovereign lady the empress "whereas our beloved son the Prince Amaryllus has been bewitched by a wicked sorceress it is our pleasure that he be confined in our highest tower until he be recovered from his unhappy infatuation" — Guards! Seize the prince!

Am: Do with me as you wish — I have kissed like a prince & am willing to die like a prince
Tor: (starting) Who are you?
Am: I am Prince Amaryllus
Tor: O father (etc as before)

Herald: Now hear further "whereas this same sorceress has proved herself to be an unhallowed witch, in that she ate of the Imperial chocolates and has not even suffered from indigestion, our command is that she be confined in our foulest dungeon there to await her doom" Guards! seize the witch

Tor: Willingly I go to die for I have killed your prince (Then follows slow finale as before)

Tor comes out of her trance crying out "the poison kiss" — pushes Am away & crouches in a corner.

Ang: and Gall: come running in & there follows (more or less) your finale. As a climax to this I have two alternative ideas

I don't know if you think this at all possible — Perhaps you will reject it altogether — But in case not I send you an awful re-hash of your text (with some additions of my own!) to which I have already set music

I fear it is rather too serious & grand opera-ish — but perhaps this won't matter if we keep all the rest quite light.

Evelyn Sharp, in her restrained way, pushes back. She writes on the above suggestion from Vaughan Williams:

I am not quite sure I agree with them all, for one thing, if we use up so much incident in Act II we have so little action left for Act III, haven't we? I mean when there is no more mystery between Tormentilla and Amaryllus, most of the excitement is gone.

Evelyn Sharp goes on to ask if she could talk over the plot with Vaughan Williams, "if only to get my mind a little clearer on it".

And so it goes on – Vaughan Williams shaping the libretto with a marked romantic quality. In a letter of 27 January 1929 he is suggesting heroic couplets for a "slow serious song".[24] In December 1929 Vaughan Williams admits that it is "all my fault that it is too heavy at present".[25] The uncertainty over how serious the opera should be persists.

By May 1936, after the first performance in Cambridge, Vaughan Williams was still worrying that the opera "is not quite amusing enough". He feels that the end of Act I is "scrappy" and whole episodes are either long winded "partly owing to the fact that we have to tell it over twice in dialogue and in song".[26] He had already cut 20 minutes of music for the first performance, and Evelyn Sharp had cut much of the dialogue, but Vaughan Williams remained dissatisfied. In a letter of memorable candour between composer and librettist, of 15 May 1936, he asks categorically for some lines to be deleted which he regards as "facetious". He admits that "the low comedy part ... alarmed me in cold print" and wonders whether one would care to hear the libretto twice. Finally, he adds "I think generally all through the opera we have too many explanations about poisons etc".[27]

These are remarkable admissions seven years after they began working on the opera. That Vaughan Williams remained dissatisfied is clear from a letter dated 4 January 1942, contained in the BBC Archives, from the composer to the conductor Stanford Robinson. In it he says:

> I wish you could find me a first class librettist. The really good playwriters won't write libretti. I recoil with horror from the hack librettist, however much he may know about stage business.
>
> Three of my operas have at all events good libretti:
>
> > Sir John in Love
> > Riders to the Sea
> > The Shepherds

The omission of both *Hugh the Drover* and *The Poisoned Kiss* is striking.[28]

The libretto was now moving to its final stage. OUP agreed to publish the opera, with a number of conditions about the libretto, which was revised by Hubert Foss's brother William. With the death of Evelyn Sharp on 17 June 1955, Vaughan Williams suggested to Alan Frank, at the OUP, that the complete rights to the text of *The Poisoned Kiss* should be purchased from her executors. This went ahead. A performance of the opera at Cheltenham Grammar School in April 1956 stimulated the composer to a further major revision of the work, this time with the help of Ursula Vaughan Williams. As Vaughan Williams put it in a letter to Alan Frank of 18 August 1956, "Ursula is toying with the idea of doing it all in alexandrines or rhyming couplets".[29] The new version was first performed at the Royal Academy of Music on 11 July 1957.

These final revisions were quite fundamental. The main changes between the 1936 edition and the 1957 version can be summarised as follows:

Act I

Deletion of section of opening chorus
Removal of opening verses of Ensemble "Father, where are you?"
Deletion of Amaryllus's song "I thought I loved Maria"
Deletion of Dipsacus's ballad "The sun it shone"
Deletion of Trio "I refuse to adopt"

Act II

Deletion of Trio "Today when all the world"
Deletion of Tormentilla's song "Let my tears flow"
Removal of opening stanza of Tormentilla's song "There was a time!"

Act III

Deletion of Ensemble "The Angry Spirit"
Deletion of chorus of Hobgoblins "Out of the morn"
Deletion of Melodrama and Dipsacus's music

Ursula Vaughan Williams cut, revised, simplified and softened the linking dialogue. Her rhymed couplets are a considerable improvement on the prose originals. The libretto is closer to Richard Garnett than before: lighter and more romantic. Most of the rather dated 1920s references have disappeared (Marconigram, London Underground, Oedipus complex, etc). Perhaps the wit of the Sharp version has gone with it but the final version is closer to what Vaughan Williams had been asking for all along. Some embarrassments remain. For example, *Love in a hut* is still there, to these revised words:

> Love in a hut,
> Is picturesque, but,
> I owe it's disaster
> Unless you've been wise.
> Insist on good heating.
> Also some adequate seating.
>   (etc)

The plot overall must not be taken seriously – it is after all a 'romantic extravaganza'. The libretto, like all good fairy stories, would work out alright in the end – and so it proved.

Conclusions

With hindsight, Evelyn Sharp was not a wise choice as librettist for *The Poisoned Kiss*. As she admitted in her autobiography of 1933, she found it easier "to write good tragedy rather than good comedy".[30] Her priorities were social and economic rather than music or opera. Edmund Rubbra, in his wonderfully under-stated way, says of Evelyn Sharp's contribution that "the libretto is not an aid to continued interest".[31]

For Vaughan Williams, it is clear (as he admitted privately to Hubert Foss[32]) that he was writing music he really liked. Michael Kennedy quotes Vaughan Williams saying that he feared to show Holst the score "because he would never have been able to understand how I could at the same time consider it trivial and yet want to write it".[33]

Increasingly, we will be grateful that he wanted to write such expressive songs as 'Blue larkspur in a garden' or 'Love breaks all rules'. This is music of a simple beauty, noble and enchanting. Alongside tangos and waltzes, this exquisite music will endure as long as we remain receptive to romance and sheer, early-morning loveliness.

'Immemorial Ind'
Elgar's score for *The Crown of India*

Robert Anderson

Elgar wrote two works for the Coronation of George V on 22 June 1911: a March that opens in an unfestive 3/4; and the Offertory 'O hearken Thou unto the voice of my calling' that is devotional yet not complacent. He and Lady Elgar were at the dress rehearsal in Westminster Abbey, when he received the congratulations of passing peers on the award of the OM. To the intense chagrin of Lady Elgar, who had purchased appropriate clothing for the occasion, he decided they should not attend the ceremony. This rather churlish gesture probably convinced him that, as far as the crowning of the new king was concerned, his duties were at an end. But he had forgotten India.

From the beginning of the year *The Times* had glowed with forecasts about the London coronation, but had stirred enthusiasm also for a December event at Delhi, which should combine the fantastic pageantry of a durbar with what was to be almost a second crowning of the King-Emperor and his Queen-Empress. Curiosity was stimulated by accounts of the ship that should carry the royal pair, a brand-new P&O vessel called the *Medina*. The state cabins were described, the King's to port, the Queen's to starboard, both equipped with a hammock in which to sway during bad weather. Should the elements prove really hostile, these cabins near the bow could be abandoned for others amidships, where movement would be less disturbing. There were 20 cabins for ladies-in-waiting, and six for secretaries. The furnishings were supplied throughout by Waring & Gillow.

The arrival at Bombay was eagerly anticipated. The *Medina* was dressed overall, immense crowds had spontaneously assembled, the King expressed pleasure at being again on Indian soil (he had visited as Prince of Wales), and the royal couple were soon entrained for Delhi. There a vast site of 25 square miles on the Raisina hill had been prepared as a durbar encampment, with 25 acres set aside for the royal party. It was where the New Delhi of Edwin Lutyens would spring up over the succeeding years. Whether the immense expense was justified is neither here nor there, nor did it matter fundamentally that the Indian princes so obviously outdid in splendour their monarch from afar. *The Times* reported the royal pair on their lofty dais as "remote but beneficent".

The magnificence of the durbar had nonetheless struck a chord at home, in a London where it was still a fact that the sun did not set on the British Empire. 'Wider and wider yet' seemed an inevitable future for the rest of the world, which was beginning to disapprove strongly. It was natural, then, that Oswald Stoll (1866–1942), creator and proprietor of the Coliseum Variety Theatre, should wish to cash in on the national mood. He approached Henry Hamilton, actor turned prolific playwright and fluent versifier, for the text of a masque based essentially on the most quixotic moment of the durbar when George V announced, for no reason apparent to those present, that the capital of India would be shifted from Calcutta to Delhi. Certainly Calcutta, the original trading emporium of the East India Company, was less well placed since the development of Bombay on the west coast, and above all since the opening of the Suez Canal in 1869. Stoll next secured, with advantageous financial terms and illusory suggestions of possible performance on the continent, that Elgar should be the composer.

Elgar's contribution was to be part of a full-length music-hall programme, the content of which made it the more remarkable that Elgar was prepared, day after day, to conduct matinée and evening performances for the whole run of *The Crown of India* from 11 to 23 March. The items were as follows: *Le Lion de St Marc* overture by G Fabiani; Five Cliftons, Gymnastic Equilibrists; Tom Stuart in Dramatic and Burlesque Impressions; Thora, a Ventriloquial Novelty; Billy Merson, the New London Eccentric Comedian; Dmitri Andreeff, the Famous Russian Solo Harpist; Miss Irene Vanbrugh and Arthur Playfair in *The Twelve-Pound Look* by J M Barrie, scene of Sir Henry Sims' study, produced by Dion Boucicault, the *Tannhäuser* overture as interval music; Rudolfo Giglio, Chanteur Néapolitain; *The Crown of India*; A Cast of Famous Continental Mimes in 'Pierrot's Last Adventure', a pantomime in one act by Victor Arnold, music by Friedrich Bermann; The Bioscope – Topical and Interesting Events. God Save the King.

Hamilton clearly relished his commission. He researched Indian history with an almost manic thoroughness, so that his allusions were sometimes obscure towards incomprehensibility. The city of Agra, for instance, sings thus of India's mystery:

> From out what Dark thy Dawn
> Arose
> None knows:
> Behind thy veil close-drawn,
> Immeshed of gossamer and gold,
> Magic its warp and Mystery its woof,
> Alone, aloft, aloof.

Elgar did his best, using as leitmotiv throughout the aria and indeed in much of the masque a theme he had used for his 1905 piano piece, *In Smyrna*, inspired by a visit to a dervish mosque in what is now Izmir. Elgar knew from the outset that Henry Hamilton had allowed his imagination to run riot over the text and introduced too many political references for any audience unprepared by a course in Indian history to comprehend. There would have to be cuts. Bernard Shaw had been merciless when reviewing such plays by Hamilton as *Cheer, boys, Cheer!*: "I have heard it all over and over again; for in the first play of this kind I ever saw, the course of events was just the same: the hero thrashed the villain; and the villain, with his accomplice, the comic Jew, was arrested by the police in a gorgeous ballroom at the end."

For the start of his music Elgar turned to one of the 'Moods of Dan', his tributes in the visitors' book to G R Sinclair's bulldog companion in Hereford. This time it was 'The Sinful Youth of Dan'. Ideas that might have gone into *The Apostles* and *The Kingdom* were to hand, and a possible 'Judas' theme appeared in 'The Crowning of Delhi'; the 'Entrance of Delhi' borrowed music near a sketch for the possible *Cockaigne no.2* overture; material for *In the South* went towards the 'Crown of India' March. What instrumentation Elgar had in mind it is impossible to say, as no full score for the Masque exists.

A piano and vocal score of the complete work was made by Hugh Blair, on sale during the performances. Only there is the full scope of the Masque clear, and only there can be experienced the playful reference Elgar made to bagpipes and *The Campbells are Comin'* when the libretto mentions the relief of Lucknow during the Indian Mutiny of 1857 by Sir Colin Campbell. A touch more serious was another quotation in St George's song, 'The Rule of England', when Elgar came to the words "Dear Land that hath no Like". The vocal line rises *allargando* to a climax while the orchestra quietly supports with two bars of *Land of Hope and Glory*. The only other material to have survived are orchestral parts for Agra's song, a monumental full score of the 'Crown of India' March, and playing parts of the Suite Elgar made from the Masque for the following Three Choirs Festival at Hereford. The case of Agra's song is curious. The MS parts, not in Elgar's hand, date from 1921, when he was planning a performance with baritone rather than alto. A note on the leader's copy records that the parts were checked by Elgar on 14 April 1921. A performance was given two days later by Herbert Heyner, who went on to sing under Elgar in the *Gerontius* recording made at the Albert Hall in February 1927.

The March score is gigantic. Though not autograph, it has some verbal cues by Elgar. It is laid out for triple wind (without cor anglais), Elgar's usual complement of brass, a fine array of percussion, as well as stage trumpets, military band on stage, and stage drums. In other words, it is on the scale of the *Coronation Ode* full score. There is evidence enough that, though Elgar seems to have used this score in the theatre, he realised such forces would never be available in the Coliseum pit. Indeed the lines for bass clarinet and double bassoon peter out soon enough, and the stage instruments are indicated only fitfully. Some idea of the orchestra's eventual size comes from the fact that Elgar took all the players out to lunch on 13 March. This suggests a group of modest size, as indeed does Lady Elgar's diary entry: "All so happy & so proud & pleased. E. the most sweet & charming host. Immense enthusiasm for E. & health drunk – 'We are the proudest Orch. in London'." The most intriguing memo by Elgar on the score is the word "Incessu". A glance at the libretto fills out the line with "Incessu patuit Imperator". Here Henry Hamilton displays his Classical learning and one would like to think his sense of humour. The original is from Virgil *Aeneid* Book I (1.405): "et vera incessu patuit dea" ("in her step she was revealed, a very goddess"). The reference is to Venus, who has just been addressing her son Aeneas. In the Masque it is George V as King-Emperor whose step must thus reveal him. Perhaps it did.

For the Suite, Elgar selected five of the Masque movements, all of them cut except for the Menuetto, which was the same length as the original 'Entrance of "John Company"'. The 'March of the Mogul Emperors' lost 39 bars. No full score of the Suite was issued. Elgar also produced a cut-down version of the 'Crown of India' March, in which the stage trumpets and military band were accommodated into the size of a normal Elgar orchestra, and there was some redeployment of the horn parts. In none of the scores, and only in the 1921 orchestral parts did the cor anglais feature. Due mainly to a misunderstanding, Novello published none of the original material; it was the shared responsibility of Enoch &

Sons and Hawkes & Son. Nor, indeed, has Novello proved in much of a hurry to assume the task in the new century.

As presented by Henry Hamilton, the contest for the capital between Delhi and Calcutta seems to have absorbed elements of the music-hall. Calcutta, harassed by affairs of government, strides in attended by Commerce and Statecraft. Delhi enters more solemnly, with Tradition and Romance in tow. Soon enough the rivals hurl insults at each other, Delhi first:

> And wilt thou vaunt to me thy mushroom pomp
> Of new-made palaces ? that wast a swamp
> One hundred years ago: when I a Queen
> For forty centuries had been:

Calcutta replies in kind:

> A strenuous Yesterday, a strong To-day
> Are better than an aeon of decay,
> Barbaric splendours and bejewelled ease
> Adorned by Despots — and by Debauchees!

Delhi marshalled her case with the help of the four greatest Mogul emperors. Akbar (r.1556–1605), enlightened and tolerant in religious matters, had the honour of a missive from Elizabeth I of England that took two years to arrive. Jehangir (r.1605–1627) adopted Thomas Roe, ambassador from James I and often harassed to find gifts rich enough for the Great Mogul, as a favourite drinking companion. In the case of Shah Jahan (r.1629–1658), Hamilton concentrated on the Taj Mahal, a building lovingly restored by Lord Curzon when Viceroy of India (1899–1905). The last of Delhi's witnesses is Aurangzeb (r.1658–1707), fanatic in faith, a warrior in the Deccan for much of his reign, who died at a great age in great disappointment.

As main seat of the East India Company, Calcutta summons for chief witness 'John Company'. She next invokes a number of the Company's most distinguished servants, at one time household names. Robert Clive (1725–1774), victor of Plassey, ultimately had to face a parliamentary enquiry when he declared, as hinted in Hamilton's text: "I stand astonished at my own moderation." Hector Munro (1726–1805) thwarted the attempt of the Mogul emperor Shah Alam to oust the British from Bengal. Warren Hastings (1732–1818) proved an able military commander, advanced the study of Sanskrit, and founded the Bengal Asiatic Society. Though threatened with impeachment, he saved India for Britain while the home government was losing America. Cornwallis and Wellesley led on to the heroes of the Mutiny, culminating in Campbell at Lucknow, though unforgivably omitting Lady Elgar's father, Sir Henry Gee Roberts.

Now came the moment of decision. The other Indian cities present declared themselves incapable of judging between Delhi and Calcutta; so Delhi played her trump card and invoked St George. Despite a boldly jingoistic song, the saint found himself too chivalrous for so invidious a choice, and transferred the task to his namesake, the King-Emperor. Decision was for Delhi, but *The Times* was uncertain whether the monarch had been quite properly portrayed: "Though we have the Durbar and the King-Emperor and his Consort, the whole is, of course, intended to be symbolical and not realistic, and it is necessary to remember this when a smooth-faced female figure heralded as 'George, by the Grace of God, of that great name the fifth,' enters in triumphal procession."

The Times ignored everything in the programme except *The Crown of India*. It more or less ignored Hamilton too, except to say that, though some cuts had been made, more were needed. Elgar's friend, Frances Colvin, saw an early performance and wrote on 13 March: "A line dear E.E. to tell you how much we enjoyed the Masque – your music is gorgeous & gave one just the right thrill. I longed to stop those women shrieking & just have the music, & the wonderful colours to look at, it would be superb!"

Elgar replied the next day that cuts would indeed be made and that the finances of the Masque gave him scope to buy books:

> So many thanks for your letter: it was understood that the thing was to be mainly pantomime & now the dialogue will be cut out — it was an inoffensive thing & some of the music is good!
>
> When I write a big serious work e.g. Gerontius we have had to starve & go without fires for twelve months as a reward: this small effort allows me to buy scientific works I have yearned for & I spend my time between the Coliseum & the old bookshops.

Since Henry Hamilton does not appear at all in Lady Elgar's diary, and there is no evidence that Elgar met him, it was the easier to arrange cuts directly with Oswald Stoll. Drastic they were, as can be seen from the libretto once owned by Elgar's niece, May Grafton, who stayed at Severn House (Elgar's new London home) during the *Crown of India* run. The sentiments of the libretto, exhilarating enough at the safe distance of the Coliseum in 1912, had a more questionable validity in the swarming realities of India itself.

Eleven symphonies : Do they travel?
If not, why not?

This is an edited transcription of the impromptu discussion held at the end of the symposium.

Andrew Neill (AN): It is now time for our panel discussion which I hope will involve not only those on the platform but you in the audience as well. We have a rather bland title but I hope it will help us develop the discussion as we progress. Joining me on the stage are:

Byron Adams (BA)
Charles McGuire (CMcG)
David Owen Norris (DON)
Lewis Foreman (LF)

The premise is that during the last two days we have been talking about two great composers who between them wrote eleven symphonies. (**Question from audience:** Twelve symphonies? **BA:** Eleven-and-a-half, if that. **AN:** The Third Symphony will not go into the Elgar Complete Edition although the sketches for it will; I'm afraid that is the distinction between something many of us have grown to know and love, and being scholarly; so I am going to stick to eleven completed symphonies.) It is arguable that Vaughan Williams produced the greatest variety of symphonies of any symphonist of the last century. If you think of the emotional range and extraordinary variety of music contained in those symphonies, it remains astonishing to me that they have yet to be appreciated by the rest of the world.

The great symphonists of the last century include Mahler, Nielsen, Sibelius, Shostakovich and Prokofiev. In this country I was able to hear some of the symphonies of those composers as I grew up. Of course, I was particularly fortunate to be able to take the music of Sibelius to my heart from a very early age. I remember going to Promenade concerts where the audience used to wave banners saying "More Nielsen", but he now seems to have found his level, more or less. Nowadays you can put on a series of symphonies by Shostakovich or Mahler and the world will rush to hear them, but put on a series of Vaughan Williams symphonies (which I think

11. Panel Discussion – Eleven Symphonies : Do They Travel?

has only been done once in my lifetime) and the BBC sniffs and coughs as to whether it should broadcast them. I am glad to say it did, but that was a one-off.

Obviously, Elgar's symphonies are also played here, but what I want to do is look abroad. It is therefore useful to have two Americans on this panel – ideally we would also have a German, a Russian, and a Frenchman, but we haven't. I have talked to Viennese musicians and said "If you were asked to play Vaughan Williams's Fourth Symphony next week, you would die of shock" and they agreed. But ask a London orchestra to play a rarely performed Prokofiev symphony and they would simply shrug their shoulders and get on with it. So what I want to try to do is to explore this issue to see if there is a problem in the acceptance of the music of Elgar and Vaughan Williams abroad. Should we agree that there is some sort of problem, then we might address what we might do to begin rectifying matters. If there isn't a problem, we can all go away today exceedingly happy and probably rather complacent, something we should never be about great art, particularly in this country.

Is our relatively gentle climate to blame – does it permeate our music and put everyone else off? Many now rush off to Spain for their vacation and then come back and moan about the weather in this country. This poses the question: in recent years have we gone through a cultural change? If so, has that altered our interest in the culture of this country and the music of our composers? Are we more prepared to be seduced by the neuroses of Mahler than the neuroses of Elgar? It is an interesting subject which has been talked through at length by others, but we have the opportunity to consider it further today. I would therefore like to ask our panellists for their own opinions: do they think there is an issue we need to address as British people in the way the music of our two great English composers is performed abroad? Byron Adams first.

BA: Let me tell you of an incident after a performance of the Pasadena Symphony Orchestra, a fine local orchestra at which I give three pre-concert talks a year. I was introduced to the young assistant conductor, who is Russian and who also conducts the Pasadena Youth Orchestra, as a musicologist who works on Elgar and Vaughan Williams. He responded "Oh, British music is so boring." For years I would have been polite in my response, but instead I said: "Do you know any?" He said: "Oh, I've heard *The Lark Ascending* – so boring." I asked: "What do you know by Elgar?" "Oh, I know the march." "Do you know the symphonies?" I asked. "No." "Do you know the Vaughan Williams symphonies?" "No." "So you're answering from a position of ignorance, aren't you?" Of course, having a University Chair doesn't hurt in these situations.

If I may say so, the problem, as an American looking from the outside, is firstly that my interest in this music is simply because it is first rate music of an international standard, and I'm not saying that because you are an English audience. I would say it in France and I would say it in Kamchatka. Elgar is a great composer; Vaughan Williams is a great composer – by European standards. I love Mahler, but I think Elgar is as great and as important a composer at Mahler, and what Elgar tells us about *fin de siècle* England, Europe and culture in general has been one of my interests for the past 15 years; he is as rich a figure as certainly any of his German counterparts. I would say Vaughan Williams is certainly one of the great symphonists (and, I would add, opera composers, although I know that is a minority view) of the 20th century. I fell in love with an atypical piece because I auditioned as a 16-year-old for a performance of *Flos Campi*.

Having said that, there are problems, the first of which is the complacency of an international corporate musical mentality that would rather record *Scheherazade* for the ten-thousandth time than record one of the Elgar symphonies or the *Wand of Youth*. Only now are we finally getting, thanks to Stephen Connock, Michael Kennedy and Hugh Cobbe, a recording of an important work of Vaughan Williams. It is great that it is now happening but simply scandalous that it didn't happen during the composer's lifetime – but it didn't. I'll conclude my remarks by saying, and I hope you'll forgive me, something I have perceived since 1985 when I started coming to England – that it partly has to do with the enormous embarrassment that I find here about your own art, especially music. As a young American, encouraged by William Austin the great musicologist who thought very highly of Elgar and Vaughan Williams, I was pointed in that direction. I was reacting violently against the academic prejudices in America at that time and when I gleefully came over here. I said: "Vaughan Williams is a great composer" and the reaction I got from everyone except Ursula Vaughan Williams was one of embarrassment: "We don't talk about those kind of things here." You can be sure the Germans all talk about their composers to this day, and the greatest propagandist for 20th century German modernism was Adorno who is accepted in every American university and studied. Well, where is the English Adorno?

AN: David, you travel a great deal and it might be helpful to get a thought or a view from you now.

11. Panel Discussion – Eleven Symphonies : Do They Travel?

DON: I perform these composers abroad when I can. When I won a prize at the beginning of the 1990s which involved me having to perform in America a lot and play piano quintets, I chose Elgar's Quintet. There was a good deal of muted grumbling that I had not chosen Brahms. But, in general, where I sneak things into my programmes they are appreciated. I think what I can most easily add to this discussion is this. I will slightly change my focus if I may. It is most interesting – Byron's challenge to an English Adorno. Of course nobody thinks like Adorno, thank goodness.

Incidentally, coming up on the train this morning, I was rather amused to notice that, in contrast with the 19th century, most of the trains come from Germany but that music tends to come from England. I have just been reading an article in a German magazine from which, it seems to me, there are much more exciting things happening musically in England and the USA than in places which live on their past reputation.

What I would like to suggest is that, in a way, we are having a discussion which time has passed by. Nicholas Cook, Professor of Music at Southampton University, is the author of *A Very Brief Introduction to Music*, one of the more arresting books in a series of 'brief introductions' to all sorts of things published by the Oxford University Press. One of his more startling comments is that he has never been able to see the social relevance of a Brahms symphony. Each week, when I pop into Southampton, I try to catch him on that one. But I personally think it is something you would expect to find written by an Englishman in today's England. My experience of America (which is brief) is that I find their classical music tradition is very strong and very proudly defended, partly, I think, because it feels under threat and has always done so. The result is both good and bad. In Chicago, they appear to believe that music must still be performed as it was in the Twenties and Thirties and can't move on at all but, on the other hand, it is performed and loved and deeply known.

In England (and I may be about to become deeply controversial although I don't mean to be), we have particular policies which are designed to force us into multiculturalism. That may be a very good thing – I have nothing to say against multiculturalism at all – but I remember having a discussion with Monica Huggett a little while ago about the difficulty of finding official support for classical music here. We came to the conclusion that classical music has been, to borrow a phrase from Douglas Hurd, "punching above its weight" for almost a century but has now been kicked back into its corner as far as British politics is concerned. Certainly I have had conversations with many people who run opera companies who tell me that it is almost impossible to get grants to perform an opera, however interesting, unless you have a bolt-on 'hot button' that will appeal to cross-cultural threads.

There are two points I would like to draw from this. The first is that, as far as the British musical establishment is concerned, the argument has gone on beyond whether symphonies continue to be performed. I think the establishment's view about that is "O well, if you must, but wouldn't it be better if we were writing crossover symphonies of multicultural appeal". The second point is this: I used to present a BBC radio programme called *The Works*, dedicated to the study and the verification of crossover, and the conclusion I came to after two years was that it was a difficult trick to work.

I once did an interview with a sitar player and the head of composition at the Birmingham Conservatoire. The sitar player had come to the UK to teach the unadulterated classical traditions of Indian music whereas the head of composition was hoping that she [the sitar player] would be a bran tub of ideas for composition students, something which was only found out on air during the interview, leading to a wonderful confrontation.

These views might be slightly off the subject but I hope they may inform the debate as it continues.

AN: Thank you David. Did anyone hear the BBC radio programme about ten days ago by Richard Morrison on Simon Rattle's first six months in Berlin? What struck me is that, first of all, Rattle is a very charismatic figure with a large number of people running after him to keep up. But an important part of the programme was about the work the Berlin Philharmonic is doing with poor school children in East Berlin. Part of the delight of the programme was that the complacent musicians of the orchestra had never done anything like this before in their lives, but many were now rather enjoying it. The first programme they had performed there for the public was a re-interpretation of Stravinsky's *Rite of Spring* which had involved putting together a ballet with the school children, who had also enjoyed the experience immensely. The (British) Secretary of State for Culture, Media and Sport attended this performance and said how much she had appreciated it. Sadly, it is very difficult to imagine her doing a similar thing in London. I may be damning her unfairly, because the London Symphony Orchestra is doing something along these lines at St Luke's in the City of London, but it would be nice to think that a similar interest is shown by British politicians, many of whom, it seems, have a vested interest in crossover music or like to be associated with someone as powerful as Rattle.

11. Panel Discussion – Eleven Symphonies : Do They Travel?

CMcG: I'm currently living outside Cleveland, Ohio, where Franz Welser-Möst has been appointed the new music director of the Cleveland Symphony Orchestra. That decision was made to continue the legacy of the orchestra in playing late 19th century Viennese works, in particular the symphonies of Mahler, which the orchestra has a long and venerable tradition of performing, partially because of the ethnic make-up of the city of Cleveland itself. One of the interesting things about programming in a North American orchestra is that we generally tend to focus on things which have been traditional since at least the 1930s, as well as on centennials, so that a number of orchestras performed *The Dream of Gerontius* – from Indiana to Illinois to New York City and San Francisco – on its centennial, generating some publicity for the work. But, even though those performances were generally well reviewed, the work has since fallen by the wayside again. We shall see whether the same happens for *The Apostles*, *The Kingdom*, and Elgar's two symphonies on their centenaries.

Two things which I have noted are, firstly, that the Elgar-Payne reconstruction, when it appeared, was very popular; a breath of fresh air in the concert hall, and that the work is still occasionally programmed by American symphony orchestras. But, for me as a teacher, having worked at a number of institutions over the past couple of years, what I find more hopeful is that every year a student approaches me wishing to undertake an honours project on one of the Vaughan Williams or Elgar symphonies. I only began teaching in 1998 so at present I have no more than a number of undergraduates' papers, but each time a student comes up to me and says "I hadn't heard this music before – I just happened to hear it on a CD and I love it. What can I do about it? Where can I find out more about it?"

One other thing which is happening is the issue, on CD, of a number of Vaughan Williams film scores, so youngsters are discovering how much the film scores they hear today draw on both Elgar and Vaughan Williams. This is also generating a lot of interest in the neo-romantic film score of the 1980s and 1990s, as well as the great film scores of the 1940s and 1950s, and in Elgar's music as well. Even though there may be what we shall call structural problems, I think there is a great deal of hope for the future and it will be through individual student enthusiasts that we win and create this audience.

AN: Thank you. Lewis?

LF: I have so many thoughts on the subject that I am not sure how to structure them. In 1997 I retired, but have since been busier than ever. Apart from some writing, I mainly spend my time advising independent record companies on repertoire: a company will ring me and ask: "Do you have any ideas for what a particular artist such as David might record?" I think of pieces which haven't been recorded or will suit a particular artist and I then construct a programme, find the orchestral parts and prepare them for the recording. To give you an example, next week I am with Hyperion recording volume 6 of the Handley-Bantock cycle. In doing this, one gets quite a lot of feedback and, reverting to our initial premise, I am not sure that it is true at all.

There is, in particular, the example of Japan. I did a Holst CD with one particular company (Classico) which included the first-ever performance of Holst's *Cotswold Symphony*. It required a lot of effort to pull the performance together and was a very slow-selling CD series, but the Holst record alone was in profit from an early stage. This was almost entirely due to sales of the CD in Japan. Last year, a leading Japanese record magazine ran a British music issue containing many articles, in Japanese, about works and records that we know and love. You may know the 1972 recording of *A Sea Symphony* made by Toshiba. Nobody persuaded them to record it; they made it because there was a major current of interest.

There is only one country from which one does not get this sort of feedback and that is France. I remember Ted Perry of Hyperion telling me about a French magazine reviewing eight recordings of Gerald Finzi, but whether the reviews sold any copies of the CDs is unclear. Recordings are now put on sale internationally. York Bowen's Symphony, for example, is available around the world. It is not performed, but it is on CD and therefore accessible. The problem may be the difficulty and cost of getting hold of the parts, a problem that lies with the music publishers. If, for example, a musical organisation holds parts for a work, they are more likely to want to play it than if they have to hire the parts for the performance.

My daughter used to play in the Hertfordshire County Youth Orchestra as third horn and the orchestra toured Switzerland playing Elgar's First Symphony. They ended up in Geneva and everyone thought it was marvellous. Once, whilst on holiday in France, we stopped in Sées and went to a concert in the cathedral where they were playing Vaughan Williams's *Pastoral Symphony*, the first and only time I have heard it without the voice, which they replaced with a clarinet – it doesn't work but it was wonderful to hear it in that acoustic. The performers were Les Jeunesses de Portsmouth but the important point is that it was a French audience. They may not have realised what they were hearing, thinking it possibly to be early Debussy, but they were listening, so I am not sure that the proposition is true.

BA: May I respond to that? What Lewis brings up is a fascinating point, which is certainly true in America. That is that the concert audience and the audience for CDs is completely different. I live in a country which is so completely capitalist that they simply don't keep CDs in stock in Tower Records unless sales meet expectation: after one year, if it has not sold the requisite number of copies, they discontinue the CD. What is extraordinary is that the range of Elgar and Vaughan Williams stock never decreases but neither does Herbert Howells nor Finzi nor Walton. I was talking with an acquaintance who is connected with the business end of the Los Angeles Philharmonic. I pointed out that the Walton centenary is approaching, suggesting that the Philharmonic should play some of his music for the occasion. Much to my amazement, my suggestion went as high as the conductor, Esa Pekka Salonen, who dismissed the idea out of hand. "Walton? Who is that? Not an important 20th century composer at all." which was the response reported back to me. I thought this was insane because, at our record store, the new Walton recording, admittedly of his string quartets, had sold out within one week. The same thing had happened with the recording of the original version of the Vaughan Williams's Second Symphony. And it continued selling.

There is a curious disconnect between symphony orchestras' programming. When Kent Nagano and the Hallé Orchestra performed Vaughan Williams's *Sinfonia Antarctica*, the only time I have heard that work performed live, in the Hollywood Bowl in July, I was with my friend who came along somewhat reluctantly but turned to me at the end and said "That is a wonderful symphony". More importantly, there were 13,000 people there who had turned out for a programme consisting of Walton's score for *Henry V* and a number of other works by English composers which had originated as a film scores. Whenever an Elgar symphony is programmed in Los Angeles, which is approximately once every three years, it is because Ernest Fleischman, the orchestra's former manager, likes them. And you will get a huge audience who usually end up weeping after a performance of Elgar's A flat Symphony because it is very moving. However, there is one terrible little notice in the *Los Angeles Times* and then nothing for another three years.

When André Previn conducted Vaughan Williams's Fifth Symphony some fifteen years ago, the place was packed and people were ecstatic, but it has never been repeated. I've convinced at least three conductors to perform Vaughan Williams: Daniel Lewis with the Pasadena Symphony Orchestra who performed Vaughan Williams's Fourth Symphony 20–30 years ago, and more recently Peter Oundjian, the Canadian conductor who has also done Vaughan Williams's Fourth Symphony with great success in the Netherlands and Houston, and is going to perform Vaughan Williams's Sixth Symphony in San Diego of all places – I'll be interested to see how that works – and in Toronto. When Sir Roger Norrington conducted Vaughan Williams's Sixth Symphony in San Francisco, it was an enormous success. It takes a certain amount of education, but there remains a strange disconnect between the concert audience and the CD audience.

AN: I don't think there is much difference in the UK. Not so long ago I was talking to someone who is closely associated with the London Philharmonic Orchestra about my perception that, if in doubt, they have another Mahler cycle, to which the response was that it was the easiest thing to do. The musicians of the orchestra are responsible for the programming and they invite a conductor to come along and conduct what they know. When you think that this is the orchestra that has recorded the Vaughan Williams symphonies with Haitink, the Parry symphonies with Bamert and many other works by lesser known British composers and yet rarely give live performances of these works; it is an extraordinary imbalance.

DON: I'm moved to speculate by some of the points made: Charles has spoken about the traditions of the Cleveland Orchestra being maintained. Once the Cleveland Orchestra's tradition has been established and it makes a decision to continue that tradition, that at least prevents people who like Mahler from wondering why nobody performs Mahler's symphonies – after all, there are only a certain number of symphonies that can be performed. Therefore, if you are not there at the beginning to help form that tradition, it is a very difficult bus to have missed. The other thing is that Byron makes me think about conductors and the extraordinary power that they wield. It's a truth that I have been very slow to come to realise: conductors have much more power than they should wield, despite being the front men of their institutions. As our politics and arts show, society deals with front men. Of course we have some wonderful British conductors, but most current internationally famous conductors are not British. It seems to me that this may be a fault in British musical education. I remember Nicholas Kenyon, when Controller of Radio 3, remarking that Britain was very good at producing orchestral musicians but absolutely useless at producing soloists, which I found very thought-provoking, particularly the fact that that was his perception. If we are bad at producing soloists, perhaps we are even worse at producing megalomaniac front men, which means we are not well placed for the inside track.

AN: Charles, would you agree with that from your perspective at Cleveland.

CMcG: Interestingly, I don't necessarily. Elgar's music was played in Cleveland and Cincinatti and Chicago until the beginning of the First World War because he was megalomaniacal in promoting his music, even though he hated coming to the USA. *The Apostles, The Kingdom* and *The Dream of Gerontius* have all been performed at the Cincinatti May Festival, and there have been performances of his music at Chicago Festivals. In the first fourteen years of the 20th century, if you look in the clippings books at Broadheath, you will find that Elgar was widely performed, with performances of *Gerontius* in Minneapolis, San Francisco and just about everywhere else in between with phenomenal regularity. And then the performances just stopped. I think there were the roots of a tradition there for a while but, for whatever reason, it was cut off at the knees, especially in the years after the First World War. This would make a very interesting research project.

AN: You could understand that in Germany, but less so in the United States.

DON: That does imply that there is a problem with the music itself. If the music was known and liked and then fell into disfavour, then is the problem in the character of the music?

LF: I have a feeling that this is a generational issue. If you look round at any concert, you will find that the audience gets progressively greyer and the orchestra gets progressively younger. When I first started attending concerts, orchestras included individuals who had been playing before the war and had the tradition in them. Today, one tends to assume that youngsters have the tradition when they don't. One interesting thing about my projects for record companies is that the companies cannot afford to use international stars at huge fees but are, instead, working with extremely talented younger British soloists who are voraciously interested in exploring the repertoire. They are forever ringing up asking if I know of a record company that would be interested in their latest project. We have just completed a project with violinist Paul Barrett who had become interested in the early works of Bax. I happened to have at home the manuscripts of two early Bax string quartets, one composed while he was a student; but I had come to the conclusion that neither was playable. Paul nevertheless asked for photocopies which he took home. He produced parts and edited them for performance. He got his own string quartet to rehearse the edited scores, one of which they performed at the Lichfield Festival. It just needed articulating, and Paul's ensemble has now recorded the pieces for Dutton with financial support from the Bax Trust.

There are numerous players in their twenties, thirties and early forties who are keen to explore unknown repertoire. There is a real tide of interest from people who didn't know the repertoire but are keen to develop their knowledge. It is only when you reach a more exalted level that players tend to become much grander. Perhaps it is the agents who are at fault – if they are not keen to talk about little known works, then neither are the artists. But, just as audiences consist of many overlapping circles, so do players. Certain orchestras have priced themselves out of the market for the type of projects with which I am largely involved, but many of the major British orchestras are very interested in this kind of repertoire. One of the orchestras with which I work regularly, the Royal Liverpool Philharmonic, has its own label. The orchestra looks to the inclusion of little known works to attract attention to a CD and my brief is to find short orchestral works which are at the same time not well known but worth recording. And Elgar is one composer they are particularly keen to record. The orchestra has a wonderful ploy whereby they play works as encores so that they do not appear in the programme but they nevertheless record them for the CD. In this way, the RLPO has recorded Stanford's Overture to *Shamus O'Brien*, the Prelude to Alexander Mackenzie's *Columba*, Parry's March from *Hypatia* and three works by Frederick Austin. But when I talk about this approach to much grander orchestras and conductors, they are not interested.

AN: Jonathan, do you wish to comment on that?

Jonathan Darnborough: I'd like to make two points. It comes as no surprise to me that, in our international symposium, two of the overseas delegates are both from the USA. I realise that, when Claire-Louise and I have been to the USA, we have only performed English music and we have always had the warmest of receptions – not just for Elgar and Vaughan Williams but also for Nicholas Maw, John Tavener and others. But Byron's comments about the corporate musical nature of things are also most important because, to perform this repertoire, we have first to get past the middle men who set things up. It is the audience, not the concert arrangers, who love it, and this is true in Russia and France as much as in San Diego. You have to communicate directly with the audience.

AN: Thank you, Jonathan; now Malcolm.

Malcolm Smith: I think we have been spoilt in the past by having a handful of marvellous British conductors who have been prepared to stake their reputation by conducting British music – Beecham, Boult, Barbirolli, Del Mar, Groves and others. They persuaded their orchestras to perform English music, in particular Elgar and Vaughan Williams, whereas today we have not got a conductor of that status who can dictate what they are going to perform. The English conductor abroad these days is usually under the age of forty and with no sway over the orchestras. They are grateful that they have been invited to conduct but are not given the opportunity to do what they would like. In contrast, Sargent went around the world conducting all sorts of music. I therefore wonder whether Sir Simon Rattle can persuade the Berlin Philharmonic Orchestra to perform a Vaughan Williams cycle in Berlin or Vienna. André Previn exercised a great influence by performing Vaughan Williams's Fourth Symphony, and we must therefore persuade more conductors to carry the banner for British music.

BA: May I address just one point wearing my hat as an American composer? What you have but we do not is your composer societies. The Elgar Society has taken on the challenge of completing the Complete Edition; the Vaughan Williams Society, thanks to Stephen's far-sightedness, has made recordings of so many pieces – such as the Choral Hymns, the *Choral Songs in Time of War*, and *Pilgrim's Pavement* – that I never thought I would hear on CD; the Finzi Trust has done an enormous amount to enhance Finzi's reputation in the US; and the smaller societies for Howells and other British composers; and indeed the Vaughan Williams Trust for many years. Do you know what happens to an American composer's manuscripts when he dies? They are thrown out; or they disappear into a library. In the case of my former teacher, Ellis Coles, they are destroyed in the 2001 attack on the World Trade Center because they had been sent to the New York Public Library which had stored them in the basement of the building. Beware of insularity. You perhaps congratulate yourselves too much that these works are performed in England when there are international audiences, including in countries such as Russia, who are hungry for this music after a very long drought of extremely recondite music after the Second World War. I was foolish to lend to someone, with whom I have since lost contact, Rodzhestvensky's recording of *A Sea Symphony*, performed in Russian. How many of you have ever heard of the recording, yet it was commercially available in the USA. There have been quite a few Russian dissertations on Vaughan Williams in the past few years. This music travels, but it takes all our efforts to make it do so because we are fighting the great forces of an entrenched international capitalist management that would prefer to have audiences hearing the same works repeatedly.

AN: I now want to start bringing this discussion to an end and I intend to finish by asking Michael Kennedy to say a few words. But before I do so, I see that Geoffrey Hodgkins would like to contribute, as does:

Paul Banks: There are three points which to some extent have been made already but which I would like to emphasize. The point about the change in culture is one. If you look at the catalogues of what is available today, they are completely different to what was available in the 1960s. That is how people are going to get to know their music in the future. The situation may be poor as far as concerts are concerned but, thanks to Lewis and other people like that around the world, we can now hear music which we couldn't dream of hearing then. The second point is that passions change. There has been a slight whiff of Mahler-bashing here which I am alert to because, though an admirer of Elgar and Vaughan Williams, I have spent most of my adult life researching Mahler as well. When I started, it was very difficult to put together a complete set of recordings of the Mahler symphonies, whereas it was possible to go out and buy both Elgar symphonies and all of Vaughan Williams's. Things change – who knows where they are going to go in the future. The third point is to emphasize the international spread that Lewis was quite rightly talking about. The Royal College of Music has recently been involved in conferences about British music and music more generally. What struck me was the number of papers being proposed for the conference on English music that originated not just from America, because we know there is a tradition of scholarly interest in British music in North America, but from Continental Europe. So I think the situation is perhaps slightly less pessimistic than one might think.

11. Panel Discussion – Eleven Symphonies : Do They Travel?

AN: Thank you. Can I just say in response to the remark about Mahler-bashing that I am not anti-Mahler but find it surprising, considering the scale and complexity of his music, how widely it is performed and how, in such a short time, it has become the staple of many orchestras world-wide.

Geoffrey Hodgkins: This is clearly a very complex issue and we should be positive – where there are sparks, we should fan them into flames. I am loth to tell the Vaughan Williams Society what to do but, in the hope of encouraging them a little, I'd like to say a few words about the Elgar Society medal, which is awarded to non-British nationals for encouraging interest in Elgar. It was first struck ten years ago and there have so far been four recipients. Apart from Jerrold Northrop Moore, they have all been foreign conductors: Leonard Slatkin, Jerzy Maksymiuck and Tadaaki Otaka. The great thing about all three is that they are enthusiastic about Elgar, Vaughan Williams and British music in general, and Otaka has conducted both Elgar symphonies widely in Japan. The Vaughan Williams Society may therefore wish to consider whether the creation of a similar medal may encourage conductors to perform more Vaughan Williams overseas.

BA: May I just pick up the point about the scholarly tradition in the USA? That essentially did not exist until around 1985 when the Carthusian Trust began the Vaughan Williams Fellowship, of which I was the first recipient. There are two others here – Charles McGuire and Deborah Heckert – and we have just put out a book of their essays. Before that, Philip Brett did Britten and there were several other fine scholars too. I was also told that I had given the first ever talk at the American Musicological Society convention on Elgar, in 1995. There are people like Jim Hepokoski, a brilliant musicologist, who would have loved to have studied Elgar but was told he couldn't. I was told at Cornell University that I couldn't do a Vaughan Williams dissertation; I had to do one on Frank Martin instead. I'd like it recognised that, without the support of Carthusian Trust, which has put up an enormous amount of money, and William Llewellyn and Robin Wells (who is here today) there would not be a healthy and developing British musicological interest in the USA, so our thanks should go to them.

AN: Thank you, Byron; now Michael.

Michael Kennedy (MK): I'd like to pick up on a point Byron made earlier. A couple of years ago, Joyce and I went to New York when Colin Davis and the LSO were performing Elgar there. The audience was terrifically enthusiastic, and there was an Elgar symposium at which James Hepokoski gave the most brilliant 30-minute talk on Elgar I have ever heard. But what appalled me was the standard of the reviews in papers such as the *New York Times* the next day. They were writing as people wrote about Elgar thirty years ago. I felt they must have looked it up in E J Dent's book. Is this a fair comment on the US critics' attitude towards Elgar, Byron?

BA: Not just Elgar, but towards almost everything. I know some of the critics on other newspapers and they are thoughtful, well-meaning, but almost completely ignorant people. The surprise was that when *Gerontius* was performed in New York, Paul Griffiths, not always friendly towards Elgar, wrote a beautiful lead article – and *Gerontius* also received very sympathetic reviews in San Francisco, some indicating a touch of surprise. I was in New York when Colin Davis performed a very eloquent First Symphony there last November and the press notices were marginally better than usual. The debate in the US is usually about whether classical music is relevant at all in a multicultural environment. As chair of a department in California, I can tell some real horror stories of what one is expected to do to obtain funding. However, English music is gradually becoming part of this accepted canon because the German canon exploded and died some years ago. Franz Welser-Möst has just conducted *Dona Nobis Pacem* in Cleveland. What did the reviewers think of that, Charles?

CMcG: The reviews were good but there is controversy over whether it is the most appropriate piece of music to perform at this time.

BA: And I say to that: nonsense.

AN: Well it was more appropriate than a performance of Brahms' *Triumphlied* to celebrate the anniversary of the defeat of the French in 1870.

MK: Can I ask why a Brahms symphony should to be socially relevant?

AN: Of course you can, but I suspect that this is a subject for another symposium! But one final comment from:

Member of Audience: At the risk of name dropping, I though I should just defend Esa Pekka Salonen. We were having a meal with Ollie Knussen

11. Panel Discussion – Eleven Symphonies : Do They Travel?

and others and Salonen asked me if I thought he should be interested in Bax. I replied "Certainly, and do you know any of the Vaughan Williams symphonies?", to which he replied "No". So he will be getting scores and recordings of the symphonies shortly. Let us see what happens.

BA: Good that you got through to him and it would be marvellous if he were to perform the Vaughan Williams Sixth Symphony.

Member of Audience: He had had a couple of pints at this stage.

BA: Well, keep him drinking. Maybe he will learn how to phrase!

Member of Audience: I also lived in Paris for ten years and it is a cultural desert. They are now discovering baroque music, but I was involved in a radio discussion which was seeking to justify why Sibelius should be performed, so what hope is there in Paris for British music, which is way down the queue.

2nd Member of Audience: And yet two years ago I attended a performance of the *Coronation Ode*, complete with brass band, in the basilica in Lourdes, and it brought the house down.

BA: It was a miracle.

Evening concert

On the Saturday evening of the symposium, a concert of works by Elgar and Vaughan Williams was given by string soloists from the City of London Sinfonia. They were joined for Vaughan Williams's song cycle *On Wenlock Edge* by tenor James Gilchrist and pianist Piers Lane, the latter returning to the platform for the Elgar Piano Quintet. The full concert programme is given below, while notes on the works and artists are reproduced on pages 153–157.

Elgar		**String Quartet in E Minor, Op. 83**
	I	Allegro moderato
	II	Piacevole (poco andante)
	III	Allegro molto
Vaughan Williams		***On Wenlock Edge***
	1	On Wenlock Edge
	2	From afar, from eve and morning
	3	Is my team ploughing?
	4	Oh, when I was in love with you
	5	Bredon Hill
	6	Clun

Interval (10 minutes)

Vaughan Williams		***Phantasy Quintet***
Elgar		**Piano Quintet in A minor, Op. 84**
	I	Moderato – Allegro
	II	Adagio
	III	Andante – Allegro

James Gilchrist – tenor   **Piers Lane** – piano
Soloists from the **City of London Sinfonia**:
Nicholas Ward, **Jane Carwardine** – violins
Stephen Tees, **Matthew Souter** – violas; **Jo Cole** – cello

The Works

Elgar – String Quartet in E minor, op83

In his early years Elgar was an ardent player of chamber music. But though he started at least one violin sonata and many string quartets, it was only wind works such as the Harmony Music that came to completion before the turn of the century. In the Autumn of 1907 it seemed as if Elgar would at last compose a string quartet when, under the inspiration of a Malvern concert by the Brodsky Quartet, he began what promised to be a large-scale work. At the beginning of December there was a dramatic change of plan, and Elgar's main creative energy was now concentrated on producing the long-delayed symphony; the embryo quartet contributed essential ideas to the middle movements, while another section went into *The Music Makers*. It was not until 1918, the last year of the First World War, that he tried again.

This time the inspiration was Brinkwells and its wooded surroundings. It seems the String Quartet was started first, but what turned out to be a veritable chamber music year finally got into its stride with the arrival of a piano at Brinkwells on 19 August. Elgar then began the Violin Sonata, which he completed within a month. With the sonata just about finished, Elgar started the Piano Quintet on 15 September. The String Quartet was resumed by 8 October, when the second-movement piacevole was taking shape. Its impetuous finale, likened by Lady Elgar to the 'Galloping of Squadrons', was done by Christmas.

Unlike the projected quartet of 1907, the completed String Quartet has three movements. It enshrines all Elgar's skill as not only a considerable violinist himself but also the composer of such idiomatic string pieces as the Op.20 *Serenade* (also in E minor) and the *Introduction and Allegro*. The cut and thrust of the writing in the outer movements, dependent as they are on a succession of pregnant thematic tags rather than any highly developed tune, makes for maximum exhilaration. It is remarkable how extensively Elgar confines his music to three parts: assenting to George Herbert's "all music is but three parts vied", he treats the next line's "And multiplied" with notable discretion. Lady Elgar's favourite movement was the central piacevole, which she likened to "captured sunshine", and that was eventually played at her funeral. Here Brinkwells exerts its strongest influence, in the quiet fragrance of the main tune and in the long-drawn, dreamlike passages where movement seems almost to cease. Throughout the work inspiration is consistently high.

Robert Anderson

Vaughan Williams – *On Wenlock Edge*

This cycle of six songs for tenor, piano and string quartet, is based on A E Houseman's *A Shropshire Lad*. Its composition followed a period of study that Vaughan Williams undertook in Paris with Maurice Ravel in 1908. Although Vaughan Williams admitted that he could not have written Ravel's music even if he had wanted to, this 3-month tuition was successful, with Vaughan Williams learning, as he put it, "how to orchestrate in points of colour rather than in lines".

If *On Wenlock Edge* benefits from an impressionistic approach to texture which shows the influence of Ravel, the impact of Houseman's poetry is of even greater significance. The poetry is sometimes bitter, occasionally ironic, infused with moments of remarkable tenderness and nobility, with the use throughout of images of those "coloured counties" bordering the River Severn under the shadow of the Malvern Hills and Wenlock Edge. Over thirty composers have been inspired by these elements of Houseman's style to set his poetry to music, including Vaughan Williams's cycle which was first performed in November 1909.

The opening song 'On Wenlock Edge' begins agitato with urgent trills and tremolos. The "gale of life" blows through the score, before the movement ends in a tranquillo section. 'From far, from eve and morning' is a song of great tenderness, with a wonderful moment of expressiveness at "Now for a breath I tarry". The third song, 'Is my team ploughing?' is a dialogue between the dead man and his living friend. Contrasting textures allow the soloist to characterise the two parts differently. 'Oh, when I was in love with you' is a simple folkish setting, which underlies the irony of the poem. 'Bredon Hill', the most significant song of the cycle, follows this. The atmospheric touches suggest Ravel, with the bell-like effects reflecting the changing mood of the poem, from happiness, to harrowing intensity and then to acceptance and reconciliation. Finally, 'Clun' returns to Vaughan Williams's contemplative mood, ending the cycle in peace and tranquillity.

Stephen Connock

Vaughan Williams – *Phantasy Quintet*

We owe to W W Cobbett (1847–1937), an industrialist and amateur violinist, the credit for inspiring Vaughan Williams's *Phantasy Quintet*. In 1905, Cobbett initiated a prize for English chamber works. He insisted that the works be modelled on the Elizabethan 'Fancy' or 'Phantasy' and that they be in one movement or in four sections played continuously. Vaughan Williams wrote his version in 1912 following a personal request from Cobbett. Scored for two violins, two violas and cello, it was first performed in March 1914, and is dedicated to W W Cobbett.

As Vaughan Williams put it in his programme note for the first performance, "there is one principal theme (given out by the viola at the start) which runs through every movement". The opening prelude, in a slow 3/2 time, establishes a meditative mood, reminiscent of the *Fantasia on a Theme by Thomas Tallis* of 1910. The scherzo follows, providing lively ostinato rhythms, before the alla sarabanda movement. Here the 'cello is silent, the other instruments are muted, in what is a gentle, contemplative passage. The burlesca finale opens in playful mood before a moment of heightened emotion heralds the return of the theme of the prelude, closing the work in noble and ecstatic style.

Stephen Connock

Elgar – Piano Qunitet in E minor, op84

Having set aside the partially completed Piano Quintet in October 1918 to work on the String Quartet, Elgar resumed work on the Quintet in January 1919, finishing it later the same month. The first public performance was in London in May 1919.

The real importance of the Piano Quintet is in its splendour as music, in particular the *adagio* which inhabits the same withdrawn and desolate world as parts of the Cello Concerto on which Elgar was working at the same time. Yet it is impossible not to imagine some kind of extra-musical programme behind the work. A monastic element is suggested in the slow introductory bars, where the piano's quasi-plainsong theme (*Salve regina*) in bare octaves is heard against the strings' staccato murmurings. Tragedy seems implicit in the plaintive chromatic passage for strings, with the 'cello rising expressively in contrast to the other instruments' falling phrases. The *allegro* section begins vigorously and soon the second subject is heard, a hesitant tune with violins in thirds over the piano's almost guitar-like accompaniment (perhaps a Spanish touch). After this comes a broad E major melody, a tempestuous development and a sinister transformation of the second subject before the movement shudders to an end.

The *adagio* is one of Elgar's sublime movements. The viola begins the long, arching main theme, extending over forty-two bars until, with piano arpeggios, there occurs a theme derived from the plaintive chromatic phrase at the start of the first movement. A passionate climax follows, then tranquillity.

The chromatic idea opens the finale, but this wistful mood is brushed aside by the strings' enunciation of the confident first subject. An equally forceful syncopated theme enters on the piano. Haunted memories of the first movement return, misty and tearful, but the bold main theme and its syncopated subsidiary end the work joyously The Piano Quintet is dedicated to the critic Ernest Newman.

Michael Kennedy

Members of the City of London Sinfonia on stage at the British Library

The Artists

James Gilchrist began his working life as a doctor and, whilst studying and practising medicine, started working as a solo singer with many of Britain's leading choirs in Britain and abroad. In 1996 he turned to a full-time career in music and currently studies with Janice Chapman and Noelle Barker. He has sung with choral societies throughout Great Britain, with many of Britain's leading orchestras, including the ECO, CLS and Northern Sinfonia, and in opera. He appeared in Vaughan Williams's *Sir John in Love* at the Barbican and on BBC Radio 3. His recordings include Rachmaninov's *Vespers*, Schütz, Rameau Cantatas, the *St Mark Passion*, Grainger songs and Kuhnau Sacred Music.

12. Evening Concert

Future plans include Britten's *War Requiem* in King's College Chapel, and Monteverdi *Vespers* and *The Messiah* with the Sixteen. He makes his Salzburg début under Sir John Eliot Gardiner in *Israel in Egypt* and his début with Ivor Bolton and the IPO in Israel in Handel's *Solomon*.

Piers Lane was born in London and grew up in Brisbane. His international career has taken him to more than forty countries. As well as touring with British violinist Tasmin Little, he performs two-piano works with Canadian pianist Marc-André Hamelin with whom he has given recitals in London and Montreal. He continues his collaboration with The Medici Quartet in performances of the Elgar Quintet. His extensive discography includes albums of d'Albert, Saint-Saëns and Johann Strauss Virtuoso Transcriptions, the complete Études and Preludes of Scriabin, the Vaughan Williams and Delius piano concertos and, most recently, a much-admired recording of Grainger Transcriptions. His BMG Conifer recording of the Delius Violin Sonatas with Tasmin Little was awarded a Diapason d'Or and featured as Record of the Month in Repertoire magazine. In Spring 2003 Hyperion released his recording of Bach Transcriptions.

In 1994 he was made an Honorary Member of the Royal Academy of Music, where he has been a professor of piano since 1989. Now a well-known broadcaster for BBC Radio 3, he wrote and presented an acclaimed 54-part series entitled *The Piano* and is currently a regular presenter of *BBC Legends*.

The City of London Sinfonia (CLS) was founded in 1971 by its Music Director, Richard Hickox. CLS performs over 80 concerts a year at many of the UK's leading festivals and concert venues, as well as touring abroad and giving regular radio broadcasts. The CLS are resident orchestra in the towns of High Wycombe, Ipswich and King's Lynn. Highlights of 2002/03 included performances sponsored by CLS Principal Sponsor, MMC, in Birmingham, Glasgow, Manchester, Northampton and Reading, among other venues, of the Orchestra's special production of Shakespeare's *A Midsummer Night's Dream*, with the Royal Shakespeare Company acting the play, and CLS performing Mendelssohn's complete incidental music.

In London, CLS regularly performs at the Barbican. In 2002/03, Music Director, Richard Hickox conducted a series featuring Mozart's last three symphonies performed alongside work by composers with significant anniversaries in 2003: Berlioz (200th anniversary of birth), Lennox Berkeley (100th of birth) and Prokofiev (50th of death).

This evening's concert features the string principals from the CLS.

Contributor Biographies

Michael Kennedy was born in Manchester and educated at Berkhamsted. He entered journalism in 1941 and then served in the Royal Navy. He was Northern Editor of the *Daily Telegraph* from 1960 to 1986 and has been a music critic since 1948. He is now chief music critic of the *Sunday Telegraph*. In 2003 he was awarded an honorary doctorate of music by Manchester University and completed his *The Life of Elgar* in 2004. His Portrait of Elgar, from 1968, remains a seminal publication behind the renewal of interest in Elgar's life and music. Equally significant is his *The Works of Ralph Vaughan Williams*. He has also written biographies of Barbirolli, Boult, Britten, Mahler, Walton and Strauss and is author of the *Oxford Dictionary of Music*. He is Honorary Vice-President of the RVW Society, a Vice-President of the Elgar Society and Elgar Foundation and Patron of the Society's North-West branch. He was appointed CBE in 1997 and is a Companion of the Royal Northern College of Music.

Andrew Neill joined The Elgar Society in 1967, becoming its Secretary in 1978 and Chairman in 1992, a position he still holds. He became a trustee of The Elgar Birthplace in 1984. As Secretary, he arranged the 1984 Royal Festival Hall concert to commemorate the fiftieth anniversary of Elgar's death, which led to his involvement in a number of recording projects including that of *Scenes from the Saga of King Olaf* which EMI made in 1985. Since then he has been closely associated with the issue of a number of Elgar's recordings, including the Elgar Edition issued by EMI between 1992 and 1994. In 2001 he was instrumental in the establishment of *The Elgar Society Edition*, a charity formed to complete the publication of a scholarly edited edition of Elgar's music. He is also a trustee of the Royal Philharmonic Society, is married with two daughters and lives and works in London.

Claire-Louise Lucas studied with Pamela Bowden at The London College of Music. She has performed extensively throughout Britain, Europe and the USA, including an appearance as a soloist in the Salzburg Easter Festival with Maurizio Pollini and the Berlin Philharmonic Orchestra under Claudio Abbado. She also lectures on opera and song for Oxford University's Department for Continuing Education.

Jonathan Darnborough studied piano and composition at Trinity Hall, Cambridge, and the Royal Northern College of Music. He was a prizewinner in the 1992 Franco-Italian Music Competition in Paris and has performed in the USA, France, Holland, Italy and Indonesia. In July he will play Rachmaninov's Second Piano Concerto in Lausanne. He is the Associate Tutor in Music at Oxford University's Department for Continuing Education.

Claire-Louise and Jonathan have worked together since 1990 and have made a particular study of English repertoire. Their CD of songs by Elgar and Vaughan Williams will be released on the Claudio label in Spring 2003. They have toured twice in the USA, recently appearing in the Dame Myra Hess concert series at the Chicago Cultural Center, and return to the USA in September to lecture for the Smithsonian Institute.

Lewis Foreman has published many books on music and musicians, including the standard biography of Arnold Bax. He edited *Ralph Vaughan Williams in Perspective* and, for Elgar Editions, *Oh My Horses! Elgar and the Great War*.

He was associated for many years (1969–1985) with the Kensington Symphony Orchestra and its opera company Opera Viva, with which he programmed over 300 revivals for the London "fringe". Since taking early retirement from the Foreign & Commonwealth Office in London (where he was Chief Librarian) in October 1997, he has become a full time writer/researcher on music and is currently advising various independent record companies on new repertoire.

His CD booklet notes for Chandos, Hyperion, ASV, Classico, Lyrita and many other companies are well-known, and he has contributed programme notes for many performing organisations, most notably the London Symphony Orchestra and the Nash Ensemble. His obituary of the late Ted Perry, founder of the Hyperion Record Company, appeared in *The Independent* newspaper.

Byron Adams is currently Chair of the Department of Music at the University of California, Riverside. He received his doctoral degree from Cornell University, having studied musicology with William Austin and composition with Karel Husa. He has published widely on the subject of 20th-century English music, giving lectures and interviews on this topic over the BBC and at the 1995 National Meeting of the American Musicological Society. He has co-edited *Vaughan Williams Essays*, which was published by Ashgate Press in February 2003; has contributed four entries to the revised edition of the *New Grove Dictionary of Music and Musicians*, including those on Husa and Walton; and his articles and reviews have appeared in *19th Century Music, Music and Letters, MLA Notes, Current Musicology*, and *The Musical Quarterly*.

His music has been performed at the Leith Hill Festival, the 26th "Warsaw Autumn" International Festival of Contemporary Music in Poland, the Conservatoire Américain in Fontainebleau, France and in America at such institutions as the Eastman School of Music, Harvard University, Yale University, the West Virginia Symphony, the Los Angeles Mozart Orchestra and the Syracuse Symphony Orchestra. He was appointed Composer in Residence of the Colonial Symphony during the 1990–91 and 1991–92 seasons. Recorded performances of his music are available on the Orion Master Recordings, Skylark, and Mark record labels.

Michael Pope was born in London and educated at Wellington College and the Guildhall School of Music and Drama, where his studies included conducting with Joseph Lewis and musical history under Peter Latham and Alec Robertson. In 1954 he joined the BBC, and subsequently produced many revivals on the Third Network, including Elgar's *Caractacus* and *King Olaf* and a number of Stanford's later compositions. He has written, lectured and broadcast on various aspects of the British musical heritage, and was Chairman of the Elgar Society from 1978 to 1988. When musical director of the London Motet and Madrigal Club he conducted Vaughan Williams's Mass in G minor at Thaxted Church in 1968. As guest conductor of the RTE Singers in 1974, he conducted a Stanford 50th anniversary programme of late *a cappella* works, including the settings of Milton's ode 'On Time' and of related poems by Mary Coleridge. He is a Vice-President of The Elgar Society.

Hugh Cobbe was Head of Music at the British Library from 1985 until January 2002 and then held the post of Head of British Collections until his retirement from the British Library in November 2002. He was awarded the OBE in the New Year Honours. He is currently President of the Royal Musical Association (and organised its conference on Vaughan Williams in 1999). He is also Chairman of the Gerald Coke Handel Foundation, Chairman of the Britten-Pears Library, and a Trustee of both the RVW Trust and the Elgar Society Edition. He is preparing an edition of the letters of Ralph Vaughan Williams for publication by OUP which is expected to be ready for the press by the end of this year.

Contributor Biographies

Charles McGuire is currently Assistant Professor of Musicology at the Oberlin College Conservatory of Music. An expert on British music of the nineteenth and twentieth centuries, his areas of interest include the music of Edward Elgar, Ralph Vaughan Williams, the British music festival, sight-singing techniques, and the intersection of choral singing and moral reform movements. His publications include the monograph *Elgar's Oratorios: The Creation of an Epic Narrative* (Ashgate, 2002) as well as essays in *Vaughan Williams Essays* (Ashgate, 2003), *Choruses and Choral Communities* (University of Nebraska Press, forthcoming), *The Elgar Society Journal*, the second edition of the *New Grove Dictionary of Music and Musicians*, and reviews in *Notes*: Quarterly Journal of the Music Library Association and *Albion*. He is currently writing a monograph with Geoffrey Hodgkins about the librettos of Elgar's *The Apostles* and *The Kingdom*, as well as a study of tonic sol-fa.

Stephen Connock is Chairman of the Ralph Vaughan Williams Society which he founded with Robin Barber and John Bishop back in 1994. In the real world he works as a director of easyJet and has written four books on business management. He received an MBE for his work in the customer service field in 1999. He is currently writing *RVW Remembered* as well as *Let Beauty Awake*, a survey of Vaughan Williams's response to poetry. In March 2004 a new edition of Vaughan Williams's photographs was published, called *There was a time...*which he jointly edited with Ursula Vaughan Williams and Robin Wells.

As Chairman of the Linda McCartney Foundation, he has raised over £2 million and helps sponsor recordings of British music, including *Sir John in Love* and Britten's *Albert Herring*.

Robert Anderson was born in India and educated at Harrow and Cambridge. He divides his time between Elgar and Egyptology. At one time Director of Music at Gordonstoun School, he became an associate editor of *The Musical Times*, a position which in turn led in 1984 to his appointment as co-ordinating editor of the Elgar Complete Edition. He is the author of three books and numerous articles on Elgar. His *Elgar in Manuscript* was published in 1990 by the British Library and he is the author of the Dent Master Musicians biography of Elgar. Most recently, his *Elgar and Chivalry* was published by Elgar Editions in November 2002.

Robert is a Vice-President of the Elgar Society. He has conducted the St Bartholomew's Hospital Choral Society in a number of Elgar performances at the Royal Albert Hall, London and has conducted major Elgar choral works in Germany.

Notes and References

Introduction

1. See Chapter 12 for details of the concert, works performed and artists.
2. See Chapter 9 for an exploration by Stephen Connock of Ralph Vaughan Williams's opera *The Poisoned Kiss*.
3. During which the Bach transcription was played.

2 Neill: "It looks all wrong, but it sounds all right"

1. Ursula Vaughan Williams & Imogen Holst (eds): *Heirs and Rebels. Letters written to each other and occasional writings on music by Ralph Vaughan Williams and Gustav Holst* [London: Oxford University Press, 1959] p 99.
2. Jeremy Dibble: *C. Hubert Parry* [Clarendon Press, 1992] p 258.
3. J Dibble, *op cit*, p 258.
4. U Vaughan Williams: *Paradise Remembered* [Albion Music Ltd, 2002] p185.
5. From BBC radio's *'The Fifteenth Variation' A Portrait of Edward Elgar*, a centenary tribute devised and presented by Alec Robertson and broadcast 12 May 1957.
6. Sir Neville Cardus: review of a Promenade Concert performance of the A flat Symphony by the BBC Symphony Orchestra conducted by Sir Adrian Boult, published in *The Guardian* [28 July 1970].
7. Sir Adrian Boult: *Tribute to Vaughan Williams* [BBC broadcast, 1958].
8. Roy Henderson: 'RVW Remembered' in *The Journal of the RVW Society* 7 [October 1996]. Roy Henderson, baritone and teacher (1899–2000).
9. *A Social History of England* [BCA, new edn, 1994].
10. U Vaughan Williams: *RVW: A biography of Ralph Vaughan Williams* [Oxford, 1964]. See, for example, p 45.
11. Jerrold Northrop Moore: *Vaughan Williams: A life in photographs* [Oxford: Oxford University Press, 1992] p 13.
12. Robin Wells: 'Vaughan Williams and Charterhouse' in *The Journal of the RVW Society* 5 [February 1996].
13. From *Elgar Country* [BBC Home Service, 1965].
14. J N Moore: *Edward Elgar: Letters of a Lifetime* [London: Oxford University Press, 1990] p 359.
15. R Vaughan Williams: 'Musical Autobiography', reprinted in *National Music and Other Essays* [Oxford: Oxford University Press, 1963].

16 Lecture given at London University, 2 February 2003.
17 Michael Kennedy: *Adrian Boult* [Hamish Hamilton, 1987] p 102.
18 N Cardus, *op cit.*
19 J Dibble, *op cit.*

4 Foreman: Battle Songs & Elegies

1 This chapter incorporates material formerly published in Foreman (ed): *Oh, My Horses! Elgar And the Great War* [Rickmansworth: Elgar Editions, 2001] used with acknowledgements.
2 Carmen Sylva & Alma Strettell (trans): *The Bard of the Dimbovitza: Roumanian folk-songs* [Vol 1] collected from the Peasants by Hélène Vacaresco [James R Osgood, McIlvaine & Co, 1892] p 38, where it is included in a section headed 'Luteplayer's Songs'. On the Hyperion recording, CDA 67065, it is sung by Christopher Maltman.
3 The present writer's obituary of Piggott (1915-1990) appeared in *The Independent* [25 May 1990].
4 From the manuscript vocal score, with acknowledgements to George Mantle Child and the Piggott Estate.
5 Vocal Score [Boosey, 1921].
6 Interview, *Woman's Hour* [BBC Radio 4, 22 September 1988].
7 First played by Granville Bantock in a student concert at Birmingham in June 1921, by Howard Carr at Harrogate in June 1922 and by Dan Godfrey at Bournemouth in December 1922, it then remained unheard until revived by Robert Tucker and the Windsor Sinfonia at a Broadheath Singer's concert at Eton in September 1988.
8 'An Imperial Composer', an unidentified cutting, probably from *The Daily Telegraph*, in the Elgar cuttings books at the Elgar Birthplace Museum, Broadheath, Worcs.
9 Issued on Columbia 2467, it appears as track 10 on the historical CD published with Foreman, *op cit.*
10 Sung by the baritone Stanley Kirkby under the baton of the composer, on Edison Bell Winner 2713 1367. A modern reissue on LP is on Rare Recorded Editions RRE 190.
11 Thanks to Laura Ponsonby for providing a copy of the Boosey edition of Parry's music.
12 British Library: The Novello Business Archive [Add Mss 69516-69702].
13 Published by Gould & Co., and also arranged for orchestra and for violin and piano.
14 Published by Lawrence Wright Music Co.
15 Robert Bridges: *The Chivalry of the Sea: Naval Ode*, set to music for five-part chorus and orchestra by C Hubert H Parry [vocal score, Novello, 1916].

16 M U Arkwright: *Requiem Mass* for soprano & baritone solo, eight-part chorus and orchestra [Cary & Co, 1914].
17 Track 1 on the historical CD published with Foreman, *op cit*.
18 John Norris: 'The Spirit of Elgar: crucible of remembrance' in Foreman, *op cit*.
19 2 July 1921. Printed in Gregory Roscow (ed): *Bliss on Music* [Oxford University Press, 1991] p 18.
20 The Nash Ensemble's recording is on Hyperion CDA 67188/9. We should not forget that Bliss also used drums alone to accompany the 'Spring Offensive' recitation in his *Morning Heroes*. Basil Maine's recording as creator of the role was issued by Decca on a 10" 78, F 5219, reissued as track 17 on the historical CD published with Foreman, *op cit*.
21 Reid Orchestral Concerts programme [Edinburgh, 19 February 1921] pp 14–15.
22 Sir Thomas Armstrong: 'George Butterworth Rhapsody: A Shropshire Lad' – introduction to the miniature score of *A Shropshire Lad* [Eulenburg, 1981].
23 The fifth song in *Ludlow and Teme* for tenor and piano quintet, the cycle completed in December 1920.
24 Martin Brabbins's recording for Hyperion of a range of Coles's music was warmly received by the press and is on CDA 67293.
25 Gloucestershire Symphony Orchestra conducted by Mark Finch on Sunday 2 March 2003 at Cheltenham Town Hall.
26 LSO conducted by Richard Hickox [Chandos CHAN 9902].
27 Re-orchestrated in true Stanford style by Jeremy Dibble, it was revived by the Broadheath Singers conducted by Garry Humphreys at Slough in September 2002. It revealed an engaging Stanford narrative cantata that could have been written any time in the previous forty years.
28 Malcolm MacDonald: *John Foulds and his Music an introduction*. [White Plains, New York: Pro/Am Music Resources Inc, 1989] p 33.
29 BBC broadcast talk [6 May 1949]. BBC disc X 13389 now issued on CD on Symposium 1336.

5 Adams: What Have We Learnt from Elgar?

1 R Vaughan Williams: 'What Have We Learnt from Elgar?' reprinted in *National Music, op cit* [2nd edn, 1987] p 251.
2 *Ibid*.
3 *Ibid*. Vaughan Williams had made a similar rhetorical move in regards to Elgar during the course of the Mary Flexner Lectures that he delivered at Bryn Mawr in 1934, but, perhaps because Elgar was still alive at the time, did so somewhat more tentatively. See R Vaughan Williams: *National Music, op cit*, pp 41–2.
4 Murray's actual words are: "Every Man who possesses real vitality can be seen as the resultant of two forces. He is first the child of a particular age, society,

Notes and References

convention; of what we may call in one word a tradition. He is, secondly, in one degree or another, a rebel against that tradition. And the best traditions make the best rebels." U Vaughan Williams & I Holst (eds): *Heirs and Rebels*, *op cit*, frontispiece.

5 Raymond Knapp: 'Brahms and the Anxiety of Allusion' in *The Journal of Musicological Research* 18 [1998] p 5.
6 Richard Taruskin: 'Revising Revision' in *Journal of the American Musicological Society* 46 [1993] p 114.
7 Knapp, *op cit*, p 5.
8 Vaughan Williams's friend and Cambridge contemporary, the historian George Trevelyan, may have further influenced him in this regard. Trevelyan expropriated the broad outlines of evolutionary theory to articulate a 'great man' theory of history, similar to that of the 'great composer' theories of both Parry and Vaughan Williams. Trevelyan's confident belief was that civilization – and specifically that of the English-speaking peoples – is constantly evolving towards the creation of great men who in turn improve and enlighten society, a belief that pervades his influential volume *The History of England*.
9 R Vaughan Williams: Mass in G minor [1922], for example, often cited as being influenced by Tudor polyphony, is as much an inspired adaptation of Debussy's harmonic innovations as it is a tribute to 16th-century English church music.
10 M Kennedy: *Portrait of Elgar* [Oxford: Oxford University Press, 1968] p 74.
11 Roland John Wiley: 'The Tribulations of Nationalist Composers: A Speculation Concerning Borrowed Music in Khovanshchina,' in Malcolm Hamrick Brown (ed): *Musorgsky: In Memoriam 1881–1981* [Ann Arbor: UMI Research Press, 1982] p 168.
12 J N Moore: *Edward Elgar: A Creative Life* [Oxford: Oxford University Press, 1984] p 342.
13 J N Moore, *op cit*, p 344.
14 Dibble: *Charles Villiers Stanford: Man and Musician* [Oxford: Oxford University Press, 2002] p 389, n. 9.
15 M Kennedy: *The Works of Ralph Vaughan Williams* [London & New York: Oxford University Press, 1964] p 137.
16 J N Moore: *op cit*, pp 343, 349. Note, however, that, in an utterly disingenuous anticipation of Vaughan Williams's more thoroughgoing use of French music to distance himself from German models, Elgar claimed to Ernest Newman that one of the main devices in Cockaigne – the "use of diminution to mark youth" – was suggested to him by Delibes's ballet *Sylvia* and not from the Apprentice's theme in Wagner's *Meistersinger* Overture. See J N Moore, *op cit*, p 345.
17 R Vaughan Williams: *National Music*, *op cit*, p 252.
18 Philip Brett: 'Musicology and Sexuality: the Example of Edward J. Dent' in Sophie Fuller & Lloyd Whitsell (ed). *Queer Episodes in Music and Modern Identity* [Urbana: University of Illinois Press, 2002] p 182.
19 R Vaughan Williams, *National Music*, *op cit*, p 122.

6 Pope: Stanford, Elgar and Vaughan Williams

1. J Dibble: *Stanford, op cit*, p 168.
2. Robert Anderson: *Elgar in Manuscript* [London: The British Library, 1990] p 51.
3. J Dibble: *Stanford, op cit*, pp 285–6.
4. Elgar Birthplace Museum: EBML 7393.
5. Percy M Young: *Elgar O.M. : A Study of a Musician* [London: Collins, 1955] p 75.
6. Sir Alexander Campbell Mackenzie: *A Musician's Narrative* [London: Cassell, 1927] p 205.
7. Paul Rodmell: *Charles Villiers Stanford* [Aldershot: Ashgate, 2002] p 245.
8. J Dibble: *Stanford, op cit*, p 313.
9. P Rodmell, *op cit*, pp 239–40.
10. Thomas F. Dunhill: *Sir Edward Elgar* [London: Blackie, 1938] p 11.
11. Charles Villiers Stanford: *Musical Composition: A Short Treatise for Students* [London: Macmillan, 1911] p 159.
12. Edward Elgar ed Percy M Young: *A Future for English Music and other Lectures* [London: Dennis Dobson, 1968] p 207.
13. Frederick Niecks: *Programme Music in the last Four Centuries: A Contribution to the History of Musical Expression* [London: Novello, 1907] pp 380–1.
14. John F Porte: *Sir Charles V Stanford* [London: Kegan Paul, 1921] p 3.
15. R Vaughan Williams: 'Musical Autobiography' in Hubert Foss: *Ralph Vaughan Williams: A Study* [London: Harrap, 1950] p 28.
16. M Kennedy: *Works, op cit*, pp 51, 408.
17. M Kennedy, *op cit*, p 45.
18. M Kennedy, *op cit*, p 129.
19. August J Jaeger: *The Dream of Gerontius: Analytical and Descriptive Notes* [London: Novello, 1901] pp 8, 11.
20. Ernest Walker: *A History of Music in England* [Oxford: Clarendon Press, 1907; 2nd edn, 1924] p 371.
21. J Dibble, *op cit*, pp 158–9.
22. *The Modern Madrigal Tradition*, 6: BBC Chorus, conducted by Alan G. Melville [BBC Radio 3, recorded 29 May 1970, broadcast 7 January 1971).
23. T F Dunhill: 'Choral and Instrumental Music' in Harry Plunket Greene: *Charles Villiers Stanford* [London: Edward Arnold, 1935] p 227.
24. Edward J Dent: *Opera* [Harmondsworth: Penguin Books, 1940; rev edn 1949] p 182.
25. J A Fuller-Maitland: *The Music of Parry and Stanford* [Cambridge: Heffer, 1934] p 93.
26. C V Stanford: 'The Case for National Opera' in *Studies and Memories* [London: Constable, 1908] pp 3–23.
27. See Hugh Ottaway: 'Ralph Vaughan Williams' in The New Grove

Twentieth-Century English Masters [London: Macmillan, 1986] p 127.
28 C V Stanford: *Studies and Memories, op cit*, p 6.
29 E Elgar: Speech at the opening of the Gramophone Company's new premises at 363 Oxford Street, 20 July 1921, reprinted in J N Moore: *Elgar on Record: the Composer and the Gramophone* [London: EMI Records, 1974] p 41.
30 R Vaughan Williams: 'The Letter and the Spirit' in *Music and Letters* I [1920] ii, p 88.

7 Cobbe: "My Dear Elgar"

1 J N Moore: *Letters of a lifetime, op cit*, p vii
2 Letter of 8 February 1944 to G R Barnes of the BBC – BBC Written Archives Centre.
3 See R Vaughan Williams: *National music, op cit*, p 41.
4 Humphrey Carpenter: *Benjamin Britten: a biography* [London, 1992] p 110.
5 Those who were at the Vaughan Williams conference at the British Library in 1999 will recall the late Philip Brett's stimulating paper which took this image as its starting point.
6 R Vaughan Williams: *National music, op cit*, p 188
7 R Vaughan Williams, *op cit*, p 41
8 Published by U Vaughan Williams & I Holst (eds): *Heirs and Rebels, op cit*, p 11. The letters between Holst and Vaughan Williams are now in the British Library. (Letters from Holst: Add MS 57953; letters from Vaughan Williams. Mus MS 158).
9 The letter, with others to Miss Charrington and her mother, is now in the British Library, Add MS 70935.
10 Original in the Vaughan Williams Memorial Library, Cecil Sharp House.
11 See Georgina Boyes: *The imagined village* [Manchester, 1993] p 42.
12 See M Kennedy: *Works, op cit* [2nd edn, London, 1980] p 148, fn 1.
13 A transcript of Vaughan Williams's talk 'The Stanford Centenary' is in the BBC Written Archives Centre. On the apocryphal connection between Parry and the first performance of the 'Enigma' Variations, see fn 39. below.
14 J N Moore: *Letters of a lifetime, op cit*, p 383
15 British Library, MS Mus 158.
16 VW's letters to Diana Awdrey, later Mrs Oldridge, remain in private hands. Before her death she very kindly allowed them to be photocopied for the Vaughan Williams Letters project.
17 Letter transcribed from a photocopy in the possession of U Vaughan Williams.
18 Elgar Birthplace Museum, EBM1.0112.
19 J N Moore: *Letters of a lifetime, op cit*, p 440.
20 I am indebted to Michael Kennedy and Anthony Boden for assistance on this.
21 See J N Moore: *A Creative Life, op cit*, p 796.

22 See M Kennedy: *Works, op cit*, p 295.
23 This was part of a short contribution to an Elgar centenary programme on the BBC in June 1957. A transcript is in the possession of U Vaughan Williams.
24 In the possession of Michael Kennedy and printed by him in *Works*, p 240.
25 Elgar Birthplace Museum, EBML9413.
26 *LLT* p 480.
27 Photocopy in the possession of U Vaughan Williams.
28 Photocopy in the possession of U Vaughan Williams.
29 Photocopy in the author's possession.
30 U Vaughan Williams: *RVW: A biography, op cit*, p 198. A photocopy of the original is in U Vaughan Williams's possession.
31 British Library, Add MS 69816.
32 Original in the possession of U Vaughan Williams.
33 Printed in U Vaughan Williams: *RVW: A biography, op cit*, pp 240–243.
34 Original in the possession of the John Ireland Trust.
35 BBC Written Archives Centre.
36 Written 27 February 1948. The later versions of the story are printed in R Vaughan Williams: *National Music, op cit*, p 182 and U Vaughan Williams & I Holst (eds): *Heirs and Rebels, op cit* (with the erroneous date of 1957) p 96.
37 University of St Andrews Library, MS Deposit 63/5/271.
38 Michael Kennedy has generously presented his letters from Vaughan Williams to the British Library where they are MS Mus 159.
39 See M Kennedy: *Portrait of Elgar, op cit* [3rd edn, 1987] pp 86–87.
40 Letter of 3 March 1957.
41 Letter of 9 May 1957.
42 In the possession of U Vaughan Williams. See above, fn 23.
43 Note dated 15 May 1957.
44 See M Kennedy: *Works, op cit*, p 195.

8 McGuire: From *The Apostles* to *Sancta Civitas*

1 Annie W Patterson: *The Story of the Oratorio* [London: The Walter Scott Publishing Co; New York: Charles Scribner's Sons, 1902] p 154.
2 Part of the great spectacle was also due to the fact that the solo singers were treated as 'superstars' of the time. See Gillian B Anderson: 'A Warming Flame' in *Music for Silent Films, 1894–1929: A Guide* [Washington, DC: The Library of Congress, 1988] p xiv.
3 A J Jaeger: *The Dream of Gerontius, op cit* ; *The Apostles by Edward Elgar: Book of Words with Analytical and Descriptive Notes* [London: Novello, 1903]; *The Kingdom: Analytical and Descriptive Notes* [London: Novello, 1906].
4 See, for instance, J N Moore: *A Creative Life, op cit*, especially pp 372–424 & 482–505; and Robert Anderson: *Elgar* [New York: Schirmer, 1993] pp 55–77.

5   Apparently he also wrote it "sitting on his bum". We know the position in which Vaughan Williams composed the work because it was a quip, responding to Hubert Foss who stated that Walford Davies wrote his *Solemn Melody* "on his knees". James Day: *Vaughan Williams* [third edition; from the series *Master Musicians* edited by Stanley Sadie; Oxford: Oxford University Press, 1998] p 55.
6   M Kennedy: *Works, op cit*, p 194.
7   Frank Howes: 'The Heather Festival at Oxford' in *The Musical Times* [1 June 1926] pp 537–541. Howes' review article is interesting for a number of reasons, least of all its tone and positioning of folk music. Besides the portrait of Hugh Allen that prefaces the article, the only illustrations contained within it are two pictures of folk dancing: 'Folk Dancing in New College Gardens' and 'The Sword Dance' – each of which display a number of individuals in Morris-style outfits. While these illustrations are provide the greatest visual interest of the article, Howes discusses the events portrayed within them only in a throw-away line at the end: "A disply of folk-dancing in New College Gardens on Sunday afternoon completed the Festival so far as Oxford was concerned." For the bulk of the article, after briefly describing the importance of William Heather to Oxford University in general and its music in particular, Howes discusses the concerts and academic events of the Festival in a strictly narrative style, laced infrequently with critical comments on the compositions and their performances. Besides concerts by the Bach Choir and concerts devoted to academic composers associated with Cambridge and Oxford, the festival included a concert Howes described as "Neo-academicism . . . gone to school in France" balanced with the addition of a Franz Joseph Haydn symphony.
8   The General Strike at the time of the Festival meant that the national press did not review concerts. At the time of writing, I have not been able to establish all of the compositions heard at this Festival.
9   Robert Stradling & Merion Hughes: *The English Musical Renaissance, 1840–1940: Constructing a National Music* [Manchester & New York: Manchester University Press, 2nd edn, 2001] p 150–151. Elements of the following discussion were taken from Alain Frogley's extremely useful discussion of the work found in his review article, 'Rewriting the Renaissance: History, Imperialism, and British Music Since 1840' in *Music & Letters* 84 no.2 [May 2003] pp 241–257.
10 Of course, Elgar's own compositional studies of the first few decades of the 20th century also included a great deal of Bach. With Ivor Atkins he completed an edition of the *St. Matthew Passion* and also orchestrated a number of Bach keyboard pieces – initially as part of a contest with Richard Strauss. See Ivor Keys: 'The *Apostles*: Elgar and Bach as Preachers' in Raymond Monk (ed) *Edward Elgar: Music and Literature* [Aldershot: Scolar Press, 1993] pp 35 et seq.
11 The arguments consist of a letter, quoted further in H C Banister: *Life of George Alexander MacFarren*, wherein the composer staunchly denies any connection of his oratorio to Wagner's *Lohengrin*, stating: "I don't know why Wagner should have the monopoly of the harmonies for the violin . . . But as

to my borrowing from him, that was impossible: my first possibility of hearing *Lohengrin* was when it was done in London in such a year (I forget the year), and by that time *St. John* was completed, rejected, and put away in brown paper on the shelf, sometime before its first performance." A W Patterson, *op cit*, p 158.

12 These leitmotivic guides are still available for purchase at the Elgar Birthplace Museum and have been recommended repeatedly as a good way to approach the compositions as either a listener or a singer. Lewis W. Headly's article 'The Dream of Gerontius: Some Memories of an Amateur Tenor' (in *The Elgar Society Journal*, vol 9 no.6 [November 1996] pp 303–304) recommends that the singer read Novello's analytical notes, and write in the names of the themes as they appear in the vocal score. Such a reading of the leitmotivs is problematic for numerous reasons, including Jaeger's own propensity to see them as the only driving narrative force within these compositions.

13 "The music explains – by means of leitmotivs & general treatment – much of the 'interdependence' of the words." Letter of Elgar to Canon Charles Vincent Gorton, cited in M Kennedy, *Portrait of Elgar* , *op cit*, p 192. It should be noted that Gorton was a musical amateur, and elsewhere Elgar was often ambivalent regarding leitmotivs and naming them. When Elgar was asked about or commented on leitmotivic structure by a professional musician or critic, he often disavowed overt Wagnerism. See Christopher Grogan: '"My Dear Analyst": Some Observations on Elgar's Correspondence with A J Jaeger Regarding the Apostles Project' in *Music and Letters* 72 no.1 [February 1991] pp 48–60. In a letter to Herbert Thompson, longtime critic at the *Yorkshire Post*, Elgar accepts the leitmotivs Jaeger identifies but rejects their names [Leeds University Library Special Collections, MS 361].

14 See Charles McGuire: *Elgar's Oratorios: The Creation of an Epic Narrative* [Aldershot: Ashgate Press, 2002] pp 142–146, and Anderson, *Elgar, op cit*, pp 212 *et seq*.

15 R Anderson: *Elgar, op cit*, p 214.

16 Michael Foster: *Elgar's Gigantic Worx: The Story of the Apostles Trilogy* [London: Thames Publishing, 1995] p 11.

17 For a refreshing study of the oratorios predicated on non-Wagnerian compositional influences, see Christopher Grogan: 'Aspects of Elgar's Creative Process in *The Apostles* [op 49], with Particular Reference to Scene II – "By The Wayside"' [PhD Thesis, London University, 1989].

18 Alan Edgar Frederick Dickinson: *An Introduction to the Music of R. Vaughan Williams* [London & Oxford: Oxford University Press, 1928] p 73.

19 H Foss: *Ralph Vaughan Williams, op cit* [New York: Oxford University Press, 1950] p 156.

20 Byron Adams: '"Doth Burn ere It Transform": Decadence, Roman Catholicism, and Elgar's *The Dream of Gerontius*' [conference paper, International Elgar Conference, Surrey, April 2002]. See also Ellis Hanson's *Decadence and Catholicism* [Cambridge, Mass: Harvard University Press, 1997].

Notes and References

21 Simona Pakenham: *Ralph Vaughan Williams: A Discovery of His Music* [London: Macmillan & Co. Limited, 1957] p 76 *et seq.*
22 F Howes: *The Music of Ralph Vaughan Williams* [London & Oxford: Oxford University Press, 1954] p 150.
23 M Kennedy: *Works, op cit,* p 195.
24 The immediate critical response to *Sancta Civitas* differs greatly from the later secondary literature. Howes' review of the première performance discusses its boldness, its use of tone clusters, and the sense of stasis it imparts, but give none of the labels typically used later to distance the composition from Elgar [Howes, 'The Heather Festival at Oxford', *op cit,* p 541]. A *Musical Times* review of the second performance in London privileges Vaughan Williams's "hard sayings" as to be easily understood, contrasting them with "the expletives of Stravinsky or the slang of young Parisians," but presents no contrast to Wagner or Elgar ['The Bach Choir Jubilee Festival', *The Musical Times* [1 July 1926] p 647]. The review of this performance in *The Times* discusses as a thoroughly 20th-century composition (focusing on "the scales and chords and parallel fifths" as "clichés of 20th century music" (H.C. Colles, *The Times* [10 June 1926]); a later article contrasts Handel and Vaughan Williams in their treatment of the oratorio ("Handel is elaborate where Vaughan Williams is simple"), and stating that Vaughan Williams is much closer to Handel's "operatic scenes" than to the "epic outbursts of Israel . . . which justifies the writing of oratorio", positing further that Vaughan Williams might be afraid of oratorio [H C Colles, *The Times,* 12 June 1926]. The review makes no comparison to Elgar or Wagner – the construction of the work as anti-Wagnerian comes from a later date.
25 Francesco Berger: 'More Wagner' in *The Chesterian* [February 1917]. This segment includes three pseudo-Wagnerian vignettes, all of a humorous and exaggerated nature. The first (and least offensive) capitalizes on Wagner's legendary egocentrism (the spellings are those from the article): "When I was born into this world, what a miserably poor, dark, uninformed world I found it! Did I say 'born?' (*gebornen*). If I did, I was in error. I should have said 'created' (*geschaffen*). For it was ordained *from the first,* that at a certain epoch, I, Richard Wagner, should appear, to enlighten the prevailing darkness, to rouse mankind from its supine worship of 'the false', to bless them with 'the true', to show them the higher, the better way, which if they believed in ME, was theirs forever after. I was reared [refer to medical treatises on baby's food; collect facts from records of early childhood of Shakespeare, Goethe, Julius Caesar, Hannibal, Dante, Napoleon Buonaparte, Isaac Newton, Columbus, Beethoven, Homer, Michael Angelo, Confucious and Mahomed; form theory, write a book on the 'Diet of Infantile Geniuses'] I was saying: I was reared on what was *then* known as 'music', but the truth is, Music was reared by Me. I invented it; I created it. There had *not been any* until I composed it. Beethoven was the only musician who had *attempted* any, and he halted on the threshold, and died before he had accomplished much . . ."

26 R W S Mendl: 'Confessions of an Anti-Wagnerian' in *The Chesterian*, vol.40 [June 1924] p 254–255. After these criticisms, the remainder of the article becomes less harsh in tone, noting with wonder Wagner's "technical abilities" for instrumental writing. Even this limited salvo, however, could not be left long unanswered. A regular contributor to *The Chesterian*, identified only as G.J.A., wrote a counter article in the same issue entitled 'Wagnerian Confessions' [*The Chesterian*, vol 40 [June 1924] pp 260–261.

27 Anthony Boden: *Three Choirs: A History of the Festival* [Phoenix Mill: Alan Sutton, 1992] p 168. The above quotations are a conflation of two letters from Lacey; Boden does not provide the canon's first name, nor does he provide the date for the first letter. The second letter was from the 18 March 1926 edition of *The Worcester Daily Times*. Elgar, in a reply printed in the same paper, called on Lacey to resign all of his paid "spiritual offices", defending Wagner's purported sensuality with the dubious assertion that all men were ordinarily sensual. Boden states that it is from the 18 March 1926 issue. J N Moore, in *A Creative Life, op cit*, p 773, states that it is from the 17 March 1926 issue. (Moore also does not identify Lacey's first name.) Moore further states this as a potential reason why Elgar was discouraged in completing *The Last Judgment* at this time. Questions regarding the suitability of Wagner within an oratorio context did not stop at the end of the period in question. In 1950, the Three Choirs rejected performing the overture to *Die Meistersingers von Nurnberg* because "the performance of such secular music was putting the Cathedral to a wrong use". [Boden, *Three Choirs, op cit*, p 198].

28 Halsey Ricardo: 'The Recent Performance of *Der Ring Des Niebelungen*' in *Music and Letters* VII [October 1926] pp 368–373; Luigi Sturzo: 'After "The Ring" – A Call to Genius' in *Music and Letters* VIII [October 1927] pp 418–424; J W Klein: 'Wagner and His Operatic Contemporaries', in *Music and Letters* IX [January 1928] pp 59–66; Gerald E H Abraham: 'The Influence of Berlioz on Richard Wagner', in *Music and Letters* V [July 1924] pp 239–246; and B G Steigman: 'Wagner's "Symphonic Poems"' in *Music and Letters* VIII [January 1927] pp 55–60.

29 Agnes Savill: 'Parsifal in Covent Garden and Elsewhere' in *Music and Letters*, VIII [Oct. 1928] pp 415–416.

30 G.J.A.: 'Wagnerian Confessions' in *The Chesterian*, vol 40 [June 1924] p 260.

31 H Ricardo: 'The Recent Performance', *op cit*, p 369.

32 George Ainslie Hight: *Richard Wagner: A Critical Biography* [London: Arrowsmith, 1925].

33 G A Hight: 'The English Press and Richard Wagner' in *The Musical Times* [1 September 1925] pp 831–832. These corrections were drawn, in Hight's own anti-Semitic words, "from the scandalous Jewish press of Germany, where the English tradition has not, so far as I can learn, been accepted by the more cultured classes". Hight particularly accuses Ernest Newman of succumbing to such influences, as a long critical exchange between the two authors within the September to December 1925 issues of the *Musical Times* shows.

Notes and References

34 One example of this occurs in R Vaughan Williams: 'Gustav Holst: An Essay and a Note' in *National Music, op cit*, wherein Vaughan Williams criticizes the music at the moment Brünnhilde leaps onto the funeral pyre as "hardly good enough for a third-rate German beer garden". The larger point is that any composer, be he Gustav Holst or Richard Wagner, can occasionally fail to impress.

35 R Vaughan Williams: 'Who Wants the English Composer?' in H Foss: *Ralph Vaughan Williams, op cit*, p 199.

36 R Vaughan Williams: 'What Have We Learnt from Elgar?' in *Music and Letters* XVI no.1 [January 1935] pp 13–19. The article is reprinted in *National Music, op cit*, pp 248–255.

37 R Vaughan Williams: 'What Have We Learnt from Elgar?', *op cit*, p 13.

38 R Vaughan Williams, *op cit*, p 17.

39 *Ibid*.

40 Peter's victory, through, is furthered by the aid of an unnamed woman. See C McGuire: *Elgar's Oratorios, op cit*, p 275 *et seq*.

41 E Elgar: *The Kingdom*, movement III, lines 168–169.

42 C McGuire: *Elgar's Oratorios, op cit*, p 236 *et seq*.

43 A J Jaeger: *The Apostles, op cit*, pp 5–7

44 A J Jaeger: *The Kingdom, op cit*, p 4.

45 See C McGuire: 'Elgar, Judas, and the Theology of Betrayal' in *19th-Century Music* XXIII [2000].

46 There is one caveat to this sort of interpretation of Elgar's characters. Deep into the preparations for the première of *The Kingdom*, Elgar wrote to Canon Gorton, the interpreter of his librettos, about the danger of paying too close attention to the words, saying: "The music of course explains much: - you will remember the words are not intended to be read – only listened to." (The letter, from Elgar to Gorton was probably sent sometime after 1 August 1906. A transcription of this letter can be found in J N Moore: *Letters of a Lifetime, op cit*, p 178–179; the original is in the Elgar Birthplace [EBML8934]. Does this mean that we should take the texts Elgar set with a grain of salt, and listen only to the words he gives us, ignoring the larger biblical context behind them easily discovered within a close reading? This off-the-cuff remark may be yet another example of a typical Elgarian self-protection measure. We know from the work of Jerrold Northrup Moore and Robert Anderson the great care Elgar took to at least appear erudite regarding the Bible and its history, with a special focus on the characters of the Apostles themselves (see, for instance, R Anderson: *Elgar in Manuscript* [Portland: Amadeus Press, 1990] ch 3). Peter, while not receiving the same thorough treatment Elgar lavished on Judas and Mary Magdalene in *The Apostles*, is still forwarded by Elgar in a structure that with only a moment's memory could show his humanity. Besides, on more than one occasion, Elgar became forceful when he thought Julius Buth was mangling the meaning of his librettos in translation. He recommended substitute words and lobbied individuals to promote his vision of the passages' meaning (see J N

Moore's *Elgar and His Publishers: Letters of a Creative Life* vol 2 [Oxford: Oxford University Press, 1987] pp 662–663). For instance, in a letter of 13 October 1906 regarding the German translation of the Virgin Mary's fourth-movement soliloquy within *The Kingdom*, Elgar insisted that the word *"Patience must* be in even if we alter the phrasing of the music completely" [Letter of Elgar to Novello, 13 October 1906; transcribed in J N Moore: *Elgar and His Publishers, op cit*, vol 2, p 663]. To Elgar's different professional audiences, the worth of the text could differ. To the audience that might know something about the text (a cleric), Elgar deemphasized its importance; to the one that would not necessarily have that knowledge (his translator and publisher) that text became all-important. Given this ambiguity, as well as Elgar's own studies of the Bible and its context, the multi-layered interpretation seems the best approach to both *The Apostles* and *The Kingdom*.

47 In this regard the oratorio is in no way unique among British compositions, and compositions popular in Britain. It places the work within a category of 'lauda' oratorio, a tradition that includes such venerable examples as Handel's *Messiah*, and lesser-known works such as Charles Jessop's *The Galilean*, and Henry Bishop's *The Seventh Day*. Such oratorios lose any character associations for a strategy of praising God without a specific narrative, working more like a prayer service than a story. They might pull their words from one section of the Bible or a swath of passages, but the communal aspects of such texts always outweigh any idea of individual characterization. *Messiah* is an excellent example of a forerunner of this oratorio, for Vaughan Williams sets some of the same text in *Sancta Civitas* as Handel did in *Messiah*, a fact often commented upon in the secondary literature. This is curious, especially since most critics and scholars attempt to distance *Sancta Civitas* from the British oratorio tradition.

48 R Vaughan Williams: *Sancta Civitas* [London: J Curwen & Sons Ltd; New York: G Schirmer Inc, 1953] p i.

49 Dickinson: *Vaughan Williams* [London: Faber & Faber, 1963] p 239. Dickinson first stated this in *An Introduction to the Music of R. Vaughan Williams, op cit*, p 73. See also H Foss: *Ralph Vaughan Williams, op cit*, p 155. Vaughan Williams took the introductory colophon to the work from Plato's *Phaedo*, identified but presented in Greek – and its translation and meaning have overshadowed most of the rest of the discussion about the text within the critical history of the composition. Michael Kennedy called the use of the opening quotation "the nearest Vaughan Williams was ever to come to an explicit avowal of his agnosticism" (M Kennedy: *Works, op cit*, p 194). In this, he seems to follow closely Ursula Vaughan Williams's own discussion of the passage in her *RVW: A biography, op cit*, pp 163–164. Many others have also commented on the use of the text. See, for instance, Alain Frogley's liner notes for the recording on EMI Classics 0777 7 54788 2 2; Frank Howes' discussion in *The Music of Ralph Vaughan Williams, op cit*, p 150; and S Pakenham: *Ralph Vaughan Williams, op cit*, p 78. H Foss: *Ralph Vaughan Williams, op cit*,

Notes and References

p 154–155 offers a differing set of priorities, but does so by re-envisioning Revelation (via the Authorized Version) as "a new English poetry" beyond that of the original.

50 "The importance to Vaughan Williams of the words of this oratorio can be assessed from the care he took to include what he considered to be the most graphic translations, often preferring the Taverner's Bible version to the Authorized." M Kennedy: *Works, op cit*, p 506. It seems that Kennedy mistakes Vaughan Williams's own editing of the texts for texts from the Taverner Bible.

51 Taverner's Bible is little discussed in the literature. It was one of the first English translations of the Bible, and perhaps the second translation published in England. While most scholars of biblical history dismissed the work as having "little or no influence on subsequent translators". [Anna C. Paues: 'Bible, English' in *The Encyclopedia Britannica* [11th edn, 1911], Harold H Huston & Harold R Willoughby argued in 1939 that it was indeed one of the primary sources for the New Testament Translation of the King James Bible (which became the Authorized Version; see 'The Ignored Taverner Bible of 1539' in *The Crozer Quarterly* [July 1939] pp 161–176).

52 Rev 7:17 from *The Most Sacred Bible, whiche is the holy scripture, conteyning the old and new testament, translated into English, and newly recognised with great diligence after most faythful exemplars* by Rychard Taverner [London: John Byddell for Thomas Barthlet, 1539].

53 As Huston & Willoughby note, the substitution of a Latin-derived word for one with a Greek cognate is not one that Taverner often used. Indeed, in their discussion of the Gospel of Matthew, Huston & Willoughby note that in two cases, Taverner substituted "chayre" and "throne" for "seate" [Matt 23:2 and 23:22; Huston & Willoughby, *op cit*, p 171].

54 R Vaughan Williams: *Sancta Civitas, op cit*, p 41–42.

55 Perhaps this is one of the reasons Elgar never completed his projected third oratorio, *The Last Judgment*. His libretto sketches for this work show him moving towards the method eventually adopted by Vaughan Williams in *Sancta Civitas*: sharing the thrust of the narrative between narrators, named characters, and the chorus, and in the process completely negating any chance to show the response of the individual. For Elgar, the trappings of religion were intriguing and even distracting, but the interpretation was all his own, and he needed individual voices to show it to the broader public.

9 Connock: "Sheer early morning loveliness"

1 Richard Capell: 'Vaughan Williams light opera' in the *Daily Telegraph* [16 May 1936].
2 Dyneley Hussey: 'The Poisoned Kiss' in *The Musical Times* [June 1936] p 553.
3 R Capell: 'Great composer's operetta' in the *Daily Telegraph* [13 May 1936].

4   Scott Goddard: 'The Poisoned Kiss' in *The Listener* [27 November 1941] p 737.
5   *Ibid.*
6   F Howes: 'The Poisoned Kiss' in *Monthly Musical Record* LXVI no.777 [June 1936] p 97.
7   R Vaughan Williams: 'British Music in the 18th and early 19th centuries' in *The Music Student*, vol 7 [1914–15] p 64.
8   British Library MS Mus: 161C letter of early August 1927.
9   British Library MS Mus: 161C letter of 18 August 1927.
10 R Vaughan Williams: *The Music Student, op cit*, p 64.
11 Nathaniel Hawthorne: 'Rappaccini's Daughter' in *Mosses from an Old Manse* [1844, reprinted in *Modern Penguin Collection*].
12 Richard Garnett: The Poison Maid' in *Twilight of the Gods* [T Fisher Unwin, 1888].
13 U Vaughan Williams: *RVW: A biography, op cit*, p 209.
14 F Howes: 'The Poisoned Kiss', *op cit*, p 97.
15 British Library MS Mus: 161C letter of early August 1927.
16 British Library MS Mus: 161C letter of early August 1927.
17 British Library MS Mus: 161C letter of 12 September 1928.
18 British Library MS Mus: 161C letter of 23 September 1927.
19 British Library MS Mus: 161C letter of 6 November 1931.
20 British Library MS Mus: 161C letter of 24 December 1935.
21 British Library MS Mus: 161C letter of 12 September 1928.
22 British Library MS Mus: 161C letter of 17 December 1929.
23 British Library MS Mus: 161C letter of 18 August 1927.
24 British Library MS Mus: 161C letter of 27 January 1929.
25 British Library MS Mus: 161C letter of 17 December 1929.
26 British Library MS Mus: 161C letter of 15 May 1936.
27 British Library MS Mus: 161C letter of 15 May 1936.
28 BBC Written Archive Centre, File 910 (under Vaughan Williams).
29 British Library MS Mus: 161C letter of 18 August 1956.
30 Evelyn Sharp: *Unfinished Adventure* [John Lane, The Bodley Head, 1933] pp 3–4.
31 Edmund Rubbra: 'The later Vaughan Williams' in *Music and Letters* XVIII [January 1937] p 6.
32 H Foss: 'VW and the stage' in *The Listener* [27 October 1949] p 74.
33 R Vaughan Williams: 'Musical Autobiography', quoted in M Kennedy: *Works, op cit*, p 143–144.

Index

Musical and literary works, including those by Elgar and Vaughan Williams, are listed under the name of their composer or author, but less specific references to the two composers, which inevitably occur throughout the book, are not indexed. Urban geographical entries appear under the town or city in which they are located. References to photographs are given in *italics*.

Adelaide, Queen 16
Adorno, Theodor 138-9
Agra, India 131-3
Ainley, Henry 62
Akbar the Great (Mogul Emperor) 134
Alam, Shah 134
Allen, Hugh 19, 74, 96, 103, 169
Allen, Kevin 8
Alverstone, Lord 88
American Musicological Society 149
Anderson, Robert 78
Andreeff, Dmitri 131
Antwerp, Belgium 60
Aristophanes 119
Arkwright, Marion: *Requiem Mass* 55, *58*, 59
Armstrong, Sir Thomas 63-4
  Friends Departed 55
Arnold, Victor: 'Pierrot's Last Adventure' 131
Atkins, Ivor 106
  St Matthew Passion 169
Aurangzeb (Mogul Emperor) 134
Austin, Frederic 117-18, 138, 146, 159
Awdrey, Diana 89, 93

Bach, Johann Sebastian 88, 99-102, 107-8, 169
  Ach blieb' bei uns, Herr Jesu Christ vi
  Brandenburg Concerto no.5 103
  Coffee and Cupid 103
  'Latin Magnifica' 103
  Orchestral Overture no.2 in D 103
  St John Passion 93
  St Matthew Passion 93, 101
  'Sing Ye to the Lord' 103
  'The Spirit also helpeth us' 103
Bach Choir 101, 103, 169
Bailey, J 90-1
Baldock, Sydney: *Angels of Mons* 56, 65
Bamert, Matthias 144

Banks, Paul 148
Bantock, Granville 47, 87, 142, 163
Barbirolli, Evelyn v
Barbirolli, Sir John 84, 147, 158
Baring-Gould, Sabine 88
Barrett, Paul 146
Barrie, James M: *The Twelve-Pound Look* 131
Bartholini, Jean:
  Wagner et le recul du temps 107
Bartók, Bela 62
Battishill, Jonathan 19
Bax, Arnold 69, 90, 95, 146, 151, 159
  Symphony no.1 66
  Fatherland 52, 55-6
  string quartets 146
Bax, Clifford 117
Bax Trust 146
Beauchamp family 16
Beecham, Sir Thomas 147
Beethoven, Ludwig van 105-8, 171-2
Benjamin, Arthur 64
Berger, Francesco 105
Berlin Philharmonic Orchestra 140, 147, 158
Berlioz, Hector 70, 157
Bermann, Friedrich 131
Besly, Maurice: *Phaedra* 103
Bethge, Hans: *Die chinesische Flöte* 44
Bible, The 173-5
  Authorized Version 112-13
  King James's Bible 175
  Taverner's Bible 112-13, 115, 175
Binyon, Laurence: *For the Fallen* 62
  The Fourth of August 62
  To Women 62
Birchwood, Herefs 78
Birmingham 2, 5, 20, 81, 97, 163
Birmingham Conservatoire 140
Birmingham Festival 42, 78, 82, 100-1, 105
Bishop, Henry: *The Seventh Day* 174

Bizet, Georges 8
Blair, Hugh 132
Bliss, Arthur 62-3, 67
   Morning Heroes 55, 62, 69, 164
   The Olympians 83
   Storm 55
   The Tempest 62
Bloch, Ernest 94
Bloom, Harold 72-3
   The Anxiety of Influence: A Theory of Poetry 71
Bombay, India 130-1
Book of Common Prayer 112, 115
Boucicault, Dion 131
Boult, Adrian 15, 20, 22, 84, 95, 102, 147, 158
Bowen, York: Symphony 142
Brabbins, Martyn 64
Brahms, Johannes 8, 19, 62, 80, 107, 139
   Ein Deutsches Requiem 59
   symphonies 150
   Triumphlied 150
Brand, Tita 61
Breitkopf & Hartel 48
Brema, Marie 97
Brett, Philip 149
Bridge, Frank: Lament for Strings 55-6
   Oration 55
   Piano Sonata 55
   A Prayer 55
Bridge, Frederick:
   The Flag of England 55
Bridges, Robert 82
Briggs, Asa 16
Brinkwells, Sussex 153
British Broadcasting Corporation 44, 52, 82, 84, 91-2, 94, 127, 137, 140, 145
British Library 74, 86, 124
British Museum 81, 121
Britten, Benjamin v, 1, 73, 87-8, 149, 158
   Phaedra v
Britten-Pears Library 86
Broadheath Singers 163-4
Brodsky Quartet 153
Brooke, Rupert 63
Browne, William Denis 63
   Diaphenia 63
   To Gratiana Dancing and Singing 63
Bruch, Max 8, 19, 74
Bruckner, Anton 21
Bryn Mawr 164

Buths, Julius 174
Butt, Clara 24, 50, 59, *60*
Butterworth, George 63-4
   The Banks of the Green Willow 102
   Bredon Hill 64
   A Shropshire Lad 55, 63-4
Byrd, William 1, 8, 13, 19
   Come, Pretty Babe 13, 22

Calcutta, India 131, 134-5
Cambridge, Cambs 6, 63, 73, 79, 101, 119, 126, 165, 169
   Gonville & Caius College 19
   Trinity College 2, 7
   University 17
Cammaerts, Emile: *Après Anvers* 60
Campbell, Sir Colin 132, 135
Cannadine, David 20
Capell, Richard 116
Cardus, Neville 14, 21
Carey, Clive 88, 119
Carpenter, Humphrey 87
Carr, Howard 163
   Three Heroes 55
Carthusian Trust 149
Carwardine, Jane 152
Charpentier, Gustave: *Louise* 76
Charrington, Ruth 88
Charterhouse School, Godalming, Surrey 17
Chesterian, The 106-7
Church of England 96
City of Birmingham Orchestra 102
City of London Sinfonia 152, 156-7
Cleveland Symphony Orchestra 141, 144
Clive, Robert 134
Cobbett, Walter W 154
Cole, Jo 152
Coles, Cecil 64
   Behind the Lines 55
Coles, Ellis 147
Colvin, Frances 135
Colvin, Sir Sydney 18, 82
Connock, Stephen 67, 147
Constable, Strickland: Symphony 102
Cook, Nicholas:
   A Very Brief Introduction to Music 139
'Corno di Bassetto' see Shaw, George B
Cornwallis, (Lord) Charles 135
Cowen, Sir Frederick Hymen 49, 66
   Fall In 50

Index

Croft, William 102
Crotch, William 102
Curzon, (Lord) George N 134
Daily Telegraph 62, 116
Dan the bulldog 132
Darling, C J 47
Darwin, Charles 16, 71-2
   The Origin of Species 16-17
Darwin, Erasmus 16
Darwin family 7
Davie, Cedric Thorpe 96
Davis, Colin 150
Debussy, Claude 8, 30, 76, 107, 143, 165
   La Mer 76
Del Mar, Norman 147
Delhi, India v, 130-1, 134-5
Delibes, Léo 13
   Sylvia 165
Delius, Frederick: *Requiem* 55
Dent, Edward J 6, 63, 74, 77, 82, 119, 150
Desmond, Astra 92-3
Dibble, Jeremy 13, 21, 81
Dickinson, A E F 104, 112
Dieren, Bernard van 94
Dohnányi, Ernst von 1
   Concertstück in D 103
Dorking, Surrey 8, 92, 93, 97
Dunhill, Thomas 79, 82
Dutton, Michael 62
Dvořák, Antonín 18, 70

East India Company 131, 134
Edison Bell 50
Ehrlich, Cyril 48
El Greco 105
Elgar, Alice 5, 85, 87-8, 130, 133, 135, 153
Elgar, Carice 7, 93
Elgar, Edward:
   A flat Symphony see Symphony no.1
   The Apostles 5, 7, 90-1, 95-7, 99-101, 104, 108-9, *110*, 114, 132, 141, 145, 161, 174
   The Banner of St George 52
   The Belgian Flag, see *Le Drapeau Belge*
   Big Steamers 54
   The Birthright 52, 54
   The Black Knight 2
   Canto Popolare 31-3
   Caractacus 2, 11-12, 22, 160
   Carillon 52, 54, 56, 60-2
   Cello Concerto 6, 66, 155

   Cockaigne overture 9, 71, 74-6, 165
   Cockaigne no.2 132
   Coronation March 130
   Coronation Ode 133, 151
   The Crown of India 131, 133, 135
   Le Drapeau Belge (*The Belgian Flag*) 54, 56, 60
   The Dream of Gerontius 2-6, 8-9, 13-14, 18, 20, 23, 42, 59, *60*, 72-4, 76-8, 81, 84, 87, 92-3, 95-7, 99, 104-5, 133, 135, 141, 145, 150
   'Enigma' Variations 1, 5, 8, 9, 13, 18, 74, 79, 81, 97
   Evening Scene 89
   Falstaff 5, 12, 22, 70, 99
   Fight for Right 54
   For the Fallen 6
   The Fringes of the Fleet 54
   Go, Song of Mine 5
   'Harmony Music' 153
   In Moonlight 31-2, 39-40
   In Smyrna 132
   In the South 31, 33, 132
   Inside the Bar 54
   Introduction and Allegro 153
   King Olaf 2, 84, 158, 160
   The Kingdom 5, 22, 91, 94-7, 99-101, 104, 108-9, *111*, 114, 132, 141, 145, 161, 173-4
   Land of Hope and Glory 9, 50, 52, 71, 132
   The Last Judgement 7, 90-1, 97, 172, 175
   The Light of Life 2, 78
   Master of the King's Musick 7, 89
   The Music Makers 153
   Nursery Suite 90
   O Hearken Thou 130
   Pageant of Empire 67
   Piano Quintet 54, 152-3, 155-6
   Polonia 54
   Pomp & Circumstance March no.1 52
   Rosemary 54
   The Sanguine Fan 54
   Sea Pictures 5, 23-6, 36-7, 79
   Serenade for Strings v, 88, 153
   Speak Music 38
   The Spirit of England 54, 59, 62
   The Starlight Express 51, 52, 54
   String Quartet 54, 152-3, 155
   Symphony no.1 9, 12, 14, 21-2, 80, 97, 141, 142, 143, 150, 153

Symphony no.2 5, 141
Symphony no.3 90-1, 136, 141
symphonies 23, 95, 137-8, 143, 148-9
Une Voix dans le Désert (*A Voice in the Desert*) 52, 54, 56, 60
Violin Concerto 5, 8
Violin Sonata 54, 153
Wand of Youth suites 22, 138
Elgar, Henry 17
Elgar, Joseph 17
Elgar, William 16
Elgar Birthplace Museum vi, 145
Elgar Complete Edition 136, 147
Elgar Society, The 147, 149
Elizabeth I, Queen 134
Elizabeth of Rumania, Queen see Sylva, Carmen
Elkington, Lilian: *Out of the Mist* 46, 47, 55
Ellis, W A: *R Wagner's Prose Works* 104
Emerson, Ralph W 120
English Hymnal 115
English National Opera 83
Enoch & Sons 133
Eton, Berks 15, 163
Evans, Edwin 75-6

Fabiani, G: *Le Lion de St Marc* 131
Falla, Manuel de 62
Farrar, Ernest 64
Field House School 17
Figueras, Montserrat 13, 22
Finzi, Gerald 64, 142-3, 147
   A Short Requiem 55
Finzi Trust, The 147
First World War 11, 42, 44, 145, 153
Five Cliftons 131
Fleischman, Ernest 143
Flexner, Mary 164
Folk Song Society 12, 88
folk-dancing/poetry/song 1, 2, 8, 12, 26, 28, 35, 42, 74-5, 87-8, 101, 103, 122, 169
Forli, Malvern, Worcs 78
Forster, Edward M 73
Foss, Hubert 104, 127, 129
Foss, William 127
Foulds, John: *A World Requiem* 55, 69
Fox-Strangways, Arthur H 88-9
France 11, 16, 18, 42, 137-8, 142, 147, 150, 159, 165, 169
Franck, César: Symphony 103
Frank, Alan 127

Frazer, James G 88
French see France
Freud, Sigmund 44, 71, 122
Fuller-Maitland, John A 82

Gaisberg, Fred 91
Gardiner, Balfour: *Overture to a Comedy* 102
Garnett, Richard 119, 121-2, 128
   'The Poison Maid' 121
   The Twilight of the Gods 119, 121
Gay, John 117
   Polly 116-18, 120
   The Beggar's Opera 116-18
General Strike 169
George V, King 18, 130-1, 133, 135
German see Germany
German, Edward:
   Have You News of my Boy Jack? 55
Germany 11, 16, 18-21, 29, 42, 44, 48, 64, 87, 108, 137-9, 145, 150, 165, 172, 174
Gibbons, Orlando 19
Giglio, Rudolfo 131
Gilbert, William S 116, 118
   & Sullivan, Arthur: *The Mikado* 118
   Yeoman of the Guard 117-18
Gilchrist, James 152, 156
Gladstone, William E 16
Gloucester, Glos 5, 86, 89-91
Gloucestershire Symphony Orchestra 164
Goddard, Scott 116
Godfrey, Dan 163
Goossens, Eugene 64, 117
Gorton, Canon Charles Vincent 100, 170, 173
Goss, John 8, 108
Grafton, May 135
Gramophone Company, The 48
Gray, Cecil 94
Greene, Maurice 19
Greene, Harold Plunket 88, 97
Grenville, Sir Richard 52
Grieg, Edvard 88
Griffith, Troyte 2
Griffiths, Paul 150
Groves, Sir Charles 147
Gurney, Ivor 10, 64
   In Flanders 55
   Lights Out 55
   War Elegy 55, 64

Hadley, Mrs W 88
Haitink, Bernard 144

Index

Hallé Orchestra 84, 143
Hamilton, Henry 131-5
   Cheer, Boys, Cheer 132
Hamilton, Mary C D: *A Hymn for Aviators* 50
Handel, George Frederic 99, 104, 108, 171
   The Messiah 156, 174
Handley, Vernon 22, 84, 142
Hardy, Thomas 88
Harris, William H 102
   Faire is the Heaven 102
Harwood, Basil 102
Hastings, Warren 134
Hawkes & Son 134
Hawthorne, Nathaniel 120, 122
   Mosses from an Old Manse 120
   'Rappaccini's Daughter' 120
   The Scarlet Letter 120-1
Haydn, Franz Joseph 15, 169
   'Oxford' Symphony 102
Head, Leslie 63
Heap, Charles Swinnerton 78
Heather Festival 101-2
Heather, William 169
Heckert, Deborah 149
Henderson, Roy 15
Hepokoski, James 150
Herbert, George 153
Hereford, Herefs 6, 133
Hertfordshire County Youth Orchestra 142
Heseltine, Philip 94
Heyner, Herbert 133
Hight, George Ainslie: *Richard Wagner: A Critial Biography* 107
Hindemith, Paul 90
Hobbs, Jack 122
Hockman, Vera 8
Hodgkins, Geoffrey 148-9
Holst, Gustav 87-9, 90, 95, 129, 142, 173
   Cotswold Symphony 142
   Ode to Death 55, 64
   The Planets Suite 67
Housman, Alfred E 63-4
   Is my Team Ploughing? 34
   A Shropshire Lad 154
Howells, Herbert 55, 143, 147
   Elegy for Bunny Warren 55-6
Howes, Frank 101, 105, 116, 122
   'The Heather Festival at Oxford' 102
Huggett, Monica 139

Hughes, Merion see Stradling R &
Humphreys, Garry 164
Hurd, Douglas 139

India 132, 134-5
HMS Invincible 56
Ireland, John 95
   Cradle Song 89
   London Overture 76
   Sarnia 95

Jacob, Anstey 64
Jacob, Gordon 64
   Symphony no.1 64
Jacobson, Maurice 82
Jaeger, August J 81, 100, 104, 109, 170
Jahan, Shah (Mogul Emperor) 134
James I, King 134
Janáček, Leoš 30
Jehangir (Mogul Emperor) 134
Jessop, Charles: *The Galilean* 174
Jutland, Battle of 56

Karajan, Herbert von 21-2
Kauffmann, Angelica 105
Kay, Margaret vi
Keller, Hans 15
Kelly, F S 63
   Elegy for Rupert Brooke 55-6, 63
Kennedy, Michael 76, 149-50
Kennet, Lord 95
Kensington Symphony Orchestra 63
Kenyon, Nicholas 145
Knapp, Raymond 71
Knussen, Oliver 150
Kreisler, Fritz 5

Lacey, Dr 106-7
Lane, Piers 152, 157
Leeds Festival 5, 79-80
Leeds Philharmonic Society 79
Leith Hill Festival 8, 77, 89, 92-3, 95, 101, 160
Leith Hill Place, Dorking, Surrey 17
Leoncavallo, Ruggiero: *I Pagliacci* 52
Lewis, Daniel 144
Ley, Henry G 102
Lichfield Festival 146
Listener, The 116
Liszt, Franz: Piano Sonata in B minor 25
Llewellyn, William 149
Lloyd, Charles H 102
Lloyd, Edward 97

London 48-9, 69, 75-6, 87-8, 131, 137
   Athenaeum, The 6, 79
   Coliseum Theatre 131, 135
   Covent Garden 106
   House of Commons 16
   Kingsway Theatre 117
   Lyric Theatre, Hammersmith 118
   Queen's Hall 49, 59, 66
   Regent's Park 15
   Royal Albert Hall 66, 133
   Royal Festival Hall 15
   St James's Hall 1
   St Luke's 140
   St Paul's Cathedral 75
   Savile Club 82
   Severn House 135
   Westminster Abbey 44, 47, 130
London Philharmonic Orchestra 22, 66, 84, 144
London String Quartet 82, 84
London Symphony Orchestra 22, 140, 150
Los Angeles Philharmonic Orchestra 143
Los Angeles Times 143
Lourdes, France 151
Lucas, E V 88
Lucknow, India 132, 135
Lutyens, Edwin 130
Lydgate, John: *Tarry no longer* 59

MacDonald, Malcolm 69
MacFarren, George: *St John the Baptist* 104
Mackenzie, Alexander 66, 79, 81
   Columba 146
   A Musician's Narrative 79
Mahler, Gustav 8, 19, 44, 136-8, 141, 144, 148-9, 158
   Das Lied von der Erde 44
   symphonies 148
Maine, Basil 164
Maksymiuk, Jerzy 149
Malvern, Worcs 18, 78, 153-4
Manchester Guardian 122
Martin, Frank 149
Marx, Karl 71
Mascagni, Pietro: *Cavallera Rusticana* 52
Masefield, John 88
Mason, Edward 63
Massenet, Jules 8, 13
Maw, Nicholas 147
McCormack, John 49
SS *Medina* 130

Mendel, R W S:
   Confession of an Anti-Wagnerian 106
Merson, Billy 131
Michaelangelo 105, 171
Milford, Robin 96
Mill, John Stuart 16
Milton, John 15
Moeran, Ernest J 64
Montgomery, Peter 90, 95
Moore, George E 19
Moore, Jerrold N 85-6, 90, 92, 101, 149
   Letters of a Lifetime 85, 89
Morris, Emmeline 90-1
Morris, Reginald O 90-1, 96
   Sinfonia in C major 91
   Toccata and Fugue 102
Morris, William 73
Morrison, Richard 140
Mozart, Wolfgang A 15, 108
   The Magic Flute 119
Munich, Germany 106
Munro, Hector 134
Murray, Gilbert 71, 73, 88
Music & Letters 70, 77, 88-9, 106, 108
Music Student, The 117
Musical Times, The 49, 95, 101-2, 116, 171, 173
Mussorgsky, Modest 30

Nagano, Kent 143
New York, NY, USA 141, 149-50
   Public Library 147
   World Trade Center 147
New York Times 150
Newman, Ernest 75, 94, 156, 165, 173
Nielsen, Carl 136
Nieuport, Belgium 60
Norrington, Sir Roger 144
Norris, John 62
Norwich Festival 24
Novello & Co 48, 52, 133-4, 170
Noyes, Alfred 67

Otaka, Tadaaki 149
Ouseley, Frederick 102
Oxford, Oxon 101-3, 169
   Christ Church College 102
   Magdalen College 102
   New College 101-3, 169
Oxford Book of English Mystical Verse 81
Oxford Orchestral Society 103
Oxford University Press 127, 139

Index

Pakenham, Simona 105
Palmerston, Lord 16
Paree, Paul: *Angel of Mons* 56
Parry, Hubert 6-7, 12, 19, 66, 72-3, 75,
    79, 81-2, 87, 89-90, 95-6, 102, 165
  A Hymn for Aviators 50, *50*
  L'Allegro ed Il Pensieroso 103
  Blest Pair of Sirens 21
  The Chivalry of the Sea 55-6, *57*
  From Death to Life 55
  Hypatia 146
  Jerusalem 50, 55
  Since thou O Fondest and Truest 89
  The Soldier's Tent 42-3
  Symphonic Variations 96
  symphonies 144
Pasadena Symphony Orchestra 137, 144
Patterson, Annie W 99
  The Story of the Oratorio 104
Pepusch, Johann C 117
Perry, Ted 142
Piggott, Patrick 44
  Rosanes Lieder 44, *45*
Plassey, India 134
Plato: *Phaedo* 101, 114, 174
Playfair, Arthur 131
Porte, John 80
Portsmouth Youth Orchestra 143
Powell, Dora: *Edward Elgar: memories of a
    Variation* 96
Previn, André 147
Prokofiev, Sergei 136-7, 157
Promenade Concerts 49
Puccini, Giacomo 27
Purcell, Henry 1, 19, 119
  The Gentleman Dancing Master 103

Quilter, Roger: *Where the Rainbow Ends* 52

Raikes, Raymond 52
Ramscapelle, Belgium 60
Raphael, Raffaello S 105
Rattle, Simon 140, 147
Ravel, Maurice 8, 20, 71, 76, 88, 154
Reed, Ernest 90
Reed, William H 90-1, 93
Richter, Hans 1, 21, 96-7
Rimsky-Korsakov, Nicolai: *Scheherazade* 138
Roberts, Sir Henry Gee 135
Robinson, Stanford 127
Roe, Thomas 134

Rootham, Cyril B 74
  For the Fallen 6, 55
Rosanes, Flora 44
Royal Academy of Music 79, 127, 156
Royal College of Music 2, 7, 17, 64, 73-5,
    79-80, 82, 90, 148
Royal Liverpool Philharmonic Orchestra 22, 146
Royal Northern College of Music 83
Rozhdestvensky, Gennadi 148
Rubbra, Edmund 128
Rubens, Paul:
  Your King and Country Want You 49
RVW Society 149

St Valentine String Orchestra 88
Saint-Saëns, Camille 8, 156
Salem, Massachusetts, USA 120
Salonen, Esa Pekka 143, 150-1
Salvation Army 75-6
Salzburg, Archbishop of 15
Sargent, Malcolm 147
Sarto, Andrea del 105
Savill, Agnes 106
Schoenberg, Arnold 108
Schott & Co 48
Schumann, Robert 19
Schwiller, Isadora 93
Second World War 66, 72, 148
Shakespeare, William 11, 15, 171
  A Midsummer Night's Dream 157
Sharp, Cecil 88, 122
Sharp, Evelyn 116-19, 121-4, 126-8
  The Spell of the Magician's Daughter 122
Shaw, George Bernard 1, 82, 89, 106, 132
Shelley, Percy Bysse 31
  To Jane 31-2
Shelley, Mary 31
Schillings, Max von 64
Shostakovich, Dmitri 136
Sibelius, Jean 94, 136, 151
Sinclair, George R 132
Sitwell, Osbert 74
Skelton, John 91
  Elinor Rumming 4, 91
Smart, Henry 8, 108
Society of Women Musicians 62
Somervell, Arthur: *Thalassa* 55
Souter, Matthew 152
Southampton University 139
Spenser, Herbert:
  The Evolution of the Art of Music 72

Stainer, John 97, 102
Stanford, Charles Villiers 2, 5-7, 13, 19, 66, 73-5, 78-83, 88-91, 95, 102,160
  At the Abbey Gate 47
  Eden 82
  Elegiac Ode 81
  Merlin and the Gleam 69
  Musical Composition 80
  O Breathe not his Name 89
  Organ Sonata no. 2 55
  Piano Trio no.3 55
  Requiem 78
  The Revenge 52, 53, 55
  Shamus O'Brien 146
  Songs of the Fleet 55-6
  String Quartet no.8 82, 84
  Studies and Memories 83
  Symphony no.2 13, 22
  Symphony no.6 80, 84
  The Three Holy Children 78
  The Travelling Companion 82
  The Veiled Prophet of Khorassan 82
  Verdun 55
  Via Victrix 55, 68, 69
Stanford, Jennifer 78
Stewart, H C 102
Stinchcombe, Glos 89
Stockley, William 78
Stoll, Oswald 131, 135
Stradling, Robert & Hughes, Merion 107
  English Musical Rennaissance 1840-1940 101
Strauss, Richard 8, 17, 62, 169
  Death & Transfiguration 2
Stravinsky, Igor 62, 171
  The Rite of Spring 140
Stuart Wortley, Alice 5
Stuart, Tom 131
Sullivan, Arthur 90, 116-18
  see also Gilbert, William S &
Sumsion, Alice 90
Sumsion, Herbert 90
Switzerland 142
Sylva, Carmen 42-3
  The Bard of Dimbovitza 42

Taj Mahal, Agra, India 134
Tallis, Thomas 1, 8, 10, 19
Tanhurst, Surrey 17
Taruskin, Richard 71

Tavener, John 147
Taverner's Bible see Bible
Tees, Stephen 152
Tennyson, Alfred, Lord 31, 52, 69
  The Splendour Falls 30
Teyte, Maggie 49
Thompson, Herbert 170
Three Choirs Festival 2, 5-7, 14, 18, 73, 86, 89, 91, 94, 105-6, 133, 172
The Times 130-1, 135, 171
Trevelyan, George M 19, 165
Tucker, Robert 163
Turner, John M W 11

Unknown Warrior 44, 48
United States of America 71, 135, 137-9, 143, 145-6, 148-9

Vanbrugh, Irene 131
Vaughan Williams, Arthur 17
Vaughan Williams, Sir Edward 17
Vaughan Williams, Ralph:
  Along the Field 26
  Blake Songs 26, 29
  Choral Songs in Time of War 147
  Dona Nobis Pacem 66, 150
  Fantasia on a Theme by Thomas Tallis 5, 9-11, 22, 86, 155
  Fantasia on Greensleeves 9
  Fear no more the heat of the sun 22
  Five Mystical Songs 5, 9
  Five Tudor Portraits 4, 9, 92
  film scores 141
  Flos Campi 138
  The 49th Parallel 20, 22
  Four Last Songs 26, 29
  Four Poems of Fredegond Shove 26, 29
  The House of Life 26
  Hugh the Drover 66,120, 127
  Job, A Masque for Dancing 66, 91, 116
  The Lark Ascending 66, 69, 91, 137
  Linden Lea 26, 35, 80
  'Motion and Stillness' 26, 27, 29
  Musical Autobiography 74, 96
  National Music 87
  The New Ghost 26,29
  On Wenlock Edge 20, 34-5, 91, 152, 154
  Phantasy Quintet 152, 154
  Piano Concerto 66, 116, 157
  Piano Trio in G major 17
  The Pilgrim's Progess 83-4, 88, 94-5, 147

Index

The Poisoned Kiss 116, 118-120, 123, 127-8, 148
Procris 29
Riders to the Sea 127
Sancta Civitas 7, 9, 13, 66, 91, 97, 99-101, 103-5, 108, 112-15, 171, 174-5
The Shepherds of the Delectable Mountains 103, 127
Sir John in Love 127, 156, 161
Songs of Travel 26
Suite in B minor 88
Symphony no.1 (*A Sea Symphony*) 4-5, 9, 21, 72, 77, 80-1, 84, 142
Symphony no.2 (*A London Symphony*) 4, 9, 66-7, 72, 74, 76, 77, 143
Symphony no.3 (*A Pastoral Symphony*) 8, 66-7, 69, 142
Symphony no.4 66, 116, 13, 144, 147
Symphony no.5 10, 66, 144
Symphony no.6 144, 151
Symphony no.7 (*Sinfonia Antarctica*) 70, 143
Symphony no.9 in E minor 15, 22
symphonies 96, 137, 141, 144, 148, 151
Toward the Unknown Region 20, 80
The Vagabond 26
The Wasps 119-20
The Water Mill 26, 36-8
'What Have We Learnt from Elgar?' 2, 108
'Who Wants the English Composer?' 107
Vaughan Williams, Ursula v, 14, 16, 26, 94-6, 122, 127-8, 138, 161
Paradise Remembered 14
Vaughan Williams Society, see RVW Society
Vaughan Williams Trust 147
Verdi, Giuseppe 13
Falstaff 13, 22
Victoria, Queen 16, 18

Wagner, Richard 3, 8, 13, 19, 35, 80, 99-101, 104-9, 170, 172-3
Götterdämmerung 119
Lohengrin 170
Die Meistersinger von Nürnberg 76, 106, 165, 172
Parsifal 2, 104, 106
Tannhäuser 131
Tristan & Isolde 12, 19, 106

Walford Davies, Henry: Short Requiem 55-6
Solemn Melody 55, 169
Walker, Ernest:
History of Music in England 81
'Sleep Song' 102
'Summer Rain' 102
Walker, Robert 51
Walton, William 87, 95, 143, 158, 160
Henry V 143
string quartets 143
Troilus & Cressida 83
Ward, Nicholas 152
Waring & Gillow 130
Warrack, Guy 103
Variations on an Original Theme 102
Watson, Joanne 47
Watts, George Frederick 80
Webern, Anton 90
Wedgwood, Josiah 16
Wedgwood, Margaret 17
Wedgwood family 7, 16
Weelkes, Thomas 8
Wellesley, Richard C 135
Wells, Robin 149, 161
Welzer-Möst, Franz 141, 150
Wesley family 19
Wesley, Samuel S:
Introduction and Fugue in C# minor 102
Whitman, Walt 31, 77, 81, 101, 120
Wiley, Roland John 74
Williams, Harold 92-3
Wilson, Steuart 92-3
Windsor Sinfonia 163
Wolzogen, Hans von 100
Wood, Charles 19, 102
Wood, Henry J 60, 88
Wood, Ursula see Vaughan Williams, Ursula
Woolworth Stores 50, 90-1
Worcester, Worcs 16, 18, 20, 87, 91
Worcester Daily Times 106, 172
The Works 140

Yellow Book 122
Yorkshire Post 170
Young, Percy 6, 78, 96
Ypres, Belgium 60

Zipes, Jack: *The Loafer and the Loaf* 122

The Elgar Society was formed in 1951 with the objective of promoting interest in the composer and his music. With a number of significant achievements to its credit, the Society is now the largest UK-based composer appreciation society with ten regional branches in Britain and about 10% of its membership resident outside the UK. In 1997 the Society launched its own Internet website (http://www.elgar.org) with the aim of spreading knowledge of Elgar around the world and, in the process, attracting a greater inter-national membership. This was followed in 1999 by Elgar Enterprises, the trading arm of the Society, whose purpose is to raise funds for the Society's charitable projects through the publication and sale of books, CDs, CD-ROMs and other material about the composer and his music, and in October 2001 by the launch of the Elgar Society Edition, a scheme to continue the uniform edition of all the composer's music.

It was as late as 1994 that the RVW Society was founded by Stephen Connock, John Bishop and Robin Barber. Mrs Ursula Vaughan Williams, the composer's widow, consented to be the Honorary President of the new Society. Since its inception the Society has grown quickly and nearly 800 members have joined worldwide.

The Society is active in promoting the composer's music in concerts and lectures. To date we have been influential in two performances of all nine symphonies in the concert hall, an important opera festival (*The Vision of Albion*) and for stimulating world première recordings of lesser known works, such as *The Death of Tintagiles*, *A Cotswold Romance* and *The Pilgrim Pavement* as well as a new version of *The Pilgrim's Progress*. Guest speakers are arranged for special events.

For both Societies, membership benefits include an acclaimed Journal published three times a year; discount purchasing of the publications and other merchandise of each Society's trading subsidiary (**Elgar Enterprises Ltd** and **Albion Music Ltd**); advance notification of future concerts and attendance at Society meetings. Both Societies' merchandise will be on sale throughout the weekend.

All enquiries about membership of **The Elgar Society** should be addressed to:

Jon Goldswain,
31 Queen's Road,
Marlow,
Bucks SL
telephone : +44 1628 475897
e-mail : membership@elgar.org

All enquiries about membership of **The RVW Society** should be addressed to:

Dr David Betts,
Tudor Cottage,
30 Tivoli Road,
Brighton BN1 5BH
telephone : +44 1273 501118
e-mail : D.S.Betts@sussex.ac.uk